The Amazing, Colossal Book of Horror Trivia

Everything You
Always Wanted to Know
About Scary Movies
But Were Afraid to Ask

JONATHAN MALCOLM LAMPLEY, KEN BECK & JIM CLARK

FOREWORD BY FORREST J ACKERMAN

CUMBERLAND HOUSE
NASHVILLE, TENNESSEE

THE AMAZING, COLOSSAL BOOK OF HORROR TRIVIA
PUBLISHED BY CUMBERLAND HOUSE PUBLISHING, INC.
431 Harding Industrial Drive
Nashville, Tennessee 37211

Cover design by Gore Studio, Nashville, Tennessee

The characters depicted on the front cover include director Tod Browning in the foreground and actors Bela Lugosi, Carol Borland, and Lon Chaney Sr. in the background.

Library of Congress Cataloging-in-Publication Data
    Lampley, Jonathan Malcolm, 1967–
        The amazing, colossal book of horror trivia : everything you always wanted to know
      about scary movies but were afraid to ask / Jonathan Malcolm Lampley, Ken Beck and
      Jim Clark.
           p. cm.
      Includes bibliographical references.
      ISBN 1-58182-045-3 (pbk.)
        1. Horror films. 2. Horror television programs. I. Clark, Jim, 1960– . II. Beck,
      Ken, 1951– . III. Title.
      PN1995.9.H6L26   1999
      791.43'6164—dc21   99-41695
                                                      CIP

Printed in Canada
2 3 4 5 6 7 8—10 09 08 07 06 05

The Amazing, Colossal Book of Horror Trivia

CONTENTS

Think where man's glory most begins and ends
And say my glory was I had such friends.
—Yeats

In memory of Gregory Paul Horan (1967–99)
—J.M.L.

To William Castle, king of the gimmicks, who scared the pants off of me when I first saw *House on Haunted Hill* at age ten.
—K.B.

To Clint Howard, a lion of the screen whose awesome performances always leave me as speechless as if I had just taken a bite of a peanut butter and jelly sandwich without a glass of milk.
—J.C.

The oldest and strongest emotion of mankind is fear, and the oldest and strongest kind of fear is fear of the unknown. These facts few psychologists will dispute, and their admitted truth must establish for all time the genuineness and dignity of the weirdly horrible tales as a literary form.

—H. P. Lovecraft, "Supernatural Horror in Literature" (1927)

FOREWORD

THE TROUBLE WITH TRIBBLES—OOPS—TRIVIAS
BY THE ACKERMONSTER

Question: Who is the Ackermonster who is writing this Forryword?

Answer: Forrest J Ackerman

Question: Where does he live?

Answer: Horrorwood, Karloffornia

Question: Why is he qualified to write this introduction?

Answer: He saw his first fantasy film (*One Glorious Day*) at age 5½ in 1922! and probably could answer every one of the 1,760 trivia questions in this book blindfolded.

But you can answer them with your eyes wide open. In fact, some of them may open your eyes to new information you've not known about before horror films, terrorvision, and imagi-movies.

Even a few sci-fi films may have, er, crept in.

All aboard for Transylvania with stops along the way in Metropolis, Frankenstein's laboratory, Zombieville, a mummy's tomb, and . . . well, I don't want to reveal tomb much, but I can promise you you'll die laughing or your money will be refunded (to the Orphanage of the Children of Fan Tom of the Opera).

So gather your wits about you and start challenging the makers of this book. If you can answer half the trivia questions, you qualify as a half-wit. If you can't answer any of them, you have led a sheltered life on the dark side of the moon and you'll learn a lot about fantastic films on earth. If you can answer every last one—go back to the beginning and start over!

Forrest J Ackerman models Bela Lugosi's Dracula *cape.*

   Suggestion: Read through this book with a friend and see which of you can give the most right answers. Who will be the trivia king of your block? neighborhood? town? country?

   And remember, as William Shockspeare said, "The pun is mightier than the sword!" Or as Lon Chaney might have said if he'd lived till now (*Question:* What year did the "Man of a Thousand Faces" die? *Answer:* 1930), "Laugh, Clone, Laugh!"

   Here's lurking at you, kid. I'll be seizing you . . . if you aren't seized by a paroxysm of laughter first.

                              Forrest J Ackerman
                              Creator of *Famous Monsters of
                              Filmland* magazine

ACKNOWLEDGMENTS

No book, not even one with three writers, can be written without plenty of outside help. The authors wish to thank Gary Conn, Mike Darrell, Jonathan Dees, Greg Greene, Alison Harmon, Jeff Harmon, Charlene Jones, Brooks Pearson, and Rebecca Redd for their advice, encouragement, and general support in the writing of this book.

We also give special thanks to Brent Baldwin for his computer acumen, to Terry Beck for sharing from his video library, to Steve Cox for some excellent photographs from his archives deep in the bowels of Burbank, to Jean Carson for her help with photographs and research materials, to Lee Ann Durham for the loan of her Godzilla video library, and to Fred Goodwin for fabulous photos from his fabulous collection of movie stills.

More special thanks go to Basil Gogos for his beautiful cover and to the incredible Forrest J Ackerman for contributing his delightful foreword.

We give a big hand (or a claw, if you prefer) to Jeff Thompson, who shared his expertise in horror and many fantastic photographs from his personal collection and who has been one of our biggest cheerleaders since this project began.

And we thank publisher Ron Pitkin for letting us take a stab at this book, Ed Curtis for providing necessary stitches during the editorial operation, and all of the high-voltage team members at Cumberland House who have contributed parts of themselves toward bringing this book to life.

Thanks to you all. You deserve a big round of applause (or aclaws, as the case may be). But would you settle for our just screaming all of your names frighteningly loud?

INTRODUCTION

WELCOME TO THE wonderful world of horror films! We're not sure of all the reasons why, but there is just something in most of us that enjoys the good shiver or fright that comes from watching scary movies. It's probably something that goes back to childhood and those original fears of darkness and the unknown, of being left alone or lost, or of being surrounded by things bigger than we are.

Scary movies are like ghost stories around a campfire—only without the mosquitoes (unless they're scheduled to appear in *Giant Radioactive Mosquitoes from the Planet Dracular*). And don't we all remember the first scary movie we saw? (Confess. You trembled that night under the covers—even with the flashlight turned on—didn't you?)

Maybe horror movies are popular simply because they are so different from any other kind of movie. After much careful research and analysis, some horror scholars have offered their considered opinions that we like horror films because, well, they're *cool*.

This book is a tribute to the great horror makers of the past century as well as to some who were not so great but at least gave us laughs jumbled with fear. And so, too, we salute those magnificent kings and queens of scream with hundreds and hundreds of trivia questions (and answers) about hundreds of horror films.

We've included short biographies of the greatest names in the fright business and more than a hundred photographs. Together, they are *The Amazing, Colossal Book of Horror Trivia*.

This collection goes back to the beginning of horror history in America with quizzes on author Edgar Allan Poe and actor Lon Chaney (king of the silent horror film) and brings you right up to date with the teen-scream flicks of the 1990s. That's almost a century of chills and thrills from the greatest horror producers of Hollywood, London, Tokyo, and even a few lost worlds somewhere in between.

Here you'll find a variety of brainteasers on Dracula and vampires, Frankenstein monsters and werewolves, ghosts and haunted houses, witches and warlocks, mad doctors and weird scientists, demons and devils, monkeys and great apes, big bugs and giant reptiles, invisible men and shrunken heads, teen monsters and TV horror, and even comedy in horror films.

There are sidebars on the greatest names in the genre—men like Boris Karloff, Bela Lugosi, Peter Cushing, Christopher Lee, and Vincent Price—and sketches on such horror helping hands and scream queens as Peter Lorre, Barbara Steele, Lionel Atwill, Fay Wray, and John Carradine.

We've designed the quizzes to be fun. But also, by the time you're finished, even if you don't know all of the answers to everything you always wanted to know about horror (but were too scared to ask!), you'll at least feel like you've graduated from Horror 101.

The quizzes are divided into seventeen chapters, but the list easily could have been expanded. While any number of films could have qualified for more than one chapter, we've tried to place them logically. Believe us, trying to sort hundreds of horror films into precise categories would drive any boy or ghoul mad.

But don't worry, the book's not *too* tidy. There's plenty of mayhem in our methods. And so it is that some films and quizzes have been left just to float among the chapters like so many ghosts— ready to pop and give you a scary challenge when you least expect it.

Enter these pages if you dare and enjoy the surprises of what just might be the most frightfully fun test of knowledge you'll ever encounter. But remember: Once you've removed this book from its shelf (Oops . . . you've already done that, haven't you? Well, *now* you've done it!), who knows what evil might befall you if you try to put it back. (What was that? Did something on the shelf just move?)

Whatever you do, don't look back. You never know what might be behind you.

See you at the movies!

THE
AMAZING, COLOSSAL
BOOK OF
HORROR
TRIVIA

The family that slays together: Bela Lugosi and Carol Borland play father and daughter bloodsuckers in Mark of the Vampire *(1935).*

1
DRACULA AND OTHER VAMPIRES

Ah, you young people, making the most out of life . . .
while it lasts!

—Count Dracula (Bela Lugosi) in *Abbott and*
Costello Meet Frankenstein (1948)

NOSFERATU (1922)

1. Who portrays Count Dracula in this film (HINT: His last name means "terror" in German)?

2. What is the title of the book on vampirism read by Jonathan Harker (Gustav von Wangenheim) and his wife, Nina (Greta Schroeder)?

3. According to the book, in what year was the first Nosferatu born?

4. What is unusual about the letter that Renfield (Alexander Granach) sends to Count Dracula?

5. TRUE OR FALSE: As the first film adaptation of Bram Stoker's *Dracula*, *Nosferatu* was enthusiastically supported by Stoker's widow, Florence.

6. Complete the film's original subtitle: *A Symphony of* _____.

7. Who directed the 1979 remake of *Nosferatu*?

8. Who played the vampire count in the 1979 remake?

9. In both versions of *Nosferatu*, how does Dracula die?

10. TRUE OR FALSE: There is a sequel to the 1979 version titled *Nosferatu in Venice*.

Answers on page 21

TOOTH IN ADVERTISING—GO AHEAD, TAKE A BITE

Match the advertising slogan with the correct film.

11. "The terrifying lover who died—yet lived!"

12. "In her eyes . . . desire! In her veins . . . the blood of a monster!"

13. "It will paralyze you with fright!"

14. "If you dare . . . taste the deadly passion of the blood-nymphs!"

15. "One night is all that stands between them and freedom. But it's going to be one hell of a night."

16. "You can't keep a good man down!"

17. "In the privacy of a girls' school, he sought his prey . . . turning innocent beauty into a thing of unspeakable horror!"

18. "Mistresses of the Deathmaster, sharing his hunger for human flesh, his thirst for human blood, his evil lusts that even Hell cannot fulfill!"

19. "Blood. The more she drinks, the prettier she gets. The prettier she gets, the thirstier she gets."

20. "Come see how the vampires do it."

A. *Black Sunday* (1960)

B. *Blood of Dracula* (1957)

C. *Brides of Dracula* (1960)

D. *Count Yorga, Vampire* (1970)

E. *Countess Dracula* (1971)

F. *Dracula Has Risen from the Grave* (1968)

G. *From Dusk till Dawn* (1996)

H. *Horror of Dracula* (1958)

I. *House of Dark Shadows* (1970)

J. *The Vampire Lovers* (1970)

Answers on page 22

Max Schreck sent shivers down the spines of silent movie-goers as the vampire in Nosferatu *(1922).*

MORE TOOTH IN ADVERTISING

Match the advertising slogan with the correct film.

21. "Drink from me and live forever."
22. "The power of an immortal. The soul of a human. The heart of a hero."
23. "Nothing human loves forever."
24. "The greatest blood-show on earth!"
25. "Sleep all day. Party all night. Never grow old. Never die. It's fun to be a vampire."
26. "Love never dies."
27. "The King of the Undead marries the Queen of the Zombies."
28. "There are some very good reasons to be afraid of the dark."
29. "The only man alive feared by the walking dead."
30. "The Count is back, with an eye for London's hotpants . . . and a taste for everything."

A. *Blade* (1998)
B. *Bram Stoker's Dracula* (1992)
C. *Captain Kronos: Vampire Hunter* (1974)
D. *Count Dracula and His Vampire Bride* (1979)
E. *Dracula A.D. 1972* (1972)
F. *Fright Night* (1985)
G. *The Hunger* (1983)
H. *Interview with the Vampire* (1994)
I. *The Lost Boys* (1987)
J. *Vampire Circus* (1972)

Answers on page 23

ANSWERS TO NOSFERATU (1922)

1. Max Schreck **2.** *The Book of the Vampires* **3.** 1443 **4.** It is covered with mystical and astrological symbols. **5.** False. Stoker's widow attempted to have *Nosferatu* destroyed, as the producers did not get her permission to make the film. **6.** *Horrors* **7.** Werner Herzog **8.** Klaus Kinski **9.** The count is destroyed by the rising sun. **10.** True

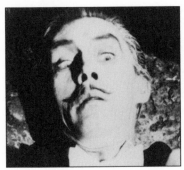

A gallery of Draculas appears on these two pages. Above, Max Schreck (left), the first Dracula, from the silent film Nosferatu *(1922); John Carradine (center), in the* House of Frankenstein *(1944); and Bela Lugosi (right), perhaps the most famous Dracula of them all, from the 1931 film.*

DRACULA (1931)

31. Who goes to Castle Dracula to conduct business with the count (Bela Lugosi)?

32. How many vampire women reside in Castle Dracula?

33. What unusual animals, native to Texas and Latin America but unknown in Transylvania, have apparently taken up residence in Castle Dracula?

34. What is the name of the ship that transports Count Dracula to England?

35. What is the name of Dracula's English residence?

36. Who plays Dr. Van Helsing in this version of *Dracula*?

37. How does Van Helsing discover that Dracula is a vampire?

38. TRUE OR FALSE: After Dracula is staked, elaborate special effects are utilized to show his uncanny disintegration into a heap of dust.

39. Although Bela Lugosi had played Dracula on Broadway, who was originally chosen to play the film role?

40. What Tchaikovsky music is heard during the opening credits of the film?

Answers on page 24

ANSWERS TO TOOTH IN ADVERTISING

11. H   **12.** B   **13.** A   **14.** J   **15.** G   **16.** F   **17.** C   **18.** D   **19.** E   **20.** I

VAMPIRE FILMS FROM THE SILENT ERA THROUGH THE 1950S

41. What is the title of the 1927 mystery movie in which Lon Chaney plays a fake vampire?

42. Under what title was this production remade in 1935, this time as a vehicle for Bela Lugosi?

43. Who plays Count Dracula in the 1931 Spanish-language version of *Dracula*?

44. In *Dracula's Daughter* (1936), why does Countess Marya Zaleska (Gloria Holden) pay a call on Dr. Jeffrey Garth (Otto Krueger)?

45. Under what alias does Count Dracula (Lon Chaney Jr.) hide his true identity in *Son of Dracula* (1943)?

46. What kind of supernatural henchman serves Armand Tesla (Bela Lugosi) in *Return of the Vampire* (1943)?

47. In what state does most of 1948's *Abbott and Costello Meet Frankenstein* (in which Count Dracula and the Wolf Man also appear) take place?

48. What causes Dr. Paul Beecher (John Beal) to turn into a bloodthirsty killer in *The Vampire* (1957)?

49. What is the occupation of vampire Drake Robey (Michael Pate) in *Curse of the Undead* (1959)?

50. In what 1959 Italian comedy does Christopher Lee play a vampire?

Answers on page 25

Below, Lon Chaney Jr. (left), in Son of Dracula *(1943); George Hamilton (center), in* Love at First Bite *(1979); and Christopher Lee (right), in* Count Dracula and His Vampire Bride *(1979).*

ANSWERS TO MORE TOOTH IN ADVERTISING

21. H **22.** A **23.** G **24.** J **25.** I **26.** B **27.** D **28.** F **29.** C **30.** E

HORROR OF DRACULA (1958)

51. TRUE OR FALSE: *Horror of Dracula* was the first vampire movie filmed in color.

52. Why does Jonathan Harker (John Van Eyssen) travel to Castle Dracula?

53. What happens to the vampire girl (Valerie Gaunt) after Harker stakes her?

54. Searching for Harker, Dr. Van Helsing (Peter Cushing) visits a nearby inn. What important clue is given to him by a serving girl?

55. When he arrives at the castle, what does Van Helsing see leaving the vampire's home?

56. What convinces Arthur Holmwood (Michael Gough) that vampires are real?

Christopher Lee may not be able to offer much relief when Carol Marsh awakens from a nightmare in Horror of Dracula *(1958).*

ANSWERS TO DRACULA (1931)

31. Renfield (Dwight Frye)   **32.** Three   **33.** Armadillos   **34.** The *Vesta*   **35.** Carfax Abbey   **36.** Edward Van Sloan   **37.** He notices that Dracula casts no reflection in the mirror of a cigarette case.   **38.** False. Dracula is staked and dies offscreen.   **39.** Lon Chaney Sr.   **40.** *Swan Lake*

57. How does Holmwood convince a reluctant border guard to share restricted government records?

58. How is it revealed that Mina (Melissa Stribling) has been victimized by Count Dracula (Christopher Lee)?

59. Where does Dracula hide his coffin?

60. How does Van Helsing destroy Dracula?

Answers on page 26

VAMPIRE FILMS OF THE 1960S AND 1970S

61. How does the bloodthirsty Baron Meinster (David Peel) meet his end in *Brides of Dracula* (1960)?

62. Who plays the vampiric Princess Asa in *Black Sunday* (1960)?

63. What is unusual about Christopher Lee's dialogue as the star of *Dracula, Prince of Darkness* (1966)?

64. Name the director of *The Fearless Vampire Killers, or Pardon Me But Your Teeth Are in My Neck* (1967).

65. Who played *Count Yorga, Vampire* (1970)?

66. Who stars as Jessica in *Let's Scare Jessica to Death* (1971)?

67. What is the real name of the vampire played by William Marshall in *Blacula* (1972)?

68. How is Count Dracula (Christopher Lee) resurrected in *Dracula A.D. 1972* (1972)?

69. In which Christopher Lee Dracula film does a motorcycle gang serve as the count's bodyguards?

70. In Andy Warhol's *Dracula* (1974), why does the count (Udo Kier) leave Transylvania to visit Italy?

71. What animal does Dr. Van Helsing (Laurence Olivier) use to locate a vampire's grave in *Dracula* (1979)?

Answers on page 27

ANSWERS TO VAMPIRE FILMS FROM THE SILENT ERA THROUGH THE 1950s

41. *London After Midnight*   **42.** *Mark of the Vampire*   **43.** Carlos Villarias   **44.** She seeks a cure for her vampirism.   **45.** He calls himself Count Alucard (HINT: Spell it backward). **46.** A werewolf   **47.** Florida   **48.** He accidentally takes pills derived from vampire bats. **49.** He is a gunslinger in this first vampire western.   **50.** *Uncle Was a Vampire*

FRIGHT NIGHT (1985)

72. Who plays Charley Brewster, the teenage horror fan with a vampire for a neighbor?

73. What is Charley's first clue that Jerry Dandridge (Chris Sarandon) is one of the undead?

74. What item does Evil Ed (Stephen Geoffreys) give Charley to ward off vampires?

75. How does Charley's girlfriend, Amy (Amanda Bearse), persuade unemployed horror star Peter Vincent (Roddy McDowall) to help her convince Charley that Dandridge is not a vampire?

76. What convinces Peter Vincent that Dandridge is a vampire?

77. Why does Dandridge develop a particular interest in Amy?

78. What animal does Evil Ed change into after being vampirized?

79. What happens to Billy Cole (Jonathan Stark), Dandridge's assistant, after Cole is shot by Peter Vincent?

80. In what room of Dandridge's home does the vampire meet his destruction?

81. According to *Fright Night Part 2* (1989), what is the relationship between the late Jerry Dandridge and the female vampire Regine (Julie Carmen)?

Answers on page 28

ANSWERS TO HORROR OF DRACULA (1958)

51. True   **52.** To kill Dracula   **53.** She crumbles into an old hag.   **54.** Harker's diary
55. A horse-drawn hearse containing a white coffin, Dracula's lair   **56.** His dead sister, Lucy, rises from the grave and attacks him. Van Helsing arrives and wards her off with a crucifix.   **57.** Holmwood bribes the guard.   **58.** Holmwood gives her a crucifix, which burns her tainted hand.   **59.** In the cellar of Holmwood's house   **60.** Van Helsing tears down some drapery, flooding Dracula's library with sunlight. The good doctor then forms a makeshift cross out of two candlesticks and forces the vampire into the sun, which disintegrates him.

VAMPIRE FILMS OF THE 1980S AND 1990S

82. In *The Hunger* (1983), what kind of doctor is Sarah Roberts (Susan Sarandon)?

83. Name the 1985 movie in which vampires from outer space menace London.

84. Name the 1986 horror-comedy in which Grace Jones owns a strip club where all the dancers are vampires.

85. In what California town is *The Lost Boys* (1987) set?

86. What kind of business does Max (Edward Herrmann) operate in *The Lost Boys*?

87. In what movie does Lance Henriksen play the leader of a group of modern-day vampires who stalk the American Southwest in an RV?

88. How many Academy Awards did *Bram Stoker's Dracula* (1992) win?

89. Who directed *Bram Stoker's Dracula*?

90. What is unusual about Marie's (Anne Parillaud) choice of victims in *Innocent Blood* (1992)?

91. What popular comedian stars in *Vampire in Brooklyn* (1993)?

92. In *The Addiction* (1995), what is coed vampire Kathleen Conklin's (Lili Taylor) major at New York University?

93. Name the 1996 horror comedy in which Dennis Miller plays a wisecracking private eye who battles the living dead.

94. According to *Blade* (1998), why is the title character (Wesley Snipes) immune to vampire bites?

95. What singer-songwriter plays Blade's friend and fellow vampire hunter Whistler?

96. For whom does Jack Crow (James Woods) work in John Carpenter's *Vampires* (1998)?

Answers on page 29

ANSWERS TO VAMPIRE FILMS OF THE 1960s AND 1970s

61. Dr. Van Helsing (Peter Cushing) manipulates the arms of a windmill into the shape of a cross, casting a deadly shadow on the vampire.   **62.** Barbara Steele   **63.** He has none.
64. Roman Polanski   **65.** Robert Quarry   **66.** Zohra Lampert   **67.** Prince Mamuwalde
68. A satanic mass   **69.** *The Satanic Rites of Dracula* (a.k.a. *Count Dracula and His Vampire Bride;* 1973)   **70.** He needs virgin's blood to survive. (Virgins have apparently become scarce in Transylvania.)   **71.** A white horse

Conducting an interview of a different kind, Horst Janson (right) duels the evil William Hobbs to the death in order to destroy the evil that has gripped a small village in Captain Kronos: Vampire Hunter *(1973).*

INTERVIEW WITH THE VAMPIRE (1994)

97. Who wrote the 1976 novel upon which this movie is based?

98. Who directed the film?

99. Who plays the vampire Lestat?

100. Near what city does Louis (Brad Pitt) become a vampire?

101. TRUE OR FALSE: Because Claudia (Kirsten Dunst) is a young girl when vampirized, her body ceases to age, even though her mind matures.

102. After they kill Lestat, why do Louis and Claudia go to Europe?

103. Name the Paris-based acting troupe whose members are all undead.

104. How is Louis finally able once again to enjoy sunrises?

105. What is the fate of Malloy (Christian Slater), the reporter who conducts the interview?

106. What Rolling Stones song plays over the closing credits, and what is the name of the group that covers the tune?

Answers on page 30

ANSWERS TO FRIGHT NIGHT (1985)

72. William Ragsdale   **73.** Charley sees Dandridge moving a coffin into his home, which is next door to Charley's house.   **74.** A cross   **75.** She gives him a $500 savings bond.
76. Vincent notices that Dandridge doesn't cast a reflection in a mirror.   **77.** She resembles his lost love, who is depicted in an old painting.   **78.** A wolf   **79.** Cole rises from the dead, only to disintegrate when Charley stakes him.   **80.** The basement   **81.** They are brother and sister.

FROM DUSK TILL DAWN (1996)

107. What actors portray the murderous bank robbers Seth and Richie Gecko?

108. What establishment is destroyed by the Gecko brothers at the beginning of the film?

109. What event has caused ex-pastor Jacob Fuller (Harvey Keitel) to lose his faith?

110. Why do the Gecko brothers kidnap Jacob and his family?

111. What is the name of the biker bar–strip club operated by the living dead?

112. What is the name of the stripper–vampire queen played by Salma Hayek in the film?

113. What weapon does Kate Fuller (Juliette Lewis) prefer to use on vampires?

114. Into what sort of monster does biker-turned-vampire-killer Sex Machine (Tom Savini) transform?

115. How many roles does comedian Cheech Marin play in this film and what are they?

116. What is the full title of the 1999 direct-to-video sequel to *From Dusk Till Dawn*?

Answers on page 31

William Marshall stepped into vampire shoes as Blacula *(1972).*

ANSWERS TO VAMPIRE FILMS OF THE 1980s AND 1990s

82. An expert on aging (geriatrics)   **83.** *Lifeforce*   **84.** *Vamp*   **85.** Santa Clara   **86.** A video store   **87.** *Near Dark*   **88.** Three: makeup, sound effects editing, and costume design   **89.** Francis Ford Coppola   **90.** She only preys upon criminals.   **91.** Eddie Murphy   **92.** Philosophy   **93.** *Bordello of Blood*   **94.** His mother was attacked by a vampire during her pregnancy.   **95.** Kris Kristofferson   **96.** The Catholic Church

VAMPIRE SPEAK

Match the quotation with the correct film.

117. "To die! To be really dead! That must be glorious!"

118. "My body can't take it anymore! The blood of these whores is killing me!"

119. "He's right. Peter Cushing does that all the time."

120. "You're so cool, Brewster!"

121. "She was beautiful when she died—a hundred years ago!"

122. "You see, Doctor, there are as many species of vampire as there are beasts of prey."

123. "Let's talk about blood, Mr. Vincent. It's very precious to me."

124. "She's going to join us, Doctor. And you are going to watch her initiation!"

125. "That's why I've come to see you. To seek release from a curse of misery and horror!"

126. "Yes, we have *Nosferatu*."

  A. Count Dracula in Andy Warhol's *Dracula* (1974)

  B. Baron Meinster in *Brides of Dracula* (1960)

  C. Dr. Grost in *Captain Kronos: Vampire Hunter* (1973)

  D. Count Dracula in *Dracula* (1931)

  E. Dr. Van Helsing in *Dracula's Daughter* (1936)

  F. Dr. Seward in *Dracula, Dead and Loving It* (1995)

  G. Evil Ed in *Fright Night* (1985)

  H. Regine in *Fright Night 2* (1989)

  I. Sex Machine in *From Dusk Till Dawn* (1996)

  J. Count Dracula in *House of Dracula* (1945)

Answers on page 32

ANSWERS TO INTERVIEW WITH THE VAMPIRE (1994)

97. Anne Rice wrote both the novel and the screenplay.   **98.** Neil Jordan   **99.** Tom Cruise   **100.** New Orleans   **101.** True   **102.** They wish to find other vampires.
103. Theatre des Vampires   **104.** He sees them in movies.   **105.** He is attacked by a revived Lestat.   **106.** "Sympathy for the Devil," performed by Guns n' Roses

MORE VAMPIRE SPEAK

Match the quotation with the correct film.

127. "She's that kind of woman. She's European."
128. "Tonight I will take Nikki away. Her soul will wander the night, and you will never find where her body rests."
129. "I want some more."
130. "Children of the night—shut up!"
131. "One lust feeds the other."
132. "The devil has sent me—twins of evil!"
133. "And when he crossed that bridge, the phantoms came to meet him."
134. "There's not room enough in this town for two doctors . . . or two vampires!"
135. "They have destroyed my servant. They will be destroyed!"
136. "Ours will be a different life, without material needs. A life that will last throughout eternity!"
137. "Every wedding needs a witness—and you will be witness to this one."

A. Dr. Blake in *Dr. Terror's House of Horrors* (1964)
B. Count Dracula in *Son of Dracula* (1943)
C. Sarah Roberts in *The Hunger* (1983)
D. Claudia in *Interview with the Vampire* (1994)
E. Count Dracula in *Love at First Bite* (1979)
F. Title card from *Nosferatu* (1922)
G. Dr. Armand Tesla in *Return of the Vampire* (1944)
H. Count Dracula in *Taste the Blood of Dracula* (1969)
I. Gustav Weil in *Twins of Evil* (1971)
J. Count Mitterhouse in *Vampire Circus* (1972)
K. Barnabas Collins in *House of Dark Shadows* (1970)

Answers on page 33

ANSWERS TO FROM DUSK TILL DAWN (1996)

107. George Clooney and Quentin Tarantino   **108.** Benny's World of Liquor   **109.** His wife was killed in an automobile accident.   **110.** The Geckos need the Fullers to cover their crossing into Mexico.   **111.** The Titty Twister   **112.** Santanico Pandemonium   **113.** A crossbow   **114.** A giant rat   **115.** Three: a border patrolman, Chet (the doorman at the club), and Carlos (a gangster associate of the Gecko brothers)   **116.** *From Dusk Till Dawn 2: Texas Blood Money*

Yvonne Monlaur and David Peel star in Brides of Dracula *(1960).*

ROLE CALL

Match the featured bloodsucker with the correct film.

138. Webb Fallon (John Abbott)	A. *Blade* (1998)
139. Martin (John Amplas)	B. *Buffy the Vampire Slayer* (1992)
140. Rachel (Jennifer Beals)	C. *House of Dark Shadows* (1970)
141. Count Dracula (John Carradine)	D. *House of Dracula* (1945)
142. Miriam (Catherine Deneuve)	E. *The Hunger* (1983)
143. Deacon Frost (Stephen Dorff)	F. John Carpenter's *Vampires* (1998)
144. Barnabas Collins (Jonathan Frid)	G. *Martin* (1977)
145. Valek (Thomas Ian Griffith)	H. *Once Bitten* (1985)
146. Lothos (Rutger Hauer)	I. *The Vampire's Ghost* (1945)
147. Countess (Lauren Hutton)	J. *Vampire's Kiss* (1989)

Answers on page 34

ANSWERS TO VAMPIRE SPEAK

117. D   **118.** A **119.** I **120.** G **121.** E **122.** C **123.** H **124.** B **125.** J **126.** F

ROLE CALL II

Match the featured vampire with the correct film.

148. Count Dracula (Louis Jourdan)
149. Count Dracula (Christopher Lee)
150. Count von Krolock (Ferdy Mayne)
151. Kurt Barlow (Reggie Nalder)
152. Count Dracula (David Niven)
153. Count Dracula (Gary Oldman)
154. Count Dracula (Jack Palance)
155. Count Lavud (German Robles)
156. David (Kiefer Sutherland)
157. Dr. Ravna (Noel Willman)

A. *Bram Stoker's Dracula* (1992)
B. *Count Dracula* (TV, 1978)
C. *Dracula* (TV, 1974)
D. *Taste the Blood of Dracula* (1970)
E. *El Vampiro* (1957)
F. *The Fearless Vampire Killers, or Pardon Me, But Your Teeth Are in My Neck* (1967)
G. *Kiss of the Vampire* (1964)
H. *The Lost Boys* (1987)
I. *Old Dracula* (1975)
J. *Salem's Lot* (1979)

Answers on page 35

The shadow of evil, cast by the infamous Count Dracula (Christopher Lee), lies over the small village of Keinenburg, where Dracula's latest victim (Carrie Baker) is found hanging from a church bell in Dracula Has Risen from the Grave *(1968).*

ANSWERS TO MORE VAMPIRE SPEAK

127. C **128.** G **129.** D **130.** E **131.** J **132.** I **133.** F **134.** A **135.** H **136.** B **137.** K

BELA LUGOSI

I AM . . . DRACULA. I bid you welcome!" This was the first line of dialogue spoken by a vampire in a talking horror film, and the actor who uttered it, Bela Lugosi, never dreamed at the time how prophetic it would be.

Even after nearly seventy years and many other interpretations, to many people, Lugosi's thick Hungarian accent and immaculate eveningwear and opera cape are permanently identified with Count Dracula.

The actor was born Bela Blasko on October 20, 1882, in the small town of Lugos, Hungary, from which he derived his stage name. His early theatrical successes were interrupted by World War I. After the conflict, Lugosi left his homeland, eventually settling in the United States in 1921. In his first American movie, *The Silent Command* (1923), he was cast as a spy, and the transformation from romantic lead to threatening heavy was under way. Lugosi worked regularly in American plays and films before his authentic accent and piercing eyes won him the title role in *Dracula* in 1927.

The play was savaged by critics, but it was wildly successful with audiences, and soon plans were afoot for a film adaptation. Universal announced that Lon Chaney would play the title role

and hired frequent Chaney collaborator Tod Browning to direct the picture, but the actor died before filming began. Many actors were considered before Lugosi finally signed on; he won the role largely because he was willing to do it very cheaply, earning only $3,500 for the most important film of his career.

Dracula's success saved Universal from bankruptcy. The studio announced

---

ANSWERS TO ROLE CALL

138. I **139.** G **140.** J **141.** D **142.** E **143.** A **144.** C **145.** F **146.** B **147.** H

that Lugosi would play the monster in *Frankenstein,* but Lugosi rejected the role. Ultimately his decision made a star and professional rival out of Boris Karloff. Lugosi never mastered English, so he quickly became typecast. Over the years he became increasingly associated with low-budget horror films.

Lugosi received good roles in *The Island of Lost Souls* (1932), *White Zombie* (1932), and several pictures in which he costarred with Boris Karloff, beginning with *The Black Cat* (1934). Among these was *Son of Frankenstein* (1939), in which Lugosi created his second-most memorable character, Ygor, the deranged hunchback. For the most part, Lugosi was consigned to Hollywood's "Poverty Row" productions. His name added marquee value to low-rent epics like *Spooks Run Wild* (1941),

The Corpse Vanishes (1942), and *Zombies on Broadway* (1945).

In 1948 Lugosi re-created his most famous role in *Abbott and Costello Meet Frankenstein.* It was the second and last time he portrayed Count Dracula on the silver screen. The film was a success and remains a classic horror-comedy, but it did nothing to reverse Lugosi's falling star. By the mid-1950s he was old, sick, and virtually unemployable.

In 1955 Lugosi became the first Hollywood star to admit publicly he had a drug problem. The actor became addicted to morphine following a painful operation, and by the mid-1950s he was an addict. After his recovery, he married Hope Lininger, a thirty-nine-year-old fan who had encouraged him during his treatment by sending him letters signed "a dash of Hope." Previously married four times, Lugosi had a son, Bela, by his fourth wife. Lugosi died on August 16, 1956. In accordance with his last wishes, he was buried with his Dracula cape.

Lugosi died just before a major resurgence of interest in horror films rekindled the careers of Karloff and several other stars of the genre. The

Bela Lugosi goes necking with Helen Chandler in Dracula *(1931).*

ANSWERS TO ROLE CALL II

148. B   **149.** D   **150.** F   **151.** J   **152.** I   **153.** A   **154.** C   **155.** E   **156.** H   **157.** G

inventive Edward D. Wood Jr. cashed in on this revival by splicing some leftover test footage of Lugosi into *Plan 9 from Outer Space* (1959). The results were laughable, to say the least; *Plan 9 from Outer Space* is now widely considered the worst movie ever made. On the other hand, the film's reputation contributed to Lugosi's posthumous legend. Martin Landau received an Oscar for his moving portrayal of Lugosi in the 1994 biopic *Ed Wood*; in his acceptance speech, Landau applauded the original Count Dracula. Hollywood had finally offered the respect and affection that Bela Lugosi so richly deserved.

DWIGHT FRYE

ALTHOUGH A VERSATILE character actor, Dwight Frye was typecast because of his performances in the most important horror films of all time, *Dracula* and *Frankenstein* (both in 1931). As the vampire's insane slave Renfield and as Dr. Frankenstein's hunchbacked assistant Fritz, Frye established horror icons that no other actor has ever surpassed.

Born in Denver, Colorado, on February 22, 1899, Frye started as a juvenile lead, first in Denver and later in New York City. He was in the Broadway production of *Dracula* with Bela Lugosi and Edward Van Sloan, which

Dwight Frye (left) was cast as a sinister assistant to Colin Clive's Henry Frankenstein (seated) and Ernest Thesiger's Dr. Pretorius (standing) in Bride of Frankenstein *(1935).*

led to his being cast in the film version. After *Frankenstein,* Frye continued to portray henchmen and other eccentrics in *The Vampire Bat* (1933), *Bride of Frankenstein* (1935), and *Dead Men Walk* (1943).

Frye originated the part of Wilmer in 1931's *The Maltese Falcon,* a role recreated by Elisha Cook Jr. in the 1941 Humphrey Bogart classic. Other credits include *The Crime of Dr. Crespi* (1935), *The Shadow* (1938), *The Man in the Iron Mask* (1939), *Drums of Fu Manchu* (1940), *Renfrew of the Royal Mounted* (1940), and *Frankenstein Meets the Wolf Man* (1943).

By the 1940s Frye was still acting but supported his family by working at Lockheed Aircraft at night. His career was at a standstill when he was cast in a substantial role in a film about the life of Woodrow Wilson in 1943. He died of a heart attack several days after winning the part on November 7, 1943, at age forty-four. Fans still visit the spot of his death—the corner of Hollywood and Vine. He was canonized by rock music's Alice Cooper in the song "Dwight Fry" (curiously without the "e") in 1971. A biography, cowritten by his son, was released in 1997.

TOD BROWNING

THE CINEMA'S FIRST director to specialize in the macabre was Tod Browning, a former circus performer and vaudeville performer born on July 12, 1880, in Louisville, Kentucky. Browning went to Hollywood to act, but he soon realized his destiny lay behind the camera. His first directing assignment was *The Lucky Transfer* (1915), a one-reel crime drama. Soon graduating to features, Browning made *The Wicked Darling* in 1919; among the cast members was Lon Chaney, soon to be immortalized as "the Man of a Thousand Faces." The director and his star collaborated on such silent hits as *The Unholy Three* (1925), *The Road to Mandalay* (1926), *The Unknown* (1927, featuring a very young Joan Crawford), and *London After*

Midnight (1927), a vampire-themed story now among the most sought-after of lost films.

In 1930, Universal hired Browning to direct *Dracula,* which was supposed to star Chaney. The actor died before shooting commenced, and ultimately Bela Lugosi played the bloodthirsty count. Released early in 1931, *Dracula* saved Universal from financial ruin during the Depression. Dracula's success motivated MGM to underwrite a new circus-themed production for Browning. The studio wanted to cash in on the sudden horror boom, but with this property they got more than they bargained for; released as *Freaks* in 1932, the picture starred actual deformed circus performers and so disturbed audiences and critics it flopped at the box office.

The failure of *Freaks,* coupled with a battle with alcohol, seriously undermined Browning's career. He made several more films, including *Mark of the Vampire* (1935, starring Lugosi) and *The Devil Doll* (1936). After directing the mystery-comedy *Miracles for Sale* in 1939, Browning retired; he died in Malibu, California, on October 5, 1962. Married to the former Alice Wilson, Browning never fathered any children and rarely commented on his film career; consequently, a lot of mystery surrounds his life and career. What information is available was gathered by David J. Skal and Elias Savada in their biography of the director, *Dark Carnival* (1995).

JAMES WHALE

IF TOD BROWNING initiated the talking horror picture, James Whale refined it. Born July 22, 1889, in Dudley, England, Whale had a varied career as a cartoonist, actor, and stage director before entering the film industry. Whale's production of *Journey's End* brought the director to Hollywood, and he directed a film version in 1930. The film was a success, as was the romantic drama *Waterloo Bridge* the following year. Whale was ready to try something different for his next project: he chose to direct *Frankenstein,* Universal's follow-up to *Dracula.*

Released late in 1931, *Frankenstein* made a star out of Boris Karloff and earned Whale a reputation as a specialist in the uncanny. Over the next four years he directed Karloff in *The Old Dark House* (1932), introduced Claude Rains to film audiences with *The Invisible Man* (1933), and oversaw the long-awaited sequel to *Frankenstein—Bride of Frankenstein* (1935). Ranked even higher by critics than the original, *Bride* is a triumph of Whale's trademark ghoulish humor; it was his greatest achievement and, sadly, his last assignment in the fantasy field. Whale helmed a number of more mainstream films, including the 1936 production of *Show Boat.* But *Bride of Frankenstein* was the high point of his career, and thereafter Whale's cinematic fortunes declined sharply. Universal changed owners in 1937, and Whale ran afoul of the new management when his *The Road Back* (1937) failed to find an audience. Whale then worked for other studios; most interesting was a popular version of *The Man in the Iron Mask* (1939), in which the director gave a future Baron Frankenstein, Peter Cushing, his first role. After making *They Dare Not Love* (1941, also with Cushing in a small role), James Whale retired. In 1957 failing health led him to drown himself in his swimming pool. Whale's career has gain increasing attention from fans and critics alike over the years. In 1998, Sir Ian McKellan received many accolades, including an Oscar nomination, for portraying Whale in the semi-biographical *Gods and Monsters.*

TOP 5 DRACULA AND OTHER VAMPIRES MOVIES

Horror of Dracula (1958)
Nosferatu the Vampyre (1979)
Brides of Dracula (1960)
Captain Kronos: Vampire Hunter (1974)
Dracula (1931)

Peter Cushing prepares to send beautiful vampire Ingrid Pitt to eternity in The Vampire Lovers *(1970).*

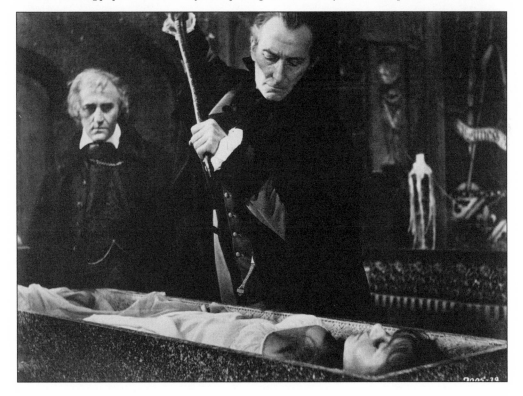

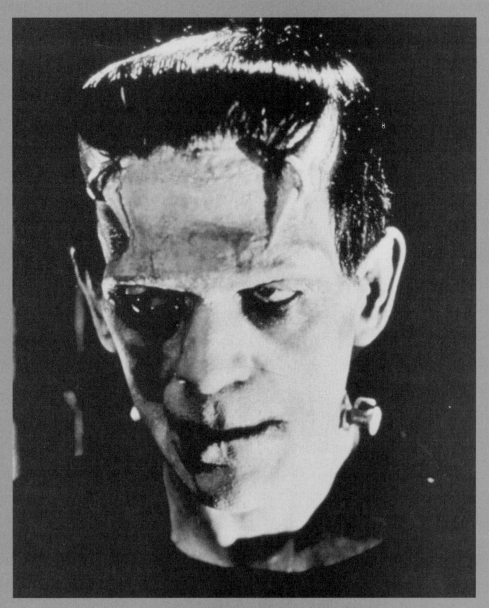

Boris Karloff stars as the monster in Frankenstein *(1931).*

2

FRANKENSTEIN'S MONSTER(S)

If the brain hadn't been damaged, my work would have been hailed as the greatest scientific achievement of all time. . . . I swore I'd have my revenge. They will never get rid of me!

—Baron Frankenstein (Peter Cushing) in *The Revenge of Frankenstein* (1958)

FRANKENSTEIN (1931)

158. Who directed this first talking version of Mary Shelley's 1818 novel?

159. Why does the hunchback Fritz (Dwight Frye) steal the brain clearly marked "criminal" instead of the "normal" one?

160. Just before Henry Frankenstein (Colin Clive) and Fritz bring their creation to life, they are interrupted by what three people?

161. What does Henry shout after realizing the experiment is a success?

162. What is unusual about the Monster's (Boris Karloff) first appearance?

163. Who promises to destroy the Monster?

164. Whom does the Monster accidentally drown?

165. Where do the angry villagers trap and (apparently) kill the Monster?

166. What toast does Baron Frankenstein (Frederick Kerr) offer at the film's conclusion?

167. TRUE OR FALSE: Bette Davis was originally considered for the role of Henry's fiancée.

Answers on page 43

BRIDE OF FRANKENSTEIN (1935)

168. What is unusual about Boris Karloff's billing in the credits of this film?

169. As the film opens, how does the Monster (Boris Karloff) survive the burning windmill?

170. Who teaches the Monster to speak?

171. Where does the Monster meet Dr. Pretorius (Ernest Thesiger)?

172. What physical defect mars the artificial life-forms created by Pretorius?

173. How does Pretorius convince Henry Frankenstein (Colin Clive) to create a female companion for the Monster?

174. What toast does the gin-sipping Pretorius offer to commemorate his partnership with Henry?

175. TRUE OR FALSE: The mad scientists use kites to attract the life-giving electricity to the female creature.

176. How does the female creature (Elsa Lanchester) react to her intended mate?

177. What does the Monster say just before pulling the lever that destroys him, his bride, and Dr. Pretorius?

Answers on page 44

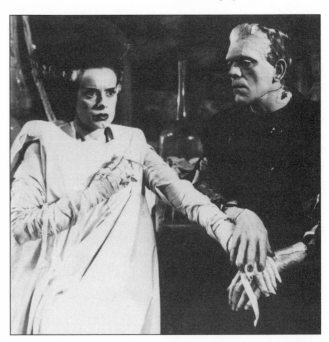

Elsa Lanchester and Boris Karloff lacked a certain "chemistry" in The Bride of Frankenstein *(1935).*

MONSTER MATCH

Match the film with the actor at right who played the Monster.

178. *Assignment Terror* (1970)	A.	Jennifer Beals
179. *The Bride* (1985)	B.	Fernando Bilbao
180. *Dracula vs. Frankenstein* (1971)	C.	John Bloom
181. *Frankenstein Created Woman* (1967)	D.	Peter Boyle
182. *Frankenstein Unbound* (1990)	E.	Nick Brimble
183. *The Ghost of Frankenstein* (1942)	F.	Lon Chaney Jr.
184. *I Was a Teen-Age Frankenstein* (1957)	G.	Gary Conway
185. *Mary Shelley's Frankenstein* (1994)	H.	Susan Denberg
186. *The Revenge of Frankenstein* (1958)	I.	Robert De Niro
187. *Young Frankenstein* (1974)	J.	Michael Gwynn

Answers on page 45

MORE MONSTER PARTS

Match the film with the actor who played the Creature.

188. *The Evil of Frankenstein* (1964)	A.	Boris Karloff
189. *Frankenstein* (1910)	B.	Kiwi Kingston
190. *Frankenstein* (1993)	C.	Bela Lugosi
191. *Frankenstein—The True Story* (TV, 1973)	D.	Charles Ogle
	E.	David Prowse
192. *Frankenstein Meets the Wolf Man* (1943)	F.	Randy Quaid
193. *Frankenstein and the Monster from Hell* (1974)	G.	Michael Sarrazin
	H.	Percy Darrell Standing
194. *Frankenstein's Daughter* (1958)	I.	Glenn Strange
195. *House of Dracula* (1945)	J.	Harry Wilson
196. *Life Without Soul* (1915)		
197. *Son of Frankenstein* (1939)		

Answers on page 45

ANSWERS TO FRANKENSTEIN (1931)

158. James Whale **159.** A loud noise startles Fritz, causing him to drop the normal brain. **160.** Victor Moritz (John Boles), Elizabeth (Mae Clarke), and Dr. Waldman (Edward Van Sloan) **161.** "It's alive! It's alive!" **162.** He enters a room backward. **163.** Dr. Waldman **164.** Maria (Marylin Harris), a little girl **165.** A windmill, which they burn with the Monster trapped inside. **166.** "Here's to a son of the house of Frankenstein!" **167.** True

THE CURSE OF FRANKENSTEIN (1957)

198. In what year does the film take place?
199. As the film opens, where is Baron Frankenstein (Peter Cushing) and why is he there?
200. What dead animal do Victor and his former tutor, Paul Krempe (Robert Urquhart), succeed in reviving?
201. Why does Cousin Elizabeth (Hazel Court) come to stay with Victor?
202. How does Victor acquire a brain for his creation?
203. Who plays the Creature?
204. How does Paul stop the Creature's initial rampage?
205. Why does Victor lock Justine (Valerie Gaunt) in the Creature's lair?
206. How is Elizabeth injured during Victor's final confrontation with the Creature?
207. How is the Creature destroyed?

Answers on page 46

THE SILENT ERA THROUGH THE 1950S

208. What famous inventor produced a version of *Frankenstein* in 1910?
209. Who plays Wolf, the title role in *Son of Frankenstein* (1939)?
210. For what purpose does Ygor (Bela Lugosi) use the Monster (Boris Karloff) in *Son of Frankenstein*?
211. What unexpected physical reaction does the Monster (Lon Chaney Jr.) suffer after receiving a brain transplant from Ygor (Bela Lugosi) in *The Ghost of Frankenstein* (1942)?
212. How do the villagers get rid of the monsters in *Frankenstein Meets the Wolf Man* (1943)?
213. Who plays Dr. Gustav von Niemann in *House of Frankenstein* (1944)?

ANSWERS TO BRIDE OF FRANKENSTEIN (1935)

168. He is billed only as "Karloff," a tribute to the drawing power of his name.   **169.** The Monster fell through the burning floor into the stream below the windmill.   **170.** A blind hermit (O. P. Heggie), who briefly provides shelter and companionship to the creature and also gives him speech lessons   **171.** They meet in an underground crypt.   **172.** Pretorius's creatures are miniature humans.   **173.** Pretorius has the Monster kidnap Henry's fiancée, Elizabeth (Valerie Hobson).   **174.** "To a new world of gods and monsters!"   **175.** True   **176.** She screams in terror.   **177.** "We belong dead!"

214. Where does the Monster (Glenn Strange) meet his fiery demise in *Abbott and Costello Meet Frankenstein* (1948)?

215. How does the condemned Baron Frankenstein (Peter Cushing) escape the guillotine in *The Revenge of Frankenstein* (1958)?

216. Where does the Baron find "spare parts" for his new creation in *The Revenge of Frankenstein*?

217. How does the baron (Boris Karloff) raise money for his strange experiments in *Frankenstein—1970* (1958)?

Answers on page 47

Peter Cushing, as Dr. Frankenstein (right), and Madeline Smith watch Shane Briant polish off the Creature's right hand in Frankenstein and the Monster from Hell *(1974).*

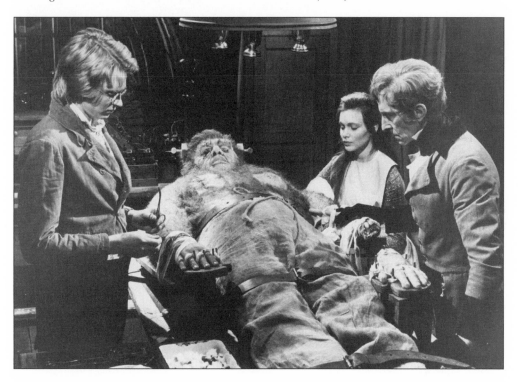

ANSWERS TO MONSTER MATCH

178. B   **179.** A   **180.** C   **181.** H   **182.** E   **183.** F   **184.** G   **185.** I   **186.** J   **187.** D

ANSWERS TO MORE MONSTER PARTS

188. B   **189.** D   **190.** F   **191.** G   **192.** C   **193.** E   **194.** J   **195.** I   **196.** H   **197.** A

In the 1973 made-for-TV movie Frankenstein: The True Story, *Leonard Whiting played the baron and Michael Sarrazin the Creature.*

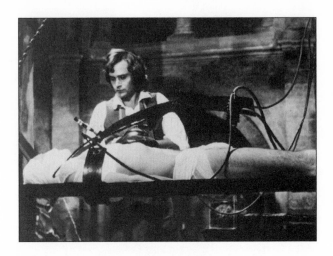

MARY SHELLEY'S FRANKENSTEIN (1994)

218. In addition to playing the role of Victor Frankenstein, what other duties does Kenneth Branaugh perform in this film?

219. As the film opens, what mission is sea captain Robert Walton (Aidan Quinn) trying to accomplish?

220. What graduation present does Victor's late mother (Cherie Lunghi) leave to him?

221. Which alum of the Monty Python comedy troupe essays a serious role as Professor Waldman, Victor's mysterious tutor?

222. What strange aquatic animals are used to help bring the creation to life?

223. What is unusual about the Creature's (Robert De Niro) eyes?

224. What musical instrument does the Creature play?

225. Why does a lynch mob hang Justine (Trevyn McDowell), the maid?

ANSWERS TO THE CURSE OF FRANKENSTEIN (1957)

198. 1860   **199.** He is in prison, awaiting execution for the crimes committed by his creation.   **200.** A puppy   **201.** She is supposed to marry him.   **202.** He causes Professor Bernstein (Paul Hardtmuth) to suffer a fatal fall so the great scholar's brain can be used. **203.** Christopher Lee   **204.** He shoots the creature in the head.   **205.** He has been having an affair with her; she now claims to be pregnant and is threatening to go to the authorities about Victor's unholy experiments.   **206.** As Victor tries to shoot the Creature, his bullets accidentally strike his fiancée.   **207.** The Creature, set ablaze by a lamp thrown by Victor, falls through the laboratory skylight and lands in a vat of acid, which dissolves every trace of him.

226. How does the Creature kill Elizabeth (Helena Bonham Carter), Victor's bride?

227. TRUE OR FALSE: Victor creates a female monster out of the bodies of Justine and Elizabeth. *Answers on page 48*

THE 1960S THROUGH THE 1990S

228. Where does Baron Frankenstein (Peter Cushing) discover the body of his Creature (Kiwi Kingston) in *The Evil of Frankenstein* (1964)?

229. In what 1966 horror-Western does a descendant of Dr. Frankenstein (Narda Onyx) turn a gunslinging outlaw (Cal Bolder) into a monster with an artificial brain?

230. How does Baron Frankenstein (Peter Cushing) meet his fate in *Frankenstein Must Be Destroyed* (1969)?

231. How is the Creature (David Prowse) accidentally destroyed in *Horror of Frankenstein* (1970)?

232. What 1973 TV production features a Frankenstein monster (Michael Sarrazin) who is quite handsome when first created, but becomes increasingly ugly as the film progresses?

233. How does Baron Frankenstein (Peter Cushing) react to the destruction of his latest project by asylum inmates in *Frankenstein and the Monster from Hell* (1974)?

234. What rock star plays Baron Frankenstein in *The Bride* (1985)?

235. Which two films produced in the late 1980s claim to tell the true story surrounding the writing of *Mary Shelley's Frankenstein*?

236. In what vehicle does Dr. Buchanan (John Hurt) travel back through time in *Frankenstein Unbound* (1990)?

237. What movie star plays the sensitive, horror movie–loving father in *Frankenstein and Me* (1996)? *Answers on page 49*

ANSWERS TO THE SILENT ERA THROUGH THE 1950s

208. Thomas A. Edison   **209.** Basil Rathbone   **210.** Ygor commands the Monster to kill the jurors who previously condemned Ygor to death.   **211.** The Monster goes blind.
212. The villagers dynamite a nearby dam, drowning the rampaging creatures.   **213.** Boris Karloff   **214.** Boat dock   **215.** Frankenstein bribes the jailers, convincing them to substitute a hapless priest in his stead.   **216.** The Baron operates a charity hospital for the poor; he acquires amputated limbs for his Creature.   **217.** He rents his castle out to an American television crew.

BORIS KARLOFF

BORIS KARLOFF, THE magnificent master of many a monster, was himself a kindly gentleman. He was born William Henry Pratt on November 23, 1887, in a suburb of London, England.

At the age of twenty-one, Karloff immigrated to Canada where he found employment as a farmhand, but he soon discovered acting and joined a touring company. He played across North America and popped into Hollywood in 1916 to be an extra in *The Dumb Girl of Portici*. By the early 1920s, Karloff alternated between acting in silent films and driving trucks. When "talking pictures" came into popularity, he had already appeared in forty movies.

The turning point of his career came in 1931, when director James Whale cast him as the Monster in *Frankenstein*. Although hidden beneath the great but gruesome guise of Jack Pierce's makeup, Karloff projected a force onto the screen with great pathos. A star was born.

"The Frankenstein monster provided him the pivotal point of his career," says daughter Sara Karloff, who was born on her father's fifty-first birthday, while he was filming *Son of Frankenstein* in 1939. "It was his signature role."

Throughout the 1930s and 1940s, Karloff and Bela Lugosi were the golden stars of American horror films. After more than 170 movies, Karloff also proved a terrific talent on television, starring as *Colonel March of Scotland Yard*, hosting *Thriller*, and providing that unforgettable voice for

ANSWERS TO MARY SHELLEY'S FRANKENSTEIN (1994)

218. He directs and coproduces the film.   **219.** Walton is trying to reach the North Pole.
220. A diary "to record the deeds of a great life"   **221.** John Cleese   **222.** Electric eels
223. They are mismatched—one is blue and the other is green.   **224.** The flute   **225.** The townspeople believe Justine has murdered Victor's younger brother, William.   **226.** He rips her heart out.   **227.** True

the Grinch in Dr. Seuss's animated *The Grinch Who Stole Christmas*. Karloff was also a star on Broadway in the 1940s in *Arsenic and Old Lace* and again in the 1950s as Captain Hook in *Peter Pan*.

During the 1960s, Karloff worked for director Roger Corman in several colorful, all-star horror spoofs. In one of his last film roles, Peter Bogdanavich's *Targets* (1968), Karloff pretty much played himself, an aging horror-film star who makes a personal appearance at a drive-in movie.

Among Karloff's many horror-movie credits are *Scarface* (1931), *The Old Dark House* (1932), *The Mask of Fu Manchu* (1932), *The Mummy* (1932), *The Ghoul* (1933), *The Lost Patrol* (1934), *The Black Cat* (1934), *The Invisible Ray* (1934), *The Bride of Frankenstein* (1935), *Charlie Chan at the Opera* (1935), *The Raven* (1935),

Boris Karloff's Frankenstein has prowled through countless movie theaters and has visited innumberable homes through television. His makeup as the Monster created a defining image for all who followed.

ANSWERS TO THE 1960s THROUGH THE 1990s

228. The Creature is frozen in a glacier. **229.** *Jesse James Meets Frankenstein's Daughter*
230. The scientist is carried into a burning house by his vengeful creation (Freddie Jones).
231. An inquisitive little girl inadvertently douses him with acid. **232.** *Frankenstein: The True Story* **233.** The dedicated (but now totally demented) scientist calmly sweeps up the mess, all the while discussing plans for his next creation. **234.** Sting **235.** *Gothic* (1986) and *Haunted Summer* (1988) **236.** A talking car **237.** Burt Reynolds

Mr. Wong in Chinatown (1937), *The Man They Could Not Hang* (1937), *Tower of London* (1939), *The Boogie Man Will Get You* (1942), *The Body Snatcher* (1945), *Bedlam* (1946), *Dick Tracy Meets Gruesome* (1947), *The Secret Life of Walter Mitty* (1947), *Unconquered* (1947), *Abbott and Costello Meet Dr. Jekyll and Mr. Hyde* (1948), *The Ghost in the Invisible Bikini* (1966), and *House of Evil* (1968).

The legendary horror star told an interviewer in late 1968, "I've been introduced to a whole new generation, thanks to my old movies being shown on television. And now, with the many TV shows I've been on in recent years, I'm really getting to be quite a public scandal."

He died February 2, 1969, at the age of eighty-one.

The great actor's daughter says that her father thought the key to giving moviegoers a good fright was to show them less, not more. "If a lot was left to the imagination of the viewer, it proved a much more personal experience for that viewer as opposed to today's films where everything is laid out in vivid color," she said. "He thought the real horror was on the streets. What was happening in our daily lives is far more terrifying that what is happening on the screen."

MAKEUP AND SPECIAL EFFECTS

DRACULA. FRANKENSTEIN. The Wolf Man. The Mummy. No matter who plays them, they must have makeup.

Lon Chaney Sr., the "Man of a Thousand Faces," did his own elaborate makeups in such films as *The Hunchback of Notre Dame* (1923) and *The Phantom of the Opera* (1925). But for most horror thespians, an expert makeup artist is required to complete the transformation from man to monster.

One of the early masters was Jack P. Pierce, the man responsible for the menagerie of Universal monsters. Most famous for designing Boris Karloff's Frankenstein monster, Pierce also turned Karloff into the Mummy in 1932, Lon Chaney Jr. into the Wolf Man in 1941, and Claude Rains into the Phantom of the Opera in 1943.

Pierce's painstaking techniques involved long hours and plenty of morticians' wax, yak hair, and spirit gum. Promoted to head Universal's makeup department in 1936, Pierce eventually had a falling out with studio executives over his costly and time-consuming practices.

Born in New York in 1889, Pierce died in 1968, neglected by all but the most devoted fantasy film fans. Nevertheless, Pierce's unforgettable creations continue to inspire makeup artists all over the world.

The current dean of American makeup artists is Dick Smith. Born in Larchmont, New York, on June 26, 1922,

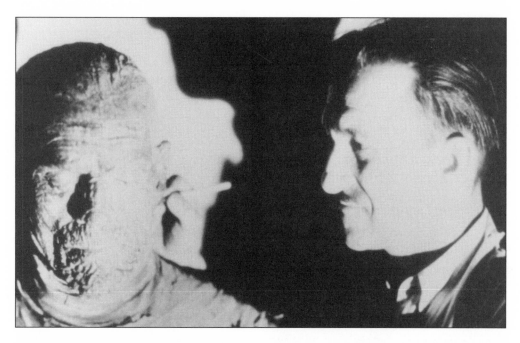

Jack Pierce (right) was the makeup master behind most of the monsters that appeared in Universal films during the 1930s and 1940s. Above, he applies the finishing touches to Boris Karloff for The Mummy *(1932).*

Smith received his start at NBC in the late 1940s. His first film assignment was a sci-fi thriller, *The Flame Barrier* (1958). Some of his most notable achievements include *Requiem for a Heavyweight* (1962), *Midnight Cowboy* (1969), *Little Big Man* (1970), and *The Godfather* (1972).

Smith's effects work can also be seen in scary movies like *House of Dark Shadows* (1970), *The Exorcist* (1973), *Ghost Story* (1981), and *Death Becomes Her* (1992). He shared a Best Makeup Academy Award for *Amadeus* (1984). Smith is most respected for his improvements in the area of old-age makeup, which allows actors greater fluidity of movement and thus contributes to a more realistic effect.

Rick Baker, born on December 8, 1950, in Binghamton, New York, apprenticed under Smith before finding professional assignments on *The Thing with Two Heads* (1972) and *It's Alive!* (1974).

Baker's first major assignment was *King Kong* (1976), in which he wound up playing the giant ape in several scenes. His elaborate full-body werewolf transformation won him an Academy Award in 1981 for *An American Werewolf in London,* the first one ever awarded in the Best Makeup category. Other Oscars followed for *Harry and the Hendersons* (1987), *Ed Wood* (1994)—in which he miraculously transformed Martin Landau into an elderly Bela

When Lon Chaney Jr. starred in The Ghost of Frankenstein *(1942), it took him four hours to have the Karloffesque makeup applied, which meant he needed to report to the studio at 4 A.M.*

Lugosi, *The Nutty Professor* (1996), and *Men in Black* (1997).

Baker's fantasy film credits include *It Lives Again* (1978), *The Howling* (1980), *The Funhouse* (1981), and *Gremlins 2: The New Batch* (1990). Some of his greatest successes have involved transforming humans into apes in *Greystoke: The Legend of Tarzan, Lord of the Apes* (1984), and *Gorillas in the Mist* (1988).

With the passing of the great horror stars, FX artists such as Tom Savini became the real stars of contemporary fright films. Dubbed "the God-father of Gore," Savini was born on November 3, 1946. Seeing the Lon Chaney biopic *Man of a Thousand Faces*

The Karloffian image dominated depictions of Frankenstein's creature well into the 1970s. Below (left), David Prowse played the Monster in The Horror of Frankenstein *(1970). In a radical departure from tradition, Michael Sarrazin (below right) played the Monster in the television production* Frankenstein: The True Story *(1973) without the usual makeup. Sarrazin's creature deteriorated over time, becoming repulsive and reclusive as he "aged."*

inspired Savini's fascination with show business in general and special effects makeup in particular.

Following a tour of duty in Vietnam, Savini began working as an actor and makeup artist. *Deathdream* (1972) was his first movie makeup job. By the late 1970s, he was doing makeup and performing in George Romero's *Martin* (1978) and *Dawn of the Dead* (1979). Savini stayed busy throughout the 1980s doing makeup and playing small parts in projects such as *Friday the 13th* (1980), *Knightriders* (1981), *Creepshow* (1982), *Day of the Dead* (1985), *Texas Chainsaw Massacre 2* (1986), and *Monkey Shines* (1988). Savini directed the remake of *Night of the Living Dead* in 1990 and continues to be active on both sides of the camera. In 1983 he published *Bizarro* (republished as *Grande Illusions*), a guide to creating makeup effects.

TOP 5 FRANKENSTEIN'S MONSTER(S) MOVIES

Frankenstein (1931)
Bride of Frankenstein (1935)
Son of Frankenstein (1958)
Curse of Frankenstein (1957)
Evil of Frankenstein (1964)

Oliver Reed's little Leon grows up to be a demonic werewolf in The Curse of the Werewolf *(1961).*

3

MAN INTO BEAST

*I tell you—we haven't begun to discover what science can
do to the mind and body of man!*

> —Dr. Jekyll (John Barrymore) in *Dr. Jekyll and
> Mr. Hyde* (1920)

DR. JEKYLL AND MR. HYDE (1932)

238. Name the actor who won an Oscar for his portrayal of the title characters.

239. Why is the good doctor referred to as "jeek-ul" in this film?

240. TRUE OR FALSE: Dr. Jekyll's face—and later Mr. Hyde's face—is first shown as a reflection in a mirror.

241. Why is Jekyll late for a dinner party hosted by Muriel, his fiancée (Rose Hobart)?

242. How does Jekyll make the acquaintance of "bad girl" Ivy Pierson (Miriam Hopkins)?

243. Why does Jekyll send Ivy fifty pounds?

244. What event triggers Dr. Jekyll's automatic and unintended transformation into Mr. Hyde?

245. How does Hyde murder Ivy?

246. What is the final fate of Dr. Jekyll?

247. How does Mr. Hyde's appearance change over the course of the film?

Answers on page 57

JEKYLL-HYDE AND OTHER TRANSFORMING MONSTERS

248. Who plays the dual roles without makeup in Paramount's silent version of *Dr. Jekyll and Mr. Hyde* (1920)?

249. Name the two leading ladies who appear opposite Spencer Tracy in the 1941 version of Robert Louis Stevenson's classic tale of terror.

250. What was the last film directed by Victor Fleming prior to his direction of the 1941 *Dr. Jekyll and Mr. Hyde*?

251. Who actually commits the murders blamed on Janet Smith (Gloria Talbot), the unfortunate *Daughter of Dr. Jekyll* (1957)?

252. What causes Robert Clarke's unfortunate reaction to sunlight in *The Hideous Sun Demon* (1959)?

253. In what state do *The Alligator People* (1959) reside?

254. In *The Two Faces of Dr. Jekyll* (1960), what physical change takes place when Dr. Jekyll (Paul Massie) drinks the serum that transforms him into Mr. Hyde?

255. What causes Anna Franklyn (Jacqueline Pearce) to transform into *The Reptile* (1966)?

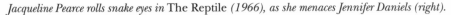

Jacqueline Pearce rolls snake eyes in The Reptile *(1966), as she menaces Jennifer Daniels (right).*

Fredric March's Mr. Hyde (left) skulked about in 1932's Dr. Jekyll and Mr. Hyde, *and Jack Palance (right) reprised the role for television in 1968.*

256. What substance turns Ralph Bates into Martine Beswick in *Dr. Jekyll and Sister Hyde* (1972)?

257. Exposure to what liquid transforms an ancient skeleton into *The Creeping Flesh* (1972)?

258. In what 1974 shocker does Dr. John Beck (Stewart Moss) transform into a literal "bat-man"?

259. Who stars as an ugly podiatrist who turns into a handsome murderer in *Dr. Heckyl and Mr. Hype* (1980)?

260. What happens when Dr. Jekyll's great-grandson (James Mathers) injects his subjects with a Nazi mind-control serum in *Dr. Jekyll's Dungeon of Death* (1982)?

261. What is the relationship between the title character (Julia Roberts) and Dr. Jekyll (John Malkovich) in *Mary Reilly* (1995)?

262. In what 1995 film does Tim Daly transform into Sean Young?

Answers on page 59

ANSWERS TO DR. JEKYLL AND MR. HYDE (1932)

238. Fredric March   **239.** That is how author Robert Louis Stevenson intended the name to be pronounced, supposedly as a pun on "hide and seek."   **240.** True   **241.** He insists on performing an operation in a hospital charity ward.   **242.** Jekyll rescues her from an irate customer.   **243.** The doctor feels guilty about terrorizing Ivy while in his Mr. Hyde persona.   **244.** While walking through a park, Dr. Jekyll witnesses a cat killing a bird.   **245.** He strangles her with his bare hands.   **246.** He is shot to death by the police after the Mr. Hyde persona once more asserts itself at an inopportune moment.   **247.** Hyde's appearance is uglier and more brutish with every transformation.

Lon Chaney Jr. as himself and in Wolf Man makeup.

THE WOLF MAN (1941)

263. Why does Welsh native Larry Talbot (Lon Chaney Jr.) speak with an American accent?

264. What scientific instrument does Sir John Talbot (Claude Rains) have mounted in his attic?

265. What does Larry purchase from Gwen's (Evelyn Ankers) antique store?

266. What famous horror star appears briefly as Bela the gypsy?

267. According to *The Wolf Man*, what symbol marks the palms of werewolves?

268. How does Larry become a werewolf?

269. TRUE OR FALSE: Larry Talbot kills almost a dozen people over the course of the film.

270. How does the unfortunate Wolf Man meet his demise?

271. What is the scientific term for werewolfism?

272. Recite the complete poem quoted in the film that begins with the line, "Even a man who is pure in heart." *Answers on page 60*

AN AMERICAN WEREWOLF IN LONDON (1981)

273. Name the comedy specialist who directed this frightening yet funny feature.

274. What pub do David Kessler (David Naughton) and Jack Goodman (Griffin Dunne) visit while backpacking across the moors of northern England?

275. Why does Jack's mutilated corpse return to haunt David?
276. In a dream sequence, what animal does David stalk and devour?
277. What Rodgers and Hart song plays on the soundtrack when David first transforms into a werewolf?
278. How many people does David kill during his first night as a werewolf?
279. Why does the undead Jack meet with David in a London porno theater?
280. What film is showing while the two friends talk?
281. TRUE OR FALSE: David is killed when heavily armed British police officers shoot him with silver bullets.
282. Name the 1997 in-name-only sequel to *An American Werewolf in London*.

Answers on page 61

WEREWOLF FILMS FROM THE THIRTIES THROUGH THE SIXTIES

283. *The Werewolf of London* (1935) actually tells the story of two wolf men; name the characters and the actors who play them.
284. Name the mysterious plant whose blossoms provide a temporary antidote in *The Werewolf of London*.
285. How does mad scientist George Zucco transform farmhand Glenn Strange into a werewolf in *The Mad Monster* (1942)?
286. How is werewolf Larry Talbot (Lon Chaney Jr.) resurrected in *Frankenstein Meets the Wolfman* (1943)?
287. Who shoots Larry Talbot (Lon Chaney Jr.) with a silver bullet in *House of Frankenstein* (1944)?
288. What causes gypsy queen Celeste La Tour (Nina Foch) to turn into a wolf in *Cry of the Werewolf* (1944)?
289. TRUE OR FALSE: Larry Talbot (Lon Chaney Jr.) is burned to death at the finale of *House of Dracula* (1945).

ANSWERS TO JEKYLL-HYDE AND OTHER TRANSFORMING MONSTERS

248. John Barrymore   **249.** Lana Turner and Ingrid Bergman   **250.** *Gone with the Wind* (1939)   **251.** Her guardian (Arthur Shields), who is a werewolf   **252.** Radiation poisoning   **253.** Louisiana   **254.** He gets younger and better looking!   **255.** She is cursed by a Borneo snake cult.   **256.** A serum derived from female hormones   **257.** Water   **258.** *The Bat People*   **259.** Oliver Reed   **260.** They become violent kung-fu fighters.   **261.** She is one of the good doctor's maids.   **262.** *Dr. Jekyll and Ms. Hyde*

290. Name the 1946 film in which murders committed by a maniac are blamed on a werewolf.

291. What causes Steve Ritch to become *The Werewolf* (1956)?

292. Who plays both a werewolf and a mummy in *Face of the Screaming Werewolf* (1959)?

293. When and where is *The Curse of the Werewolf* (1961) set?

294. What temporarily keeps Leon (Oliver Reed) from turning into a wolf in *The Curse of the Werewolf*?

295. Who is the *Werewolf in a Girl's Dormitory* (1962)?

296. Name the Spanish horror star who made his debut as reluctant werewolf Waldemar Daninsky in *Frankenstein's Bloody Terror* (1967).

297. Besides werewolf Waldemar Daninsky, what other monsters are gathered by alien invader Dr. Warnoff (Michael Rennie) to help him conquer the world in *Assignment Terror* (1969)?

Answers on page 62

WEREWOLF FILMS FROM THE SEVENTIES THROUGH THE NINETIES

298. Name the biker gang in *Werewolves on Wheels* (1971).

299. In what 1973 film does Dean Stockwell play a werewolf who spreads his curse to the president of the United States?

300. Who plays the hairy father of *The Boy Who Cried Werewolf* (1973)?

301. What 1974 production stars Calvin Lockhart as a wealthy hunter who suspects one of his weekend guests is a werewolf?

302. In what city is *Legend of the Werewolf* (1975) set?

303. Name the reluctant werewolf played by Earl Owensby in *Wolfman* (1979).

304. What 1981 film features a scene of two people turning into werewolves while having sex?

ANSWERS TO THE WOLF MAN (1941)

263. He spent eighteen years in the United States.   **264.** A telescope   **265.** A cane with a silver wolf's head mounted on the tip   **266.** Bela Lugosi   **267.** A pentagram   **268.** He is bitten in a fight with a werewolf, who turns out to be Lugosi.   **269.** False. Besides Lugosi, Talbot kills only one other person—an unlucky gravedigger.   **270.** Talbot is clubbed to death with his own silver-tipped cane, wielded by his father.   **271.** Lycanthropy   **272.** Even a man who is pure in heart / And says his prayers by night / May become a wolf when the wolfsbane blooms / And the autumn moon is bright.

305. What do the names of many characters in *The Howling* (1981) have in common?

306. Which 1984 film about werewolves is partially inspired by the fairy tale of Little Red Riding Hood?

307. Upon which Stephen King novella is *Silver Bullet* (1985) based?

308. How is young Marty Coslaw (Corey Haim) handicapped in *Silver Bullet*?

309. In what sport does Scott Howard (Michael J. Fox) suddenly excel after becoming *Teen Wolf* (1985)?

310. According to werewolf hunter Stefan Crosscoe (Christopher Lee) in *The Howling II* (1986), what is the only thing more fatal to werewolves than a silver bullet?

311. Name the 1991 film in which a heroic werewolf gets involved with a circus full of monsters.

312. What does Will Randall (Jack Nicholson) do for a living in *Wolf* (1994)?

Answers on page 63

ANSWERS TO AN AMERICAN WEREWOLF IN LONDON (1981)

273. John Landis   **274.** The Slaughtered Lamb   **275.** Jack tells David that the spirits of a werewolf's victims cannot rest until the wolf's bloodline is severed; since David has become a werewolf, he must kill himself to end the suffering of the living dead.   **276.** A deer   **277.** "Blue Moon"   **278.** Six   **279.** Jack wants David to meet the restless spirits of his victims; they also suggest ways in which David can best kill himself.   **280.** *See You Next Wednesday* (This is a running joke in John Landis's films; this title appears in some form in all the movies he directs.)   **281.** False. This film points out that regular bullets are sufficient to kill werewolves; interestingly, silver has nothing to do with genuine werewolf legends. The lore of using silver bullets, knives, etc., to kill them is an invention of the movies.   **282.** *An American Werewolf in Paris*

LON CHANEY

THE FIRST NAME in the history of early American horror films is simply Chaney. Born Leonidas Chaney on April 1, 1883, in Colorado Springs, Colorado, Chaney was the son of deaf-mute parents. (His grandmother founded the Deaf and Blind State Institute of Colorado.) Chaney communicated with his mother and father through facial expressions and pantomime, a talent that was to take him to the heights of fame in the era of silent films.

As a youth, Chaney, who had three siblings, worked at the Grand Opera House in Colorado Springs, where he did odd jobs and filled in on the stage in small roles. During tourist season, he and his brother guided sightseers to Pikes Peak via the thirty-odd burros they owned.

In his late teen years, Chaney left Colorado to perform a play he had co-written. He later worked with other acting troupes, barnstormed the country, eventually married, and by 1912 had made his way to Hollywood.

Over the next eighteen years, the actor appeared in more than 150 movies and earned his nickname "the Man of a Thousand Faces" because of his ability to play a wide variety of roles and because of his expertise with makeup and his skill at inventing prosthetic devices. His characters often featured physical defects made all the

---

ANSWERS TO WEREWOLF FILMS FROM THE THIRTIES THROUGH THE SIXTIES

283. Dr. Wilfrid Glendon (Henry Hull) and Dr. Yogami (Warner Oland)   **284.** The mariphasa *lupino lumino*   **285.** The doctor uses a transfusion of wolf's blood.   **286.** Grave robbers accidentally expose his corpse to the rays of the full moon.   **287.** His lover, the gypsy (Elena Verdugo)   **288.** She inherits the curse from her mother.   **289.** False. For once the Wolf Man is actually cured of his affliction by the end of the movie!   **290.** *She-Wolf of London*   **291.** He is injected with an experimental treatment for radiation poisoning.   **292.** A slumming Lon Chaney Jr.   **293.** Eighteenth-century Spain   **294.** His family's unconditional love   **295.** Mr. Swift (Curt Lowens), the school superintendent   **296.** Paul Naschy   **297.** Count Dracula, the Frankenstein Monster, and a mummy

more real by Chaney's method of working in pain because of the wires, ropes, or other tricks he used to portray these poor tortured souls.

While his roles were often those of villains and people with bizarre or grotesque physical features, Chaney enamored filmgoers with his acting prowess for eliciting their empathy. He first gained attention in 1919 for a part in *The Miracle Man.*

Chaney wrote scripts and directed films for Universal, starting in 1915, but his indelible characterizations are those for which he is most remembered, notably such roles as a legless master criminal in 1920's *The Penalty,* tormented bellringer Quasimodo (Chaney wore seventy pounds of gimmickry to appear realistic) in *The Hunchback of Notre Dame* in 1923, *The Phantom of the Opera* in 1925, and *London After Mid-*

Two of Lon Chaney's most famous roles are the Hunchback of Notre Dame (below left, whisking away Patsy Ruth Miller in 1923) and the Phantom of the Opera (below right, with Mary Philbin in 1925).

ANSWERS TO WEREWOLF FILMS FROM THE SEVENTIES THROUGH THE NINETIES

298. The Devil's Advocates   **299.** *The Werewolf of Washington*   **300.** Kerwin Matthews
301. *The Beast Must Die,* co-starring Peter Cushing   **302.** Paris   **303.** Colin Glasgow
304. *The Howling*   **305.** They are named after directors of previous werewolf movies.
306. *The Company of Wolves*   **307.** *Cycle of the Werewolf*   **308.** He is paralyzed and confined to a wheelchair.   **309.** Basketball   **310.** A titanium bullet   **311.** *Howling VI—The Freaks*
312. He is a book editor.

night in 1927. Some of his greatest roles were made under the guidance of director Tod Browning for MGM.

Chaney made only one sound film, a remake of his 1925 silent flick *The Unholy Three*, which was released in 1930, a mere month before his death of throat cancer that year. His life was retold on film in 1957 when James Cagney starred as Chaney in *Man of a Thousand Faces*.

Among Chaney's other film credits are *Treasure Island* (1920), *Oliver Twist* (1921), *The Monster* (1925), *He Who Gets Slapped* (1926), *Tell It to the Marines* (1927), *The Unknown* (1927), *Mockery* (1928), and *While the City Sleeps* (1928).

LON CHANEY JR.

L ON CHANEY JR. was born Creighton Chaney on February 10, 1906, in Oklahoma City, Oklahoma, while his acting parents were on tour. He made his first stage appearance as a babe of six months in one of his parents' plays.

Chaney Jr. worked all sorts of jobs, mainly as a plumber, before finally entering films, the field that had made his father a star during the silent era. In

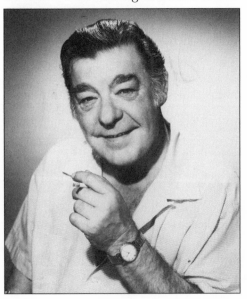

the 1930s, Chaney played lots of small parts and was billed as Creighton, but by 1935 he began calling himself Lon Chaney Jr. in order to boost his career.

His first role of importance was that of Lennie to Burgess Meredith's George in *Of Mice and Men* in 1940. Afterward, Universal signed the actor with the intent of casting him in horror films. Chaney's earliest major role was as the title character in 1941's *The Wolf Man*, but he then appeared as a variety of horror characters.

"I've played 'em all," the actor told an interviewer in the early 1960s. "Most of 'em were the second time around— Frankenstein, the Mummy, Dracula, but the Wolf Man was mine, all alone. I played him six times.

"All the best of the monsters played for sympathy," Chaney said. "That goes for my father, [Boris] Karloff, myself, and all the others. They all won the audience's sympathy. Why, the Wolf Man didn't want to do all those bad things; he was forced into them."

Lon Chaney Jr. growled his way (above left) through Dracula vs. Frankenstein *(1971), but his trademark persona was that of the Wolf Man (above right).*

In his later years, Chaney provided many good character roles, including that of the retired sheriff in *High Noon* (1952). He also made a number of guest appearances on episodic television shows (mainly westerns) of the 1950s and 1960s. Chaney died in 1973 from throat cancer, the same disease that claimed his father's life. His last film was *Dracula vs. Frankenstein* (1971).

Among the actor's other noteworthy films are *The Ghost of Frankenstein* (1942), *The Mummy's Tomb* (1943), *Frankenstein Meets the Wolf Man* (1943), *Son of Dracula* (1943), *House of Frankenstein* (1944), *Abbott and Costello Meet Frankenstein* (1948), *I Died a Thousand Times* (1955), *The Cyclops* (1957), *The Alligator People* (1959), and *Dr. Terror's Gallery of Horrors* (1965).

Top 5 Man into Beast Movies

Dr. Jekyll and Mr. Hyde (1932)
The Werewolf of London (1935)
The Wolf Man (1941)
The Howling (1980)
The Curse of the Werewolf (1961)

Claire Bloom and Julie Harris share screams in The Haunting *(1963).*

4

GHOSTS AND HAUNTED HOUSES

Once the door is locked, there is no way out. The windows have bars a jail would be proud of, and the only door to the outside locks like a vault.

—Frederick Loren (Vincent Price) in *House on Haunted Hill* (1958)

THE HAUNTING (1963)

313. What is the name of the haunted mansion in this film?

314. How many people spend the entire night in the house?

315. What actor plays Luke, who is due to inherit the place?

316. Which room is "the cold, rotten heart of the house"?

317. How old is the mansion?

318. In what room did Abigail's companion hang herself?

319. What actress plays a character whose thoughts are heard ("the house wants me") as the film progresses?

320. What frightens the two women the most the first night they spend in the house?

321. Which character's name is written on the wall by an unseen force?

322. What is Dr. John Markaway's profession?

Answers on page 68

THE UNINVITED (1944)

323. What is the name of the haunted mansion?

324. How did the former owner, Mary Meredith, die there?

325. What sound is heard at night in the house?

326. What is the profession of Rick Fitzgerald, who buys the house with his sister, Pamela?

327. Who plays the haunted young Stella, for whom Rick writes "Stella by Starlight"?

328. What fragrance of perfume fills a room when a particular ghost is near?

329. For what reason does the doctor come one night to visit Stella, Rick, and Pam?

330. What object does Rick throw at a ghost?

Answers on page 70

GENERAL QUESTIONS (SILENTS THROUGH THE 1950S)

331. In *The Bat* (1959), which former *Little Rascals* star gets spooked with Agnes Moorehead and Vincent Price?

332. There are four films with this title, but the 1927 silent version is the granddaddy of the "old dark house mysteries," according to movie critic Leonard Maltin. What is the title?

333. Adapted from J. B. Priestley's novel *Benighted, The Old Dark House* (1932) features what actor as Morgan the butler in his first starring role?

334. What was the first sound horror film?

335. What role do Charles Laughton, John Gielgud, and Patrick Stewart have in common?

336. Who played the spine-breaking Creeper in *House of Horror* in 1946?

337. What disfiguring disease did this actor have?

338. What was this actor's last film as the Creeper?

Answers on page 70

ANSWERS TO THE HAUNTING (1963)

313. Hill House   **314.** Four   **315.** Russ Tamblyn   **316.** The nursery   **317.** Ninety years old   **318.** The library   **319.** Julie Harris   **320.** Loud pounding on the wall and door **321.** Eleanor   **322.** Parapsychologist

Vincent Price has his sinister look down to perfection for House on Haunted Hill *(1958).*

HOUSE ON HAUNTED HILL (1958)

339. How many people does Vincent Price invite to spend the night in the haunted house?

340. What is their cash reward if they can stay all night long?

341. What actor portrays Watson Pritchard, the owner of the house?

342. Who plays the pilot hero of the film?

343. What is "Emergo"?

344. How many people have been murdered in the house in previous years?

345. What does Frederic offer his wife, Annabelle, if she will leave him?

346. What are the party favors?

347. What are the hours the guests have to stay in the house to collect their rewards?

348. Who is listed in the closing credits as being played "by himself"?

Answers on page 71

Patrick Swayze plays a ghost who realizes that he can be heard by psychic Oda Mae Brown (Whoopi Goldberg), a charlatan who discovers her powers are authentic, in Ghost *(1990).*

GENERAL QUESTIONS (1960S THROUGH 1990S)

349. Who plays the host of radio show *Manhattan Mystery Theater* in 1986's *Haunted Honeymoon*?
350. Where do most of the killings take place in *Ruby* (1978)?
351. What is the name of the female killer in *Ruby*?
352. Who portrays the governess in *The Innocents* (1961)?
353. On what novel is *The Innocents* based?

ANSWERS TO THE UNINVITED (1944)

323. Windwood   **324.** She fell off a cliff onto the rocks below.   **325.** A woman crying **326.** Music critic and composer   **327.** Gail Russell   **328.** Mimosa   **329.** To hold a séance **330.** A candlelabrum

ANSWERS TO GENERAL QUESTIONS (SILENTS THROUGH THE 1950s)

331. Darla Hood   **332.** *The Cat and the Canary*   **333.** Boris Karloff   **334.** *The Terror* (1928), with "spine-chilling Vitaphone effects" that included the moaning wind, screeching doors, eerie organ music, and piercing screams   **335.** All three were *The Canterville Ghost* (1944, 1986, 1996).   **336.** Rondo Hatton   **337.** Acromegaly   **338.** *The Brute Man*

354. What Southern writer worked on the screenplay for *The Innocents?*

355. What child star in *The Innocents* was an adult star in *The Legend of Hell House* (1973)?

356. Who plays Julia in *The Haunting of Julia* (1977)?

357. What TV star had the title role in *The Haunting of Helen Walker,* a 1995 TV remake of *The Innocents?*

358. Who plays a bewitching housekeeper in 1960's *13 Ghosts?*

359. What did patrons have to wear in order to see the ghosts in *13 Ghosts?*

360. What is William Katt's occupation in *House* (1986)?

361. Who plays the parapsychologist who comes to see George C. Scott's place in *The Changeling* (1980)?

362. Who plays the scam artist who chases ghosts out of haunted houses in *The Frighteners* (1996)?

363. What actors play the four old men, members of the Chowder Society, who share a dark secret in *Ghost Story* (1981)?

364. In *Lady in White* (1988), where does Frankie (Luke Haas) witness the ghostly murder?

365. What employee beckons Professor Ash (Aidan Quinn), an exposer of frauds and spiritualists, to come check out the sights and sounds of Edbrook in *The Haunted* (1995)?

Answers on page 73

THE AMITYVILLE HORROR (1979)

366. In what state is Amityville located?

367. Who plays Father Delaney?

368. The theme music for *The Amityville Horror* (1979) was originally written for (but not used in) what horror classic?

369. In which of the *Amityville* films does Meg Ryan appear?

370. Who wrote the novel *The Amityville Horror,* basis for the movies?

Answers on page 73

ANSWERS TO HOUSE ON HAUNTED HILL (1958)

339. Five **340.** $10,000 **341.** Elisha Cook Jr. **342.** Richard Long **343.** A flying skeleton that came hovering over the heads of patrons as this film ran in certain theaters (director William Castle's gimmick) **344.** Seven **345.** $1 million **346.** Miniature coffins with loaded pistols inside **347.** Midnight until 8 A.M. **348.** The skeleton "Emergo"

POLTERGEIST (1982)

371. Who cowrote the story and was a producer for *Poltergeist* (1982)?

372. What is Carol Anne's catch phrase in *Poltergeist?*

373. What is Carol Anne's catch phrase in *Poltergeist II* (1986)?

374. What 1940s movie is on the bedroom television early in *Poltergeist?*

375. What is the name of actress Zelda Rubinstein's character in all three *Poltergeist* films?

376. Who plays Carol Anne in all three *Poltergeist* films?

377. What is Carol Anne's last name?

378. What happens to the family house at the end of *Poltergeist?*

379. How old is Carol Anne in *Poltergeist?*

380. Which actor was stabbed to death after the filming of *Poltergeist?*

Craig T. Nelson and JoBeth Willliams are baffled by a mysterious force that irresistibly draws their young daughter (Heather O'Rourke) to the television set in Poltergeist *(1982).*

381. Which actor died between the filming of *Poltergeist II* and *Poltergeist III* (1988)?

382. Which actor died after the filming and just prior to the release of *Poltergeist III*?

383. What is the name of Noble Craig's character in *Poltergeist II*?

384. What was the film's campaign slogan?

Answers on page 74

A NIGHTMARE ON ELM STREET (1984)

385. Who wrote and directed *A Nightmare on Elm Street*?

386. Who plays Freddy Krueger?

387. What color is Freddy's blood?

388. What are Freddy's theme colors (even down to his suspenders)?

389. Who plays Nancy Thompson in *A Nightmare on Elm Street* and two sequels?

390. In what two films in the *Nightmare* series does Johnny Depp appear?

391. What performer plays Freddy Krueger's father?

392. In which *Nightmare* film does Wes Craven play himself?

393. In which *Nightmare* film do Roseanne and Tom Arnold (horror of horrors!) appear?

394. Complete this little ditty: One, two, Freddy's coming for you / Three, four, better lock your door / Five, six, grab your crucifix . . .

Answers on page 75

ANSWERS TO GENERAL QUESTIONS (1960s THROUGH 1990s)

349. Gene Wilder **350.** A drive-in theater that shows horror films **351.** Leslie **352.** Deborah Kerr **353.** Henry James's *Turn of the Screw* **354.** Truman Capote **355.** Pamela Franklin **356.** Mia Farrow **357.** Valerie Bertinelli **358.** Margaret Hamilton **359.** Ghostviewers **360.** Horror novelist **361.** Barry Morse **362.** Michael J. Fox **363.** Fred Astaire, Melvyn Douglas, Douglas Fairbanks Jr., and John Houseman **364.** In the shool cloakroom **365.** The Nanny (Anna Massey)

ANSWERS TO THE AMITYVILLE HORROR (1979)

366. New York (Long Island) **367.** Rod Steiger **368.** *The Exorcist* **369.** *Amityville 3-D* (a.k.a. *Amityville: The Demon*) **370.** Jay Anson

WILLIAM CASTLE

NO ONE HAS ever liked to scare the public more than inimitable film-maker William Castle. Born in New York City on April 24, 1914, Castle was acting on Broadway by the time he was fifteen. At eighteen, Castle was directing a revival of *Dracula* on Broadway, and before heading for Hollywood, he wrote and directed for radio in the 1930s.

In 1944 Castle won the New York Film Critics Award for the year's best mystery with *The Whistler*. More than one hundred other feature films followed. Among them were *The Crime Doctor's Warning (1945)*, *The Fat Man (1951)*, *The Mark of the Whistler (1944)*, and several westerns.

Finally, in 1955, Castle started his own film company and began producing and directing the films that would make him the gimmick king of all time—motion pictures such as *Macabre* (1958), *House on Haunted Hill* (1958), *The Tingler* (1959), *Thirteen Ghosts* (1960), *Homicidal* (1961), *Zotz!* (1962), *The Old Dark House* (1962), *Strait-Jacket* (1964), *The Night Walker* (1964), *I Saw What You Did* (1965), *The Spirit Is Will-*

ing (1966), *Rosemary's Baby* (1968), *Shanks* (1974), and *Bug* (1975).

He told an interviewer in the early 1970s that his ghoulish ways all began after he saw the French frightener *Diabolique:* "I came out of the theater and there was a line around the block. I realized then that people like to be scared."

At that point, he mortgaged his house to make 1958's *Macabre*, a quickie but a spooky film. When he realized it was far from a masterpiece,

---

ANSWERS TO POLTERGEIST (1982)

371. Steven Spielberg **372.** "They're here." **373.** "They're back." **374.** *A Guy Named Joe,* which Spielberg remade as *Always* (1989) **375.** Tangina (Barrons) **376.** Heather O'Rourke **377.** Freeling **378.** It's pulled into a black hole. **379.** Five years old **380.** Dominique Dunne **381.** Julian Beck (Kane) **382.** Heather O'Rourke **383.** Vomit Creature **384.** "It knows what scares you."

Castle came up with the idea of insuring audience members for $1,000 each against being scared to death. The film brought in $2 million.

Castle, the "Gimmick Genius," was known for loading theater houses with fright-producing gadgets such as hot-wired seats, floating glow-in-the-dark skeletons above the audience, and offering Lloyd's of London insurance policies and Ghostviewers.

He was paid due tribute (including a movie within a movie) in *Matinee* (1993) as John Goodman portrayed Lawrence Woolsey, a Castle-like moviemaker. *Mant,* the movie-within-the-movie, was a flattering imitation of the genius of scary flicks exploitation.

Before his death of a heart attack on May 31, 1977, Castle shared his story in the autobiographical *Step Right Up! I'm Gonna Scare the Pants Off America* (1976).

KING OF THE CASTLE QUIZ

395. For which of his films did William Castle give out Ghostviewers?

396. Who was the first big-time star to work with Castle (in the movie *Strait-Jacket*)?

397. In what Castle film does a character tell the audience that, in order to survive, they need to scream for their lives?

398. What Castle movie featured Emergo?

399. In what film did Castle ask the audience at the end if the culprit onscreen should live or die?

400. What 1975 film featured Castle portraying a director?

Answers below

TOP 5 GHOSTS AND HAUNTED HOUSES MOVIES

The Haunting (1963)
House on Haunted Hill (1958)
Poltergeist (1982)
House of the Long Shadows (1982)
The Innocents (1961)

ANSWERS TO A NIGHTMARE ON ELM STREET (1984)

385. Wes Craven **386.** Robert Englund **387.** Green **388.** Red and green **389.** Heather Langenkamp **390.** *A Nightmare on Elm Street* (as Glen Lantz) and *Wes Craven's New Nightmare* (in a TV commercial) **391.** Alice Cooper **392.** *Wes Craven's New Nightmare* **393.** *Freddy's Dead: The Final Nightmare* **394.** Seven, eight, better stay up late / Nine, ten, never sleep again.

ANSWERS TO KING OF THE CASTLE QUIZ: **395.** *13 Ghosts* **396.** Joan Crawford **397.** *The Tingler* **398.** *House on Haunted Hill* **399.** *Mr. Sardonicus* **400.** *The Day of the Locust*

Barbara Steele is both victim and villain in Black Sunday *(1961).*

5

WITCHES AND WARLOCKS

We are *the weirdos, mister.*

—Nancy (Fairuza Balk) in *The Craft* (1996)

GENERAL QUESTIONS

401. What horror superstar plays Professor Driscoll in *Horror Hotel* (1960)?

402. What do the three witches in *Hocus Pocus* (1993) fly on instead of brooms?

403. Where do the children (Thora Birch and Omri Katz) live in *Hocus Pocus*?

404. *The Witches* (1990) was the final feature film project for what great puppeteer?

405. Who plays the hapless husband in *Weird Woman* (1944)?

406. Three witch movies, *Weird Woman* (1944), *Burn, Witch, Burn* (1962), and *Witches' Brew* (1980), were all based on what short story?

407. In Lana Turner's final feature film she plays a witch. Name the film.

408. What short actor plays the Imp in *The Undead* (1957)?

409. Who made her final feature film appearance in *The Witches* (1966)?

410. What is Tawny Kitaen's "witchboard" in *Witchboard* (1985)?

Answers on page 79

WARLOCKS, WIZARDS, AND MAGICIANS

411. Who stars as a witch-hunter in *Conqueror Worm* (1968) and *Cry of the Banshee* (1970)?

412. Who stars in *Simon, King of the Witches* (1971), as he curses "the establishment" and lives in a Los Angeles sewer?

413. Who stars as the mad doctor in the 1926 silent *The Magician*?

414. What magical role have both Sam Neill and Edward Woodward played thirteen years apart?

415. Who plays warlock Joseph Curwen in *The Haunted Palace* (1964)?

416. Who plays the warlock in pursuit of Sandra Dee in *The Dunwich Horror* (1970)?

417. What two famous actors are pursued by a witch in *Witchery* (1989)?

418. Who finds out his wife is a witch in *Daughters of Satan* (1972)?

419. Who plays the head of a coven that builds occult toys in a small town in *Necromancy* (1972)?

Jimmy Stewart meets up with a fetching witch in Kim Novak and her feline, Pyewacket, in Bell, Book, and Candle *(1958).*

In true testimony to the makeup artist's skill, Anjelica Huston plays the Grand High Witch Miss Ernst in The Witches *(1990).*

420. Who stars as the evil Roxor in *Chandu the Magician* (1932), and then returned two years later to portray the heroic Chandu in a sequel?
421. Who plays the philandering wife Vincent Price seeks revenge upon in *The Mad Magician* (1954)?
422. Who fakes death as a magician-hypnotist in *The Strange Mr. Gregory* (1946)?
423. Sandra Bullock and Nicole Kidman star as witch sisters in which 1998 film?
424. What is the name of the dummy in 1978's *Magic?*

Answers on page 80

THE WITCHES OF EASTWICK (1987)

425. Whose novel by the same name inspired *The Witches of Eastwick?*
426. What three actresses play the conniving witches?
427. Who plays Daryl Van Horne?
428. In what region of the United States is Eastwick located?
429. What actress, who once played Daniel Boone's daughter on television, plays Felicia Alden?

Answers on page 81

ANSWERS TO GENERAL QUESTIONS

401. Christopher Lee **402.** Vacuum cleaners **403.** Salem, Massachusetts **404.** Jim Henson **405.** Lon Chaney Jr. **406.** "Conjure Wife," by Fritz Leiber **407.** *Witches Brew* (1980) **408.** Billy Barty **409.** Joan Fontaine **410.** A Ouija board

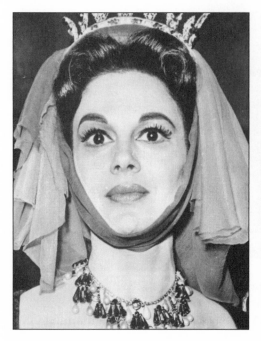 

Witches could be a tricky lot, as these two photographs show. Patricia Medina changes from queen to witch in Snow White and the Three Stooges *(1961).*

THE CRAFT (1996)

430. What are the first names of the four girls who experiment with witchcraft?

431. What is the name of Neve Campbell's character?

432. In what city do the young would-be witches attend school?

433. *The Craft* won a 1997 MTV Movie Award in what category?

434. What actress-director played Grace in *The Craft* and also played Carolyn in *The Amityville Horror*?

Answers on page 82

ANSWERS TO WARLOCKS, WIZARDS, AND MAGICIANS

411. Vincent Price   **412.** Andrew Prine   **413.** Paul Wegener   **414.** Merlin; Woodward in *Arthur the King* (TV, 1985) and Neill in *Merlin* (TV, 1998)   **415.** Vincent Price   **416.** Dean Stockwell   **417.** David Hasselhoff and Linda Blair   **418.** Tom Selleck   **419.** Orson Welles **420.** Bela Lugosi   **421.** Eva Gabor   **422.** Edmund Lowe   **423.** *Practical Magic*   **424.** Fats

Julian Sands (left) and Richard E. Grant are magical rivals in Warlock *(1991).*

WARLOCK (1991)

435. Who plays Warlock in 1991's *Warlock?*

436. Who directed *Warlock?*

437. In what city does the modern-day portion of *Warlock*'s activity take place?

438. In what city does *Warlock*'s time travel begin?

439. In what year does Warlock begin his time travel?

440. Who is Warlock's pursuer through the centuries of time travel?

441. What is it that Warlock wants?

442. What might happen if the Warlock succeeds in his quest?

443. What is the name of the sequel to *Warlock?*

444. What legendary character actor, who played Pruneface in 1990's *Dick Tracy,* appears in the 1993 sequel to *Warlock?*

Answers on page 83

ANSWERS TO THE WITCHES OF EASTWICK (1987)

425. John Updike's   **426.** Cher, Michelle Pfeiffer, and Susan Sarandon   **427.** Jack Nicholson
428. New England   **429.** Veronica Cartwright

WITCH ONE IS SHE?

Match the actress to her bewitching role.

445. Evelyn Ankers
446. Kay Walsh
447. Janet Blair
448. Billie Burke
449. Teri Garr
450. Margaret Hamilton
451. Allison Hayes
452. Anjelica Huston
453. Patrica Jessel
454. Tawny Kitaen
455. Veronica Lake
456. Angela Lansbury
457. Robyn Lively
458. Patricia Medina
459. Bette Midler
460. Kim Novak
461. Jan White
462. Kelly Preston
463. Winona Ryder
464. Barbara Steele

A. *The Witches* (1966)
B. *Bedknobs and Broomsticks* (1971)
C. *Bell, Book, and Candle* (1959)
D. *Burn, Witch, Burn* (1962)
E. *The Crucible* (1996)
F. Glinda, the Good Witch of the North in *The Wizard of Oz* (1939)
G. *Hocus Pocus* (1993)
H. *Season of the Witch* (1973)
I. *Horror Hotel* (1960)
J. *I Married a Witch* (1942)
K. *The She-Beast* (1965)
L. *Snow White and the Three Stooges* (1961)
M. *Spellbinder* (1988)
N. *Teen Witch* (1989)
O. *The Undead* (1956)
P. *Weird Woman* (1944)
Q. *The Witches* (1990)
R. *Witches' Brew* (1980)
S. *Witchboard* (1985)
T. The Wicked Witch of the East in *The Wizard of Oz* (1939)

Answers on page 84

ANSWERS TO THE CRAFT (1996)

430. Sarah, Nancy, Bonnie, and Rochelle   **431.** Bonnie   **432.** Los Angeles   **433.** Best Fight (between witches Sarah and Nancy, with knives)   **434.** Helen Shaver

THE WICKER MAN (1973)

465. What famous British mystery writer wrote the screenplay of *The Wicker Man*?

466. What prompts police officer Neil Howie (Edward Woodward) to visit Summerisle?

467. How does Sergeant Howie travel from the mainland to the island?

468. For what fruit is Summerisle most famous?

469. Who plays Willow McGregor, the innkeeper's daughter?

470. According to Lord Summerisle (Christopher Lee), who brought new strains of crops—and paganism—to the island in 1867?

471. What does Sergeant Howie find in the grave of Rowan Morrison?

472. What fate does Sergeant Howie believe is in store for Rowan?

473. TRUE OR FALSE: Lord Summerisle wears a woman's wig and skirt while leading the May Day parade.

474. According to Lord Summerisle, what "rare gift" will the pagans bestow upon Sergeant Howie?

Answers on page 85

ANSWERS TO WARLOCK (1991)

435. Julian Sands   **436.** Steve Miner   **437.** Los Angeles   **438.** Boston   **439.** 1691
440. Redferne   **441.** The Grand Grimoire, the devil's bible   **442.** The creation of the world could be undone.   **443.** *Warlock: The Armageddon* (1993)   **444.** R. G. Armstrong

VINCENT PRICE

PROBABLY THE MOST famous horror star since the glory days of Boris Karloff and Bela Lugosi, Vincent Price's velvety voice and sinister smile made him a natural choice to play villains of all kinds. But unlike his peers in the terror game, Price's fearsome screen persona was somewhat tempered with an element of fun. Indeed, the "Merchant of Menace" is remembered as much for his dark humor and onscreen mugging as for the murder and mayhem he committed in many of his one hundred films.

Vincent Leonard Price Jr. was born on May 27 (he shares a birthday with Christopher Lee), 1911, in Saint Louis. His father was president of the National Candy Company, and young Vincent grew up in upper-middle-class prosperity. He earned a degree in art history at Yale and began work on a master's thesis at the University of London, but an interest in acting changed his life. He made his professional debut in a British production of *Chicago* in 1935. Later that same year he was cast as Prince Albert in *Victoria Regina* and re-created the role on Broadway, opposite Helen Hayes.

Price headed for Hollywood in 1938, where he made his film debut in the screwball comedy *Service De Luxe*. Although Price was at first groomed for leading-man status, character parts, including the title role in *The Invisible Man Returns* (1940), quickly followed. In 1944 he portrayed Gene Tierney's slimy fiancé in *Laura*, a classic murder mystery that became Price's favorite among his own movies. Typed as a heavy, the actor starred in the 3-D horror hit *House of Wax* in 1953. Throughout the 1950s a variety of roles came his way, but he made his greatest impact in thrillers like *The Fly* (1958) and two William

---

ANSWERS TO WITCH ONE IS SHE?

445. P   **446.** A   **447.** D   **448.** F   **449.** R   **450.** T   **451.** O   **452.** Q   **453.** I   **454.** S
455. J   **456.** B   **457.** N   **458.** L   **459.** G   **460.** C   **461.** H   **462.** M   **463.** E   **464.** K

Castle projects: *House on Haunted Hill* (1958) and *The Tingler* (1959).

In 1960 Price's association with American International Pictures and Roger Corman began with *The House of Usher*, the first in a long line of Edgar Allan Poe adaptations, the best of which was the last, *Tomb of Ligeia* (1964). As early as 1963 Price was spoofing his macabre image in *The Raven*, a horror comedy that teamed him with fellow fear icons Boris Karloff and Peter Lorre as well as an up-and-coming thespian, Jack Nicholson.

But there was no trace of comedy in *Witchfinder General,* also known as *The Conqueror Worm,* a grim 1968 piece of historical horror in which Price portrayed Matthew Hopkins, a witch-hunter who sadistically tortures innocent people in seventeenth-century England. Meanwhile, Price appeared in a number of mainstream pictures. Among his non-genre efforts were a western, *More Dead Than Alive* (1968), and the Elvis Presley vehicle *The Trouble with Girls* (1969).

In 1971 Price starred in the title role of *The Abominable Dr. Phibes.* This darkly campy tale about a disfigured musician's campaign against the doctors responsible for his wife's death initiated a series of similarly droll revenge thrillers, including a sequel, *Dr. Phibes Rises Again* (1972), *Theater of Blood* (1973), and *Madhouse* (1974, opposite Peter Cushing). By this time Price was

Vincent Price could play any role in any number of ways, from "serious" horror to parodying his image as a master of horror.

ANSWERS TO THE WICKER MAN (1973)

465. Anthony Shaffer, author of *Sleuth*   **466.** An anonymous letter requests Howie to investigate the disappearance of a young girl, Rowan Morrison.   **467.** He arrives in his sea plane.   **468.** Apples   **469.** Britt Ekland   **470.** His grandfather, a Victorian scientist and "freethinker"   **471.** The body of a hare   **472.** Howie believes she will be sacrificed to appease the harvest gods.   **473.** True   **474.** "A martyr's death"

firmly established as the modern terror king, not only in the nation's cinemas, but on television as well. He often tweaked his gruesome reputation on comedy programs like *Rowan and Martin's Laugh-In* and *The Carol Burnett Show.* In 1977 he began touring in *Diversions and Delights,* a one-man show about the life of Oscar Wilde, which met with great acclaim. Along with his wife, Coral Browne, Price starred in a short-lived sci-fi television series, *Time Express* (1979). His most notable work on the small screen, however, was the PBS anthology *Mystery!* which he hosted for ten years, beginning in 1980.

Price worked with Christopher Lee, Peter Cushing, and John Carradine in *The House of the Long Shadows* (1982), an old-fashioned haunted house flick. In 1987 he appeared with Bette Davis, Lillian Gish, and Ann Sothern in *The Whales of August,* a sen-

Vincent Price was at his wicked best as Frederick Loren, a fabulously wealthy man who invites several strangers to stay at an eerie house that's been the site of seven murders. From its bloodcurdling opening shriek to its twist-upon-twist finale, the movie became legendary among the genre.

sitive drama about aging sisters coming to terms with their mortality. His last feature film role was one of his best: He was the inventor of Johnny Depp in *Edward Scissorhands* (1990).

Price was married three times. He fathered a son, Vincent Barrett Price, by his first wife, Edith Barrett, and a daughter, Victoria, by his second wife, Mary Grant. In 1974 he married Coral Browne, an acclaimed British actress whom he met on the set of *Theater of Blood*. They remained together until her death on May 29, 1991. His own health impaired by Parkinson's disease and lung cancer, Price died on October 25, 1993.

A Renaissance man of sorts, Price wrote several books, primarily about cooking and art, but he never published a formal autobiography. Several books about Hollywood's "Merchant of Menace" have been published over the years, most recently Lucy Chase Williams's *The Complete Films of Vincent Price* (1995) and *Vincent Price* (1998), edited by Gary and Sue Svehla.

TOP 5 WITCHES AND WARLOCKS MOVIES

The Conqueror Worm (1968)
Black Sunday (1960)
The Witches of Eastwick (1987)
The Dunwich Horror (1969)
Warlock (1991)

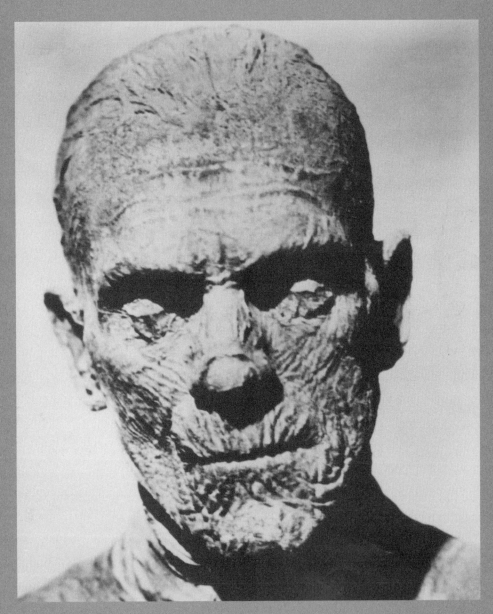
Boris Karloff stars as the central character in The Mummy *(1932).*

6

THE
UNDEAD

He went for a little walk!

—Ralph Norton (Bramwell Fletcher) in
The Mummy (1932)

THE MUMMY (1932)

475. In the opening of the film, the title is seen inscribed on what landmark?

476. Imhotep steals what sacred scroll?

477. What is the curse for opening the casket?

478. How does Bramwell Fletcher's character eventually die (not shown onscreen)?

479. What is Imhotep's punishment?

480. In what city is most of the action set?

481. With what device can Ardeth Bey see the present as well as the past?

482. What does Edward Van Sloan give David Manners to keep him safe?

483. Helen is the reincarnation of whom?

484. With what item does Ardeth Bey wield hypnotic power over humans?

Answers on page 91

MORE MUMMY

485. Name the four sequels to the original Universal production of *The Mummy*.
486. What was the Mummy's name in the sequels?
487. Who played the Mummy in the first sequel?
488. Who played the Mummy in the other three sequels?

Answers on page 92

THE MUMMY (1959)

489. Who plays Kharis, the Egyptian high priest who is mummified for attempting to revive his beloved, Princess Ananka?
490. Besides mummification, how is Kharis punished for his crime?

The Curse of the Mummy's Tomb *(1964) features Dickie Owen as the great bandaged one.*

491. Who warns the expedition led by archaeologist Stephen Banning (Felix Aylmer) not to desecrate the tomb of Ananka?

492. Why doesn't John Banning (Peter Cushing) enter the tomb with his father?

493. What causes Stephen Banning to go insane?

494. Name the facility where Stephen Banning is incarcerated.

495. How does the crate containing Kharis's undead remains wind up in an English swamp?

496. How is Isobel (Yvonne Furneaux) able to save her husband, John, from Kharis?

497. How is Kharis finally destroyed?

498. TRUE OR FALSE: Karnak, the god worshiped by Kharis and Ananka, is actually one of the most important deities in Egyptian mythology.

Answers on page 93

THE MUMMY (1999)

499. What is the name of the Mummy in this 1999 version of the story?

500. What is the name of the treasure hunter played by Brendan Fraser?

501. When was the Mummy buried?

502. In what decade is the grave of the Mummy disturbed from his rest?

503. In what city was the Mummy buried?

Answers on page 93

ANSWERS TO THE MUMMY (1932)

475. One of the Egyptian pyramids   **476.** The Scroll of Thoth   **477.** Death   **478.** He dies laughing in a straitjacket.   **479.** He is buried alive.   **480.** Cairo   **481.** His pool of remembrance   **482.** A charm of Isis   **483.** Princess Anck-es-en-Amon   **484.** A ring on his left hand

NIGHT OF THE LIVING DEAD (1968)

504. As the film opens, where are Johnny (Russell Streiner) and Barbara (Judith O'Dea) going?

505. With what line does Johnny taunt his sister just before he is attacked by a flesh-eating ghoul (Bill Hinzman)?

506. TRUE OR FALSE: Barbara enthusiastically helps Ben (Duane Jones) board up the isolated farmhouse where they both take refuge from the ghouls.

507. Where have Harry Cooper (Karl Hardman) and the others been hiding since before Ben and Barbara arrived at the farmhouse?

508. How does the group learn that the recent dead are coming back to life and attacking the living?

509. What happens to Tom (Keith Wayne) and Judy (Judith Ridley) when they try to escape from the zombie-besieged house?

510. According to Sheriff McLelland (George Kosana), how does one best defend oneself against the living dead?

511. How is Helen Cooper (Marylin Eastman) killed?

512. Who is the only one of the group to survive the night of horror?

513. What is this character's fate?

Answers on page 94

ZOMBIE MOVIES FROM THE 1930s THROUGH THE 1960s

514. Name the zombie master portrayed by Bela Lugosi in *White Zombie* (1932).

515. What Egyptian artifact allegedly grants immortality to Professor Morlant (Boris Karloff) in *The Ghoul* (1933)?

516. In what Southeast Asian country are zombie soldiers being created in *Revolt of the Zombies* (1936)?

517. Why does Dr. von Altermann (John Carradine) create zombies in *Revenge of the Zombies* (1943)?

518. Name the comedy team that runs afoul of Bela Lugosi in *Zombies on Broadway* (1945).

519. What do the *Zombies of Mora Tau* (1957) guard?

ANSWERS TO MORE MUMMY

485. *The Mummy's Hand, The Mummy's Tomb, The Mummy's Ghost,* and *The Mummy's Curse*
486. Kharis   **487.** Tom Tyler   **488.** Lon Chaney Jr.

In I Walked with a Zombie *(1943), Christine Gordon remains in a catatonic state while James Ellison escorts her about.*

520. Who plays the cemetery caretaker who discovers that moving around pins on a graveyard map causes people either to die or to return from the dead in *I Bury the Living* (1958)?

521. What 1959 thriller involves shrunken heads and an Ecuadorian zombie?

522. Why is Kieron Moore murdering innocent bystanders for their hearts in *Dr. Blood's Coffin* (1961)?

523. Why does Squire Hamilton (John Carson) revive the bodies of his deceased neighbors in *Plague of the Zombies* (1966)?

Answers on page 95

ANSWERS TO THE MUMMY (1959)

489. Christopher Lee **490.** His tongue is cut out. **491.** Mehemet Bey (George Pastell), a disciple of Karnak **492.** John's leg is broken, so he can't enter the tomb. **493.** After reading from the Scroll of Life, Banning is confronted by the revived Kharis and goes mad. **494.** Engerfield Nursing Home for the Mentally Disordered **495.** It falls off the wagon hauling it to Mehemet's lair. **496.** Isobel resembles Ananka, so she orders Kharis to leave John alone. **497.** After being shot up by villagers, the Mummy sinks into the swamp. **498.** False. Karnak is a location in Egypt, not a deity.

ANSWERS TO THE MUMMY (1999)

499. Imhotep **500.** Rick O'Connell **501.** 1290 B.C. **502.** 1920s **503.** Hamunaptra

DAWN OF THE DEAD (1978)

524. In what state is *Dawn of the Dead* filmed and set?

525. Name the television station for which Francine (Gaylen Ross) and Stephen (David Emgee) work.

526. Why does a SWAT team attack an urban housing project?

527. What type of vehicle do Francine, Stephen, Peter (Ken Foree), and Roger (Scott H. Reiniger) use to escape the city?

528. What is the name of the mall in which the foursome set up house?

529. According to Stephen, why are the living dead attracted to the mall?

530. What physical condition complicates matters for Francine?

531. In what major department store does the group find most of the material they need for their "homestead"?

532. What do Peter and Roger do with the bodies of zombies killed in the mall?

533. How does director George Romero make a Hitchcock-style cameo appearance in *Dawn of the Dead*?

Answers on page 97

Undead comrades roam the countryside in the 1968 Night of the Living Dead *(left), which was remade in 1990 with a more upscale wardrobe (right).*

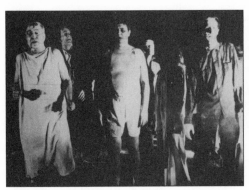 

ANSWERS TO NIGHT OF THE LIVING DEAD (1968)

504. To a rural cemetery to visit their father's grave   **505.** "They're coming to get you, Barbara!"   **506.** False. She lapses into catatonic shock.   **507.** The farmhouse's cellar
508. From television news reports   **509.** They are burned alive in Ben's exploding truck, and then their remains are devoured by the ghouls.   **510.** "Beat 'em or burn 'em; they go up pretty easy."   **511.** She is stabbed to death by her daughter, Karen (Kyra Schon), who has become a zombie.   **512.** Ben   **513.** He is mistakenly shot to death by one of the zombie-hunting posse.

ZOMBIE MOVIES FROM THE 1970S THROUGH THE 1990S

534. What do *The Corpse Grinders* (1971) make out of human remains?

535. What causes corpses to revive in *The Living Dead at the Manchester Morgue* (1974)?

536. Why does the title character need voodoo priest Baron Samedi (Don Pedro Colley) to provide her with an army of zombies in *Sugar Hill* (1974)?

537. Who plays the S.S. officer who commands Nazi zombies in *Shock Waves* (1977)?

538. In what 1979 film does an underwater zombie do battle with a shark?

539. In the "Father's Day" episode of *Creepshow* (1982), what does the corpse of Nate Grantham (John Amplas) demand as he kills his family?

540. Where does most of *Day of the Dead* (1985) take place?

541. TRUE OR FALSE: George Romero directed the horror-comedy *Return of the Living Dead* (1985).

542. Why does zombie victim Julie Walker (Mindy Clarke) mutilate herself with glass shards and other sharp objects in *Return of the Living Dead III* (1993)?

543. Who stars as a caretaker who is responsible for killing the living dead again in *Cemetery Man* (1995)?

544. Who wrote the story on which *The Body Snatcher* (1945) is based?

545. What famous horror stars appeared together for the last time in *The Body Snatcher*?

546. What war is the backdrop for *Isle of the Dead* (1945)?

547. How is the vision of Dr. Knox (Peter Cushing) impaired in *Mania* (1959)?

548. In what European city does *Mania* take place?

549. How does the motorcycle gang achieve immortality in *Psychomania* (1972)?

Answers on page 98

ANSWERS TO ZOMBIE MOVIES FROM THE 1930s THROUGH THE 1960s

514. Murder Legendre   **515.** The Eternal Light, which is a valuable jewel   **516.** Cambodia   **517.** He wants to raise an army of the undead to serve the Nazi cause.   **518.** Wally Brown and Alan Carney   **519.** An underwater treasure   **520.** Richard Boone   **521.** *The Four Skulls of Jonathan Drake*   **522.** The hearts will be used to revive the recently deceased "great men" of the world.   **523.** He uses them to work in his tin mine.

HAMMER STUDIOS

FOUNDED AS Exclusive Films in 1935 and initially devoted to the distribution of short subjects and reissued features, Hammer Film Productions began emphasizing original material in 1948. The majority of these were feature versions of popular English television shows, competently made but of little interest to audiences outside of Great Britain. But the unexpected popularity of a science fiction thriller called *The Quatermass Xperiment* (1955; U.S. title, *The Creeping Unknown*) convinced the company to explore other fantasy projects.

The Curse of Frankenstein (1957) broke new ground in screen terror. The plot centered around the scientist rather than the monster, and the film (in glorious Technicolor) featured an amount of gore and violence much greater than any seen in the old Boris Karloff *Frankenstein*. Furthermore, Hammer discovered two new horror stars in Peter Cushing (the baron) and Christopher Lee (the Creature).

Although the initial critical reception was hostile (one reviewer wrote, "I put it among the half dozen most repulsive films I have ever encountered"), *The Curse of Frankenstein* was an immediate popular sensation, eventually earning more than seventy times the cost of its production. Six sequels followed, all but one starring Cushing as the cold-eyed maker of monsters. But Hammer's most successful series was inaugurated in 1958 when *Dracula* (U.S. title, *Horror of Dracula*) grossed even more money than *The Curse of Frankenstein*. Through his association with the character of the count, Lee found a role he would make his own. And as vampire expert Dr. Van Helsing, Cushing revealed an even greater talent for destroying evil rather than creating it. Lee essayed the part six more times for Hammer. (The company also supplemented its earnings with nine non-Lee vampire pictures over the next fifteen years.)

Hammer made its reputation through glamour, horror, and mixing the two. One Million Years B.C. (1966) was a breakout movie for one of the studios first stars, Raquel Welch, but the studio found its best success through horror.

"Hammer Glamour" included such stars as Martine Beswick (left) and Caroline Munroe (right).

Hammer produced other shockers, such as *The Mummy* (1959), *The Hound of the Baskervilles* (1959), *The Two Faces of Dr. Jekyll* (1960), *Curse of the Werewolf* (1961), *Maniac* (1963), *The Gorgon* (1964), *The Plague of the Zombies* (1966), and *The Devil Rides Out* (1968). For a while, the studio continued to produce more mainstream films, but it soon became apparent that "Hammer Horror" was what the public demanded. In fact, the company's international success earned it the prestigious Queen's Award to Industry in 1968, an achievement that made even the harshest critics take notice.

In spite of relatively low budgets, Hammer's films were (in the early days, at least) produced with care and sophistication. The same technicians and actors were reunited time and again, including directors like Terence Fisher, Freddie Francis, and Val Guest; screenwriters Jimmy Sangster and Anthony Hinds (son of co-founder Will Hinds); and makeup artists Phil Leakey and Roy

---

ANSWERS TO DAWN OF THE DEAD (1978)

524. Pennsylvania **525.** WGON, Philadelphia **526.** The residents refuse to surrender their dead relatives to the authorities. **527.** Helicopter **528.** Monroeville Mall **529.** The ghouls instinctively return to places that were of great significance to them when they were alive. **530.** She is pregnant. **531.** J. C. Penney's **532.** They store the bodies in a large industrial freezer. **533.** He plays a television director at WGON.

Ashton. Production designer Bernard Robinson ingeniously redressed the same sets over and over, consistently making Hammer films look more expensive than they were. And composer James Bernard wrote magnificent scores for the Frankenstein and Dracula series, among others.

But arguably Hammer's most valuable assets were the actors. Cushing and Lee remained the firm's primary stars, but supporting performers like Michael Ripper, Thorley Walters, Andre Morell, Ralph Bates, and Shane Briant did their share to make patently absurd plots seem plausible. The company also gave future stars Oliver Reed and David Prowse (Darth Vader in *Star Wars*) good roles early in their careers. "Hammer Glamour," bestowed by such lovely leading ladies as Barbara Shelley, Martine Beswicke, Veronica Carlson, Ingrid Pitt, and Caroline Munro, also contributed to Hammer's longevity. Internationally renowned actresses like Ursula Andress, Raquel Welch, and Joan Collins also joined Hammer's ranks.

By 1970 the company was in its twilight. Many of the most creative minds behind Hammer Films had retired or passed away. A general decline in British film production affected the firm's ability to raise the necessary capital for new ventures. But perhaps Hammer's greatest shortcoming was an inability to change with the times. What was considered shocking in the late 1950s seemed tame by the standards of the 1970s. Instead of breaking new ground, Hammer tried unsuccessfully to recycle earlier formulas in films like *Scars of Dracula* (1970) and *Frankenstein and the Monster from Hell* (1974). Although Hammer's later efforts were often entertaining and inventive, they remained variations on familiar themes. The failure of *To the Devil—A Daughter* in 1976 spelled the end of Hammer Horror.

Hammer did, however, produce some interesting television shows in the 1980s. Rumors also continue to circulate that the company will return to feature-film production. New merchandising and video releases of the old movies provide some visibility for the company's current management. Perhaps like its most famous fiends, Count Dracula and Baron Frankenstein, Hammer will once again rise from the grave.

ANSWERS TO ZOMBIE MOVIES FROM THE 1970s THROUGH THE 1990s

534. Cat food   **535.** A government-sponsored pest-control machine that uses ultrasonic waves accidentally brings the dead to life   **536.** She uses them for revenge against the gangsters who murdered her boyfriend.   **537.** Peter Cushing   **538.** *Zombie* (a.k.a. *Zombie Flesh Eaters*)   **539.** "I want my cake!"   **540.** An underground military installation **541.** False   **542.** The pain delays her transformation into a brain-eating ghoul. **543.** Rupert Everett   **544.** Robert Louis Stevenson   **545.** Boris Karloff and Bela Lugosi **546.** Balkan war of 1912   **547.** He has a lazy eye.   **548.** Edinburgh, Scotland   **549.** They commit suicide and then roar out of their graves on their bikes.

HAMMER HORRORS

550. Perhaps foreshadowing things to come, one of the company's first productions was a horror film entitled *The Mystery of the Mary Celeste* (1935). What famous screen bogeyman starred in this picture?

551. Name the converted manor house at which most of Hammer's films were shot from 1951 to 1968.

552. Name the director most closely associated with Hammer's best films, including *Curse of Frankenstein* and *Horror of Dracula* (1958).

553. Name the rarely seen film in which Hammer addressed the serious subject of child molestation.

554. What is the connection between Hammer producer Anthony Hinds and screenwriter John Elder?

555. Provide the title of the Hammer film that starred Raquel Welch.

556. Hammer produced a feature version of the popular British television program *Man About the House* in 1974. What American sitcom was also based on this show?

557. What popular American movie star appeared in two films for Hammer— *The Nanny* (1965) and *The Anniversary* (1968)?

558. Who plays Peter Cushing's wife in *Fear in the Night* (1972)?

559. Other than Dracula films, what Hammer production was based on a novel by Bram Stoker?

560. What pop singer recorded a song entitled "Hammer Horror"?

561. How many films based on the novels of Dennis Wheatley did Hammer produce?

Answers on page 101

CHRISTOPHER LEE

Born Christopher Frank Carandini Lee on May 27 (he shares a birthday with Vincent Price), 1922, this actor holds a special distinction in the motion picture industry: He is truly the last of the great horror stars. It is a title that Lee has somewhat reluctantly accepted, having spent much of the last three decades attempting to escape his fearsome image. The effort has been fairly successful, but to the baby-boomer generation of fright fans, he will always be the screen's greatest Dracula.

Lee made his stage debut in a school production of *Julius Caesar* at the age of nine. Also in the cast was Patrick Macnee, future star of television's *The Avengers*. During World War II, Lee served as an intelligence officer in the Royal Air Force. An Italian cousin, actually Italy's ambassador to Great Britain, suggested Lee become a film actor. The young man's mother was not impressed. "Think of the appalling people you will meet!" was her shocked reaction.

Lee had one line in his motion picture debut, *Corridor of Mirrors* (1948). More bit parts followed over the years, including roles in *Hamlet* (1948) and *Moulin Rouge* (1952), films which also featured a young Peter Cushing in the cast, although the actors did not actually meet until years later. Lee's dark looks and towering six-foot-four-inch height, how-

ever, were liabilities that prevented him from getting major parts.

Matters improved substantially when Hammer Film Productions cast Lee as the Creature in *The Curse of Frankenstein* (1957), in which Cushing played Baron Frankenstein. The spectacular results revived the Gothic horror movie. Hammer paired its new stars again in *Dracula* (1958, a.k.a. *Horror of Dracula*). Lee's performance in the title role was so well received that he returned to it in six sequels for Hammer, plus he would imitate or parody the character in other films.

Over the next few years, Hammer cast Lee in numerous thrillers, often alongside Cushing. Among the best are *The Mummy* (1959), *The Hound of the Baskervilles* (1959), *The Terror of the*

Tongs (1961), *The Gorgon* (1964), and *The Devil Rides Out* (1968). Lee did not work exclusively for Hammer; he appeared in several films for rival studios, and he also made five appearances as Sax Rohmer's Oriental menace Fu Manchu, beginning with *The Face of Fu Manchu* in 1965.

Unhappy with the kinds of roles he was being offered and particularly weary of Hammer's treatment of the Dracula character, Lee focused his efforts on more mainstream fare in the 1970s. He was Scaramanga in the James Bond adventure *The Man with the Golden Gun* (1973) and made high-profile

On the facing page, Christopher Lee sinks his fangs into Isla Blair in Taste the Blood of Dracula *(1970), one of Lee's favorite and most well-known roles.*

ANSWERS TO HAMMER HORRORS

550. Bela Lugosi **551.** Bray Studios **552.** Terence Fisher **553.** *Never Take Sweets from a Stranger* (1961) **554.** They're one and the same. Hinds used Elder as a pseudonym.
555. *One Million Years B.C.* (1966), Hammer's most financially successful film **556.** *Three's Company* **557.** Bette Davis **558.** Joan Collins **559.** *Blood from the Mummy's Tomb* (1971), based on Stoker's *The Jewel of the Seven Stars* **560.** Kate Bush **561.** Three: *The Devil Rides Out* (U.S. title: *The Devil's Bride*, 1968), *The Lost Continent* (based on Wheatley's *Uncharted Seas*, 1968), and *To the Devil—A Daughter* (1976)

appearances in *The Three Musketeers* (1973), *Airport '77* (1977), and *Circle of Iron* (1979). But it was a horror-mystery film that gave the actor what remains his best role ever: the pagan aristocrat Lord Summerisle in *The Wicker Man* (1973). Alternately humorous and horrifying, Lee's contribution to this classic thriller clearly demonstrated he was capable of much more than baring his fangs and menacing screaming starlets.

The ordinarily somber actor demonstrated a taste for comedy, best exhibited in Steven Spielberg's *1941* (1979), *Serial* (1980, playing a gay motorcycle gang leader), *Gremlins 2: The New Batch* (1990), and *The Stupids* (1996). But he has not abandoned the genre that made him famous. Lee appeared with Price, Cushing, and John Carradine in *The House of the Long Shadows* (1982) and then hunted werewolves in *The Howling II* (1985). Yet perhaps his best recent film is *A Feast at Midnight* (1995), a charming "coming of age" comedy set in a British prep school. In 1999 Lee returned to familiar territory, making guest appearances in *Talos the Mummy* and Tim Burton's *Sleepy Hollow.*

Married since 1961 to the former Birgit Kroencke (their daughter Christina was born in 1963), Lee has remained active in his late seventies. He has written *Tall, Dark, and Gruesome,* an engaging 1977 autobiography that finally found an American publisher in 1999.

TOP 5 UNDEAD MOVIES

Dawn of the Dead (1979)
Night of the Living Dead (1968)
The Mummy (1932)
I Walked with a Zombie (1943)
The Mummy (1959)

PETER CUSHING

ALTHOUGH MOST HORROR-MOVIE stars were associated with the monsters and madmen they portrayed, England's Peter Cushing actually fought on the side of the angels more often than not. It is true that he came to cinematic prominence by making a monster out of Christopher Lee in *The Curse of Frankenstein* (1957), and he played to his widest audience as Grand Moff Tarkin, the evil Death Star commander in 1977's *Star Wars*. But for decades he was also the screen's definitive vampire hunter, Dr. Van Helsing, and he was the first actor since Basil Rathbone to play Sherlock Holmes in a full-length motion picture (*The Hound of the Baskervilles*, 1959).

In a film career that stretched over six decades, Cushing specialized in battling all manner of things that go bump in the night. He even played Doctor Who, Britain's most popular sci-fi television character, in two features. It is therefore fitting that his fans remember him as "the Gentle Man of Horror."

Born Peter Wilton Cushing on May 26, 1913, in Surrey, England, the future horror star became interested in acting by watching the onscreen exploits of silent cowboy star Tom Mix. Like many aspiring thespians before him, Cushing had to overcome his parents' objections to an acting career. He at first compromised by

working for a local surveying company by day and acting in amateur plays by night.

With his father's blessing and a one-way passage to America, however, Cushing sailed for Tinseltown in 1939. He found work almost immediately on James Whale's version of *The Man in the Iron Mask*. In all, Cushing appeared in seven features during his Hollywood sojourn. MGM seemed interested in grooming the young actor for stardom, but with the outbreak of World War II, he decided his place was back in England. He found work almost immediately, entertaining troops in a touring production of Noel Coward's *Private Lives*. He also found the love of his life

Peter Cushing in Count Dracula and His Vampire Bride *(a.k.a.* The Satanic Rites of Dracula, *1973).*

in his costar, actress Helen Beck, whom he married in 1943.

Cushing entered the British film industry in 1947, playing Osric in Laurence Olivier's adaptation of *Hamlet.* In the early 1950s Cushing became one of England's first major television stars, appearing most notably as the doomed Winston Smith in a terrifying version of *1984.* It was this performance that led to his casting as Victor Frankenstein in Hammer's landmark remake of the Mary Shelley classic. Ultimately Cushing re-created the character for Hammer in five more films, and for many people it remains the actor's most famous role.

The phenomenal worldwide success of *The Curse of Frankenstein* altered dra-matically the direction of Cushing's career. There were a few exceptions, but over the next twenty years, his primary source of income was derived from horror movies, often for Hammer. The company cast him as Van Helsing five times, beginning with 1958's *Dracula* (released in the U.S. as *Horror of Dracula*). Other Hammer horrors included *The Mummy* (1959), *Night Creatures* (1962), *The Gorgon* (1964), and the underrated *Twins of Evil* (1972). Cushing's other chillers included *Mania* (1959), *Dr. Terror's House of Horrors* (1964), *Scream and Scream Again* (1969), and *Tales from the Crypt* (1972).

Cushing's appearance in *Star Wars* introduced the actor to a new genera-tion of fans, but advancing age and failing health prevented his working

Above left, Cushing inspects the ankle chains that once held a vampire captive in The Brides of Dracula *(1960). On the right, he deals out five powerful hands in* Dr. Terror's House of Horrors *(1964).*

much longer. He joined fellow horror vets Christopher Lee, Vincent Price, and John Carradine for *The House of the Long Shadows* (1982) and spoofed his mad-scientist image in *Top Secret!* (1984), but after a supporting role in the time-travel fantasy *Biggles* (1986), he retired from acting.

In 1994 he reteamed with long-time friend and costar Lee to narrate *Flesh and Blood,* a British television documentary on Hammer Films. Cushing lost a long battle with cancer on August 11, 1994.

Perhaps because he rarely played monsters, Cushing's career has not received as much attention as those of Vincent Price and Christopher Lee. Deborah Del Vecchio and Tom Johnson examined his work in *Peter Cushing: The Gentle Man of Horror and His Ninety-One Films* (1992), and Mark A. Miller published *Christopher Lee and Peter Cushing and Horror Cinema* in 1995. Cushing's two volumes of memoirs, published in Great Britain in the late 1980s, finally appeared in America in 1999.

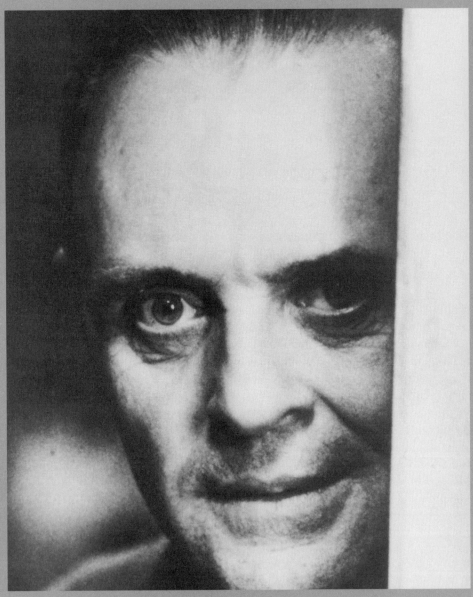

Anthony Hopkins notched an Oscar for his portrayal of Hannibal "the Cannibal" Lecter in 1991's Silence of the Lambs. *And apparently Hannibal will be back for more.*

7
PSYCHOS, SLASHERS, AND SERIAL KILLERS

We all go a little mad sometimes.

—Norman Bates (Anthony Perkins) in *Psycho* (1960)

MANIAC MOVIES THROUGH THE 1960S

562. Who directed *M* (1931)?

563. What tune does Beckert (Peter Lorre) whistle before attacking his victims in *M*?

564. What does psychotic murderer Danny (Robert Montgomery) carry around in a hat box in *Night Must Fall* (1937)?

565. What do the victims of serial killer Professor Warren (George Brent) have in common in *The Spiral Staircase* (1946)?

566. In *Lured* (1947), how does a homicidal maniac find his victims?

567. Who wrote the novel upon which *Screaming Mimi* (1958) is based?

568. What does psychotic killer Mark Lewis (Carl Boehm) do for a living in *Peeping Tom* (1960)?

569. What has turned Mark into a homicidal maniac in *Peeping Tom*?

570. What does Grant Williams use to murder his victims in *The Couch* (1962)?

571. What musical instrument does maniac Simon Ashby (Oliver Reed) play in *Paranoiac* (1963)?

572. In what Southern town would one find *2,000 Maniacs* (1964)?

573. What drives magician Duke Duquesne (Cesar Romero) mad in *Two on a Guillotine* (1965)?

574. Name the 1965 Roman Polanski film that stars Catherine Deneuve as Carol, a young woman slowly being driven mad by sexual repression.

575. What does the title character leave at each murder scene in *The Psychopath* (1966)?

576. What kind of victims does John Harrington (Stephen Forsyth) target in *Hatchet for a Honeymoon* (1969)?

Answers on page 109

PSYCHO (1960)

577. Name the author of the novel upon which this film is based.

578. What infamous real-life murderer inspired the character of Norman Bates (Anthony Perkins)?

579. An early subtitle reveals that *Psycho* begins in Phoenix, Arizona; what date and time are also noted at this point in the film?

580. How much money does Marian Crane (Janet Leigh) steal?

581. What is the license plate of the car she buys on her way to California?

582. In what town does Marian find the Bates Motel?

583. What alias does Marian use when she registers at the Bates Motel?

584. What does Marian's boyfriend, Sam Loomis (John Gavin), do for a living?

585. What kind of animal does Norman stuff and display in the motel office?

586. Where is Mrs. Bates supposed to be buried?

587. TRUE OR FALSE: Anthony Perkins provides the voice of Mrs. Bates.

588. For what type of musical instrument did Bernard Herrmann compose the score to *Psycho*?

589. How does director Alfred Hitchcock make a cameo appearance in *Psycho*?

590. TRUE OR FALSE: *Psycho* was the first mainstream motion picture to show a fully functioning bathroom—including a toilet!

591. Who plots to drive the released Norman Bates (Anthony Perkins) mad again in *Psycho II* (1983)?

592. Who directed *Psycho III* (1986)?

593. Who plays the twisted Mrs. Bates in the television movie *Psycho IV: The Beginning* (1990)?

Perhaps one of the most well-known icons of horror cinema: Anthony Perkins tops the stairway leading to the home behind the Bates Motel in Psycho *(1960).*

594. Who stars as Norman Bates in the 1998 remake of *Psycho*?

595. In the 1998 version, how much money does Marian (Anne Heche) steal?

596. Name the composer who faithfully re-creates Bernard Herrmann's original score for use in the 1998 version.

Answers on page 110

ANSWERS TO MANIAC MOVIES THROUGH THE 1960s

562. Fritz Lang   **563.** "In the Hall of the Mountain King" from *Peer Gynt*   **564.** The head of his victim   **565.** They are all disfigured or handicapped in some way.   **566.** Through the personal ads of a London newspaper   **567.** Frederic Brown   **568.** He is a photographer.
569. When Mark was a boy, his father (Michael Powell, the film's director) used him as a test subject for cruel psychological experiments.   **570.** An ice pick   **571.** The organ   **572.** Pleasant Valley   **573.** He accidentally beheads his wife (Connie Stevens) with his trick guillotine.
574. *Repulsion*   **575.** A doll of each victim   **576.** He kills brides on their wedding nights.

THE TEXAS CHAINSAW MASSACRE (1974)

597. Who directed this film?

598. What future television funnyman provides the opening narration to the movie?

599. On what date does the film take place?

600. A shot of what dead animal follows the opening credits?

601. How does the Hitchhiker (Edwin Neal) wound wheelchair-bound Franklin Hardesty (Paul A. Partain)?

602. Who plays the murderous psychopath Leatherface?

603. Where does Leatherface store the body of Pam (Terri McMinn)?

604. What do Leatherface and his deranged brothers feed Grandpa (John Dugan)?

605. How does Sally Hardesty (Marilyn Burns) finally manage to escape from Leatherface?

606. In *The Texas Chainsaw Massacre Part II* (1986), who plays Texas Ranger "Lefty" Enright?

607. Why does Enright seek revenge on Leatherface (Bill Johnson) and his family?

608. What does Stretch (Caroline Williams) do for a living?

609. Provide the full title of the third film in the series.

610. What now-famous actress attempted to block the release of *Texas Chainsaw Massacre: The Next Generation* (1994) after her career in Hollywood took off?

611. TRUE OR FALSE: Another rising star, Matthew McConaughey, landed his first leading role in *Texas Chainsaw Massacre: The Next Generation*.

Answers on page 112

ANSWERS TO PSYCHO (1960)

577. Robert Bloch   **578.** Ed Gein   **579.** December 11, 2:43 P.M.   **580.** $40,000
581. NFB-418   **582.** Fairvale, California   **583.** Marie Samuels   **584.** He runs a hardware store.   **585.** Birds   **586.** Greenlawn Cemetery   **587.** False   **588.** Stringed instruments
589. He can be glimpsed standing in front of Marian's office early in the film.   **590.** True
591. Lila Crane (Vera Miles), who still blames Norman for the death of her sister twenty-two years earlier   **592.** Anthony Perkins   **593.** Olivia Hussey   **594.** Vince Vaughn
595. $400,000   **596.** Danny Elfman

HAPPY HALLOWEENS

612. Who composed the memorable theme music for *Halloween*?

613. Where does most of the film take place?

614. What kind of Halloween costume is young Michael Myers (Will Sandin) wearing when he kills his sister (Sandy Johnson)?

615. What song is playing while Laurie (Jamie Lee Curtis) and Annie (Nancy Loomis) are driving to their baby-sitting gigs?

616. What two sci-fi movies are showing on television during *Halloween*?

617. Where does Annie meet her doom?

618. What is Lynda (P. J. Soles) trying to do when she is murdered?

619. When Laurie goes looking for Annie, what does she find?

620. What does Laurie first use to kill The Shape (Nick Castle)?

621. Where does Laurie attempt to hide from her attacker?

622. How does Dr. Sam Loomis (Donald Pleasence) figure out in which house to look for Michael?

623. How does Loomis save Laurie?

624. As the film ends, what happens to the body of Michael Myers?

625. TRUE OR FALSE: *Halloween II* (1981) takes place five years after the events of the first movie in the series.

626. What does Laurie find out about her relationship to Michael Myers in *Halloween II*?

627. How many of the next four films in the series pertain to Michael Myers?

628. How does Laurie (Jamie Lee Curtis) fake her death prior to the events of *Halloween H20: Twenty Years Later* (1998)?

629. What is unusual about the car driven by Norma (Janet Leigh), Laurie's secretary?

630. How does Laurie finally rid herself of Michael Myers?

631. To whose memory is *Halloween H20* dedicated?

Answers on page 113

IT'S YOUR LUCKY DAY!

632. Name the campground where most of *Friday the 13th* (1980) takes place.
633. What nickname have the locals given the campground?
634. Who shows up to warn the new camp counselors to leave—before it is too late?
635. What game do three of the counselors play during a thunderstorm?
636. Which counselor is killed while lying on a cot?
637. Which counselor gets an ax through the head?
638. Name the actress who plays the psychotic Mrs. Voorhees.
639. For what 1950s game show is this actress best known?
640. Why is Mrs. Voorhees slaughtering the camp counselors?
641. How does Alice (Adrienne King) finally kill Mrs. Voorhees?
642. What happens to Alice during a dream sequence near the film's conclusion?
643. Who is killed at the beginning of *Friday the 13th Part 2* (1981)?
644. How does the demonic Jason Voorhees disguise himself in most of the films in this series?
645. What is the subtitle of the eighth film in the series, released in 1989?
646. Name the actor who has most often portrayed Jason Voorhees.

Answers on page 114

OH, THIS QUIZ IS JUST CHILD'S PLAY

647. Who provides the voice of Chucky in all of the *Child's Play* films?
648. Who receives Chucky as a gift in *Child's Play* (1980)?
649. What is the name of the toy factory in the films?
650. Who provides the voice of Tommy Doll in *Child's Play 2* (1990) and Good Guy Doll in *Child's Play 3* (1991)?
651. Who plays Tiffany in *Bride of Chucky* (1998)?
652. What future *Lois and Clark* actor plays Andy Barclay in *Child's Play 3* (1991)?
653. Who wrote all four *Child's Play* movies?

Answers on page 114

ANSWERS TO THE TEXAS CHAINSAW MASSACRE (1974)

597. Tobe Hooper   **598.** John Larroquette   **599.** August 18, 1973   **600.** An armadillo **601.** He cuts him with a knife.   **602.** Gunnar Hansen   **603.** In a freezer   **604.** Some of Sally's blood   **605.** She flags down a passing pickup truck.   **606.** Dennis Hopper **607.** He is the uncle of the unfortunate Sally and Franklin from the first film.   **608.** She is a DJ.   **609.** *Leatherface: Texas Chainsaw Massacre III*   **610.** Renee Zellweger   **611.** True

THE SILENCE OF THE LAMBS (1991)

654. What actor won an Oscar for his unforgettable portrayal of cannibalistic psychopath Dr. Hannibal Lecter?

655. Why does FBI agent Jack Crawford (Scott Glenn) choose trainee Clarice Starling (Jodie Foster) to ask the incarcerated Dr. Lecter for help?

656. According to Lecter, what did he once do to a census taker?

657. Why have the media dubbed serial killer Jame Gumb (Ted Levine) "Buffalo Bill"?

658. Where does Gumb keep Catherine Martin (Brooke Smith) imprisoned?

659. Why is Dr. Lecter transported to Memphis, Tennessee?

660. How does Lecter disguise himself during his escape from Memphis?

661. At the film's conclusion, what is Lecter's excuse for cutting short a telephone call to Clarice?

662. TRUE OR FALSE: *The Silence of the Lambs* is based on a novel by Stephen King.

663. What is the title of the novel's sequel, which was published in the summer of 1999?

Answers on page 115

ANSWERS TO HAPPY HALLOWEENS

612. John Carpenter, the film's director   **613.** Haddonfield, Illinois   **614.** A clown suit
615. "Don't Fear the Reaper," by Blue Oyster Cult   **616.** *The Thing* and *Forbidden Planet*
617. In her car   **618.** She is trying to call Laurie on the telephone.   **619.** Annie's body, accompanied by a leering jack-o'-lantern, and the tombstone of Judith Myers   **620.** Knitting needles   **621.** In a closet   **622.** He sees Lindsey (Kyle Richards) and Tommy (Brian Andrews) run screaming from the house.   **623.** He shoots Michael.   **624.** It vanishes—he is still on the loose.   **625.** False. *Halloween II* picks up exactly where the first film ends.
626. They are brother and sister.   **627.** Only three—*Halloween III* (1982) involves deadly Halloween masks.   **628.** An auto accident   **629.** The car is the same one Leigh (Curtis's mother) drove in Alfred Hitchcock's *Psycho* (1960).   **630.** She decapitates him.
631. Donald Pleasence, who died in 1995

Robert Englund does his thing as Freddy Krueger
in A Nightmare on Elm Street *(1984).*

MANIAC MOVIES FROM THE 1970S THROUGH THE 1990S

664. What is the setting of *Blood and Lace* (1971)?

665. What disease causes hippies to go mad and kill people in *I Drink Your Blood* (1971)?

666. What unusual task must Dr. Martin (Robert Powell) accomplish in order to get a job as assistant director of the *Asylum* (1972)?

ANSWERS TO IT'S YOUR LUCKY DAY!

632. Camp Crystal Lake   **633.** Camp Blood   **634.** A local eccentric called Crazy Ralph (Walt Gorney)   **635.** Strip Monopoly   **636.** Jack (Kevin Bacon)   **637.** Marcie (Jeannie Taylor)   **638.** Betsy Palmer   **639.** "I've Got a Secret"   **640.** She blames teenage counselors for the drowning of her son, Jason, in 1957.   **641.** Alice manages to decapitate Mrs. Voorhees.   **642.** She is attacked by the undead remains of Jason.   **643.** Alice, the only survivor of the first film.   **644.** He uses a hockey mask.   **645.** *Jason Takes Manhattan* **646.** Kane Hodder. He has played the part since the seventh film, which was released in 1988.

ANSWERS TO OH, THIS QUIZ IS JUST CHILD'S PLAY

647. Brad Dourif   **648.** Andy Barclay (Alex Vincent)   **649.** Good Guy   **650.** Edan Gross **651.** Jennifer Tilly   **652.** Justin Whalin, who played Jimmy Olsen   **653.** Don Mancini

667. Where does deranged actor Edward Lionheart (Vincent Price) find inspiration for the elaborate murders he commits in *Theater of Blood* (1973)?

668. What 1976 film about a deranged theater owner and his incredible torture show was allegedly filmed in "Ghoulovision"?

669. Who plays the baby sitter terrorized by a madman in *When a Stranger Calls* (1979)?

670. What does crazed killer Frank Zito (Joe Spinnell) do with the scalps of his victims in *Maniac* (1980)?

671. What 1981 slasher film features a score by rock musician Rick Wakeman?

672. How does a group of maniacs escape from a mental institution in *Alone in the Dark* (1982)?

673. What 1982 slasher film features the rare distinction of being written and directed by women?

674. What city is terrorized in *Maniac Cop* (1988)?

675. What real-life serial killer inspired *Henry: Portrait of a Serial Killer* (1990)?

676. How does Henry (Michael Rooker) earn a living in *Henry: Portrait of a Serial Killer*?

677. Around what theme are the murders based in *Se7en* (1995)?

678. Who plays serial killer John Doe in *Se7en*?

Answers on page 116

ANSWERS TO THE SILENCE OF THE LAMBS (1991)

654. Anthony Hopkins **655.** Crawford believes an inexperienced young woman will attract Lecter's attention, therefore ensuring his cooperation in the hunt for "Buffalo Bill." **656.** "I ate his liver with some fava beans and a nice chianti." **657.** Like Buffalo Bill Cody skinned animals, Jame skins his victims. **658.** In a pit in the basement of his house **659.** He has been promised better conditions by Catherine's mother, a U.S. senator, if he will help find "Buffalo Bill." **660.** He wears the face of one of his victims. **661.** He tells her, "I'm having an old friend for dinner," as he observes the arrival of his next meal—an unsuspecting Dr. Chilton (Anthony Heald), Lecter's psychiatrist while the madman was incarcerated. **662.** False. Thomas Harris wrote the original novel. **663.** *Hannibal*

ROBERT ENGLUND

ROBERT ENGLUND WAS born June 6, 1949, in Glendale, California. The son of an engineer (his father helped design the U-2 spy plane), Englund developed an interest in acting at the age of twelve. He studied at the Royal Academy of Dramatic Arts and entered the limelight with a touring company production of *Godspell.*

Englund specialized in Shakespearean comedy onstage before making his film debut in *Buster and Billie* in 1974. Other film and television roles followed, usually minor parts in films such as *Stay Hungry, A Star Is Born,* and *Big Wednesday* (all three released in 1976). He made his first horror film, Tobe Hooper's *Eaten Alive,* in 1976. He later played one of the good-guy aliens in the popular 1980s television miniseries *V,* but he jumped to international fame as the demonic murderer Freddy Krueger in Wes Craven's *A Nightmare on Elm Street* in 1984. Six sequels followed—making Englund the most popular horror icon of the 1980s and early 1990s.

For a while, Englund appeared to be the new "king of horror"—taking over for the likes of Boris Karloff, Bela Lugosi, and company. He directed *976-EVIL* in 1988, and the following year he starred in a remake of *The Phantom of the Opera.* In addition to the phenomenally successful *Nightmare* series, Englund turned up in such shockers as *C.H.U.D. II* (1989), Tobe Hooper's *Night Terrors* (1990), *The Mangler* (1990), and *Wishmaster* (1997).

Englund hosted the syndicated *Freddy's Nightmares* television show and then starred as Blackie in a short-lived NBC-TV series called *Nightmare Cafe.* Perhaps inevitably, the Freddy Krueger franchise ran out of steam, and during the mid-1990s Englund spent most of his time in mainstream television and film roles. He has lately returned to the horror genre in such offerings as *Strangeland* (1998) and *Urban Legend* (1998). The 1999 release of the long-delayed *Freddy vs. Jason,* a tag-team of the greatest cinema monsters of the 1980s, was poised to scare moviegoers into the new millennium.

ANSWERS TO MANIAC MOVIES FROM THE 1970s THROUGH THE 1990s

664. An orphanage   **665.** Rabies   **666.** He must identify which of the patients is the former director, using only information gleaned in interviews with four inmates.
667. Shakespeare's plays   **668.** *Bloodsucking Freaks*   **669.** Carol Kane   **670.** He keeps the scalps on the heads of mannequins.   **671.** *The Burning*   **672.** A power failure allows them to escape.   **673.** *The Slumber Party Massacre*   **674.** New York   **675.** Henry Lee Lucas
676. He is a pest exterminator.   **677.** The seven deadly sins   **678.** Kevin Spacey

DONALD PLEASENCE

VOTED THE WORLD'S busiest actor in the late 1980s, Donald Pleasence knocked out seventeen films between 1987 and 1989. Horror fans will not forget his performance as Dr. Sam Loomis, the obsessed shrink who pursues the homicidal Michael Myers in five of the *Halloween* series movies.

The actor was born on October 5, 1919, in Worksop, England. He made his stage debut in 1939 and joined the Royal Air Force three years later—only to be shot down and confined to a POW camp.

Pleasence's career made its way to film with *The Beachcomber* in 1954. With his bland expression, bald head, and creepy voice, he was a natural for wicked and horrific parts. His path toward horror began with *The Flesh and the Fiends* in 1959. He played the infamous bodysnatcher Hare, who, with a partner, supplied Peter Cushing's Dr. Robert Knox with fresh corpses for research.

After 1960, Pleasence alternated between horror and other fare. Among the former were *The Hands of Orlac* (1960), *Circus of Horrors* (1967), *From Beyond the Grave* (1974), *Dracula* (1979), *Prince of Darkness* (1987), *House of Usher* (1990), and *Buried Alive* (1990). His non-horror efforts included *The Great Escape* (1963), *Fantastic Voyage* (1966), *Will Penny* (1966), *You Only Live Twice* (1967), *Escape to Witch Mountain* (1975), *Escape from New York* (1981), and *Shadows and Fog* (1992).

No matter how low the budget or how prestigious the project, Pleasence never gave less than his best. His legacy of work in film and television includes his actress-daughter Angela, whose resemblance to her father is uncanny. The pair costarred in *From Beyond the Grave* (1974). The actor died on February 2, 1995, at the age of seventy-five.

TOP 5 PSYCHOS, SLASHERS, AND SERIAL KILLER MOVIES

Psycho (1960)
Halloween (1978)
The Silence of the Lambs (1991)
Henry: Portrait of a Serial Killer (1990)
Peeping Tom (1960)

Vincent Price has a campy blast as The Abominable Dr. Phibes *(1971).*

8

MAD DOCTORS AND WEIRD SCIENTISTS

We'll start with a few murders—big men, little men—just to show we make no distinction.

> —Dr. Griffin (Claude Rains) in *The Invisible Man* (1933)

THE INVISIBLE MAN (1933)

679. Who makes his film debut as Jack Griffin, the scientist who turns himself invisible?

680. How is this character billed in the credits?

681. What is the name of the rural English inn where Jack Griffin goes to research a cure for invisibility?

682. What drug is primarily responsible for turning Griffin invisible—and driving him insane?

683. TRUE OR FALSE: At one point the invisible Griffin, clad only in trousers, skips down a road singing, "Here we go gathering nuts in May!"

684. According to Griffin, why can't he go outdoors for at least an hour after meals?

685. Who plays Flora Kemp, Griffin's terrified fiancée?

686. Where do the police finally corner Griffin?

687. What natural phenomenon allows the police to track and shoot the invisible villain?

688. In what film does Vincent Price play Jack Griffin's brother, who turns himself invisible after being wrongly accused of murder, in order to find the real killer?

689. What cast member also showed up screaming in director James Whales's *Bride of Frankenstein*?

690. What Oscar-winning actor has an unbilled role in this film as a man whose bicycle is stolen?

Answers on page 122

Claude Rains kisses the hand of Gloria Stuart in The Invisible Man *(1933).*

THE TRANSPARENT INVISIBLE MOVIE QUIZ

Match the title with the plot or characters.

691. *Abbott and Costello Meet the Invisible Man* (1951)
692. *The Amazing Transparent Man* (1960)
693. *The Body Disappears* (1941)
694. *Fiend Without a Face* (1958)
695. *The Invisible Agent* (1942)
696. *The Invisible Boy* (1957)
697. *The Invisible Dr. Mabuse* (1961)
698. *The Invisible Invaders* (1959)
699. *The Invisible Man's Revenge* (1944)
700. *The Invisible Woman* (1941)
701. *Mad Monster Party?* (1967)
702. *The Man Who Wasn't There* (1983)
703. *Memoirs of an Invisible Man* (1991)
704. *Mr. Superinvisible* (1973)
705. *Now You See Him, Now You Don't* (1972)
706. *Phantom From Space* (1954)
707. *The Invisible Kid* (1988)

A. Invisible alien attacks Los Angeles and inhabits Griffith Observatory.
B. Invisible aliens from the moon vex John Carradine and John Agar.
C. Chevy Chase comedy-drama
D. John Barrymore's professor makes Virginia Bruce disappear.
E. John Carradine pulls a vanishing act on Jon Hall.
F. Animation features voices of Boris Karloff and Phyllis Diller.
G. Joey Faust is a bank robber in search of radioactivity.
H. Kurt Russell vaporizes with invisible spray.
I. Richard Eyer finds a friend in Robby the Robot.
J. Arthur Franz has a super-quick punch.
K. Dean Jones disappears.
L. Edward Everett Horton makes Jeffery Lynn go poof.
M. Watch out for flying brains with spinal cords.
N. Lex Barker tangles with evil Wolfgang Priess.
O. Jon Hall, as the grandson of the original invisible guy, goes after Nazis.
P. Steve Guttenberg gets invisible in 3-D.
Q. Sophomoric humor with Jay Underwood and Karen Black

Answers on page 123

WEIRD SCIENTIST QUOTATIONS

Match the quotation with the correct mad scientist

708. "You'll never get credit for my discoveries—who'd believe a talking head? Get a job in a sideshow!"

709. "Speak! You've got a civil tongue in your head. I know you have because I sewed it in myself!"

710. "I meddled in things that man must leave alone!"

711. "I took a gorilla and, working with infinite care, I made my first man!"

712. "Superstitious—perhaps. Baloney? Perhaps not!"

713. "Alone you have created a man. Now together we will create his mate!"

714. "Think of it! The brain of a dead man waiting to live again in a body I have made with my own hands!"

715. "Mad? I who have solved the secret of life, you call me mad?"

716. "Don't cry upon God, Dr. Vesalius. He is on my side."

717. "If I've succeeded this time, then every sacrifice will have been worthwhile."

A. Henry Frankenstein in *Frankenstein* (1931)

B. Professor Frankenstein in *I Was a Teenage Frankenstein* (1957)

C. Dr. Moreau in *Island of Lost Souls* (1932)

D. Jack Griffin in *The Invisible Man* (1933)

E. Herbert West in *Re-Animator* (1986)

F. Dr. Pretorius in *Bride of Frankenstein* (1935)

G. Dr. Vitus Verdegast in *The Black Cat* (1934)

H. Baron Frankenstein in *Frankenstein and the Monster from Hell* (1974)

I. Dr. Otto Von Niemann in *The Vampire Bat* (1933)

J. Dr. Anton Phibes in *The Abominable Dr. Phibes* (1971)

Answers on page 124

ANSWERS TO THE INVISIBLE MAN (1933)

679. Claude Rains   **680.** "The Invisible One"   **681.** The Lion's Head   **682.** Monocaine   **683.** True   **684.** "The food inside me is digested."   **685.** Gloria Stuart, future Academy Award nominee for *Titanic* (1997)   **686.** An old barn   **687.** Fresh snow reveals Griffin's footprints, which let the police hunt him down   **688.** *The Invisible Man Returns* (1940)   **689.** Una O'Connor (she played Jenny Hall)   **690.** Walter Brennan

The only thing more ominous than one mad scientist is two, especially if their laboratory is electrified. This was never more true than in The Bride of Frankenstein *(1935), when Colin Clive (above, left) joined forces with Ernest Thesiger (above, right).*

PHANTOMS OF THE OPERA

718. Where is the setting for the original *Phantom of the Opera* (1925)?

719. As what character does the Phantom come disguised to the costume party?

720. What instrument does Lon Chaney play in this film?

721. What is Chaney's phantom's first name?

722. What scene made audiences swoon with fear?

723. Who played Christine Daae in the original silent film?

724. Who portrays the singing hero in the first talkie version of *Phantom of the Opera* in 1943?

725. Who plays the Phantom, Claudin, in the 1943 film?

726. Who plays Christine Dubois in the 1943 version?

ANSWERS TO THE TRANSPARENT INVISIBLE MOVIE QUIZ

691. J **692.** G **693.** L **694.** M **695.** O **696.** I **697.** N **698.** B **699.** E **700.** D
701. F **702.** P **703.** C **704.** K **705.** H **706.** A **707.** Q

727. In what city is the 1962 *Phantom of the Opera* set?

728. Who plays Christine Charles in this third version?

729. Who plays the Phantom, Professor Petrie?

730. How is the Phantom killed in this film?

731. In 1989's *Phantom of the Opera,* who plays Christine?

732. Who portrays the Phantom?

Answers on page 126

MORE PHANTOMS TO FATHOM

733. Who plays the title role in *Phantom of the Opera* (1998)?

734. Who raises the Phantom from childhood?

735. Who portrays Christine?

736. Who is the heroine of the 1983 television movie *The Phantom of the Opera?*

737. What two actors fight over the heroine?

738. Who is the Phantom in the 1990 television movie version?

739. Who plays the opera singer the Phantom desires?

740. Who is the director of the Parisian Opera in this work?

741. Who stars in the title role of *The Phantom of Hollywood,* a 1974 television-movie set on the MGM backlot as it was being demolished in real life?

742. Who plays the evil scientist in the 1978 television movie *KISS Meets the Phantom of the Park?*

743. Who stars as an evil rock 'n' roller in director Brian De Palma's 1974 flick *The Phantom of the Paradise?*

744. Who portrays Dr. Hohner, physician to the Vienna Royal Theater, in 1944's *The Climax?*

745. Who stars as the opera heroine in *The Climax?*

746. Who plays the hero of *The Climax?*

747. What film teams Karloff and Lugosi as Karloff's scientist discovers "Radium X"?

Answers on page 126

ANSWERS TO WEIRD SCIENTIST QUOTATIONS

708. E **709.** B **710.** D **711.** C **712.** G **713.** F **714.** A **715.** I **716.** J **717.** H

MYSTERY OF THE WAX MUSEUM (1933)

748. In what extraordinary process (for its day) was this movie filmed?

749. Who directed *Mystery of the Wax Museum*?

750. What actor speaks the lines, "I am going to give you immortality. In a thousand years you'll be as lovely as you are now. Your beauty will be preserved forever"?

751. The film opens in London 1921, but where does it continue in 1933?

752. How is the wax artist disfigured?

753. What is the name of the mad Wax Man?

754. What historical character does actress Joan Gale's body turn up as in the wax museum?

755. Who stars as a reporter for the *New York Express*?

756. The madman wants Fay Wray's Charlotte for what historical figure?

757. How does the wax maniac meet his demise?

Answers on page 127

Self-images and their problems are themes explored by the marvelous Lon Chaney (below, left) as the pathetic Phantom in the 1925 silent film classic and by Vincent Price as the "abominable" Dr. Phibes (below, right).

MORE HOT WAX

758. Who stars as the madman in *House of Wax* (1953)?

759. What is the most famous object used to good effect in this 3-D flick?

760. What actress turns up as Marie Antoinette?

761. Who plays the heroine?

762. Who costars as the Wax Man's sidekick, Igor?

763. What 1923 silent film stars Conrad Veidt as Ivan the Terrible and Werner Krauss as Jack the Ripper?

764. Who waxes crazy in *Nightmare in Wax* (1973)?

765. What is the name of the house of wax in this film?

766. Where does the Wax Man find his "clients"?

767. What is the Wax Man's former occupation?

768. Who stars as a killer with a hook for a hand in *Chamber of Horrors* (1966)?

769. What famous movie sleuth stars in what 1940 film in which he uncovers crime in a wax museum that features a statue of our hero?

770. What is the setting for a 1936 film about an explorer, played by James Carew, who bets he can spend the night in a wax museum?

771. In what 1988 film does Zach Galligan meet up with Dracula, Frankenstein, the Mummy, a werewolf, the Phantom of the Opera, and Audrey II in a wax museum?

772. What is so ironic about the 3-D *House of Wax* (1953) and its director?

Answers on page 128

ANSWERS TO PHANTOMS OF THE OPERA

718. The Paris Opera House　**719.** The Red Death　**720.** Pipe organ　**721.** Erik
722. The Phantom's unmasking　**723.** Mary Philbin　**724.** Nelson Eddy　**725.** Claude
Rains　**726.** Susanna Foster　**727.** London　**728.** Heather Sears　**729.** Herbert Lom
730. He is crushed by a falling chandelier.　**731.** Jill Schoelen　**732.** Robert Englund

ANSWERS TO MORE PHANTOMS TO FATHOM

733. Julian Sands　**734.** Rats　**735.** Asia Argento　**736.** Jane Seymour　**737.** Maximilian
Schell and Michael York　**738.** Charles Dance　**739.** Teri Polo　**740.** Burt Lancaster
741. Jack Cassidy　**742.** Anthony Zerbe　**743.** Paul Williams　**744.** Boris Karloff
745. Susanna Foster　**746.** Turhan Bey　**747.** *The Invisible Ray*

THE ABOMINABLE DR. PHIBES (1971)

773. Who directed this classic comedy-horror film?

774. Why has musician-theologian Dr. Anton Phibes (Vincent Price) targeted nine prominent medical professionals for death?

775. What Old Testament phenomenon inspires Phibes's elaborate methods of murder?

776. What event has caused Phibes's horrible disfigurement and led the world at large to believe he is dead?

777. What is the specialty of Dr. Hargreaves (Alex Scott), the physician whose head is crushed by a frog-shaped mask?

778. Name the American character actor who plays Dr. Vesalius, leader of the surgical team stalked by Dr. Phibes.

779. How does Dr. Phibes escape capture by Scotland Yard's Inspector Trout (Peter Jeffrey)?

780. What song is played over the closing credits?

781. Who plays the beloved but deceased wife of Dr. Anton Phibes in *The Abominable Dr. Phibes* and *Dr. Phibes Rises Again* (1972)?

782. TRUE OR FALSE: A third film in the *Phibes* series was planned but never filmed.

Answers on page 129

ROUTINE DOCTOR EXAMINATIONS

783. What is the name of the villain who chases Maria through the underground maze of tunnels in *Metropolis* (1926)?

784. In *The Cabinet of Dr. Caligari* (1919), the first true horror film, Caligari is head of what type of institution?

785. Who plays the mad doctor in *Devil Bat* (1941)?

786. Lionel Atwill is the scientist, but who plays the title role in *Doctor X* (1932)?

787. What film superstar is Dr. Xavier in *The Return of Dr. X* (1939)?

ANSWERS TO MYSTERY OF THE WAX MUSEUM (1933)

748. In two-color Technicolor **749.** Michael Curtiz, director of *Casablanca* and *Mildred Pierce* **750.** Lionel Atwill **751.** New York City **752.** In a fire **753.** Ivan Igor **754.** Joan of Arc **755.** Glenda Farrell **756.** Marie Antoinette **757.** A cop shoots Igor, who falls into a vat of boiling wax.

Werner Krauss (left) is the wayfaring Dr. Caligari, and Conrad Veidt is his sleepwalking henchman in the groundbreaking silent feature The Cabinet of Dr. Caligari *(1919).*

788. What caused mad *Mr. Sardonicus* (1961) to have a permanent smile upon his face?
789. In what film does Albert Dekker play a mad scientist who shrinks people?
790. Who played *The Body Snatcher* (1945)?
791. Who starred as *The Mad Doctor of Market Street* (1941)?
792. What was the objective of the crazed surgeon in *The Brain That Wouldn't Die* (1958)?
793. Who plays the doctor who makes Boris Karloff look really bad in *The Raven* (1935)?

ANSWERS TO MORE HOT WAX

758. Vincent Price   **759.** A paddleball   **760.** Carolyn Jones   **761.** Phyllis Kirk
762. Charles Bronson   **763.** *Waxworks*   **764.** Cameron Mitchell   **765.** The Hollywood Wax Museum   **766.** They are actors "missing" from the studio.   **767.** Studio makeup man
768. Patrick O'Neal   **769.** Charlie Chan in *Charlie Chan at the Wax Museum*   **770.** Madame Tussaud's in London, in *Midnight at Madame Tussaud's*   **771.** *Waxwork*   **772.** Andre de Toth had only one eye; thus, he could not see the 3-D effects of film, which is probably the most popular of its genre.

794. What happens to Biderbeck (Robert Quarry) at the conclusion of *Dr. Phibes Rises Again* (1972)?

795. Who wreaks havoc, as the evil doctor, with Lon Chaney Jr. in *Man Made Monster* (1941)?

796. Mike Connors is the good guy, but who's the mad scientist in *Voodoo Woman* (1957)?

797. What B-film good guy defeats the mad doctor of *Curse of the Swamp Creature* (1966)?

798. What is the name of the dentist-gone-insane in 1996's *The Dentist*?

799. Who plays Dr. Lawrence Caine in 1998's *The Dentist II*?

Answers on page 130

ISLAND OF LOST SOULS (1932)

800. What famous science fiction author wrote *The Island of Dr. Moreau,* the basis for this film and its remakes?

801. TRUE OR FALSE: This author considered *Island of Lost Souls* an excellent adaptation of his novel.

802. What do the "beast-men" call the laboratory where Dr. Moreau (Charles Laughton) conducts his terrible experiments?

803. What famous horror-movie star plays a supporting role as the apelike Sayer of the Law?

804. What evil plan does Dr. Moreau have in mind for shipwreck victim Edward Parker (Richard Arlen) and Lota, the Panther Woman (Kathleen Burke)?

805. Who comes to Moreau's island in search of Parker?

806. What fate befalls Dr. Moreau at the film's conclusion?

807. Name the 1959 remake of this classic tale of terror.

808. Who starred as Dr. Moreau in the 1977 remake, *The Island of Dr. Moreau?*

809. Who plays Montgomery, the drug-addled assistant to Dr. Moreau (Marlon Brando), in the 1996 version of the story?

810. What interesting plot developed concerning *Island of Lost Souls* when it was released in England?

Answers on page 131

ANSWERS TO THE ABOMINABLE DR. PHIBES (1971)

773. Robert Fuest   **774.** Dr. Phibes blames them for his wife's death on the operating table.   **775.** The G'tach—the ten curses visited upon Pharaoh before the Hebrew Exodus   **776.** A car accident   **777.** He is a psychiatrist—a head shrinker.   **778.** Joseph Cotten   **779.** Phibes buries himself and his wife in a secret underground tomb.   **780.** "Over the Rainbow"   **781.** Caroline Munro, one of the first so-called scream queens   **782.** True

PETER LORRE

PETER LORRE WAS one of the greatest character actors of the Golden Age of Hollywood. Best remembered for his roles in three Bogart films—*The Maltese Falcon* (1941), *Casablanca* (1942), and *Beat the Devil* (1953)—he jumped to international fame as a psychopathic child killer in Fritz Lang's *M* in 1931.

Lorre was born in Rosenberg, Hungary, on June 26, 1904, and grew up in Vienna, where he trained for the stage. He ran away from home at the age of seventeen and worked as a bank clerk before making his acting debut in Zurich. Briefly engaged in about a dozen German films, he went to England and appeared in two Hitchcock films, *The Man Who Knew Too Much* and *The Secret Agent* (both in 1934).

After he came to America in 1935, Lorre played a crazed surgeon in *Mad Love*. In 1937 he tackled the laborious but lucrative Mr. Moto series, but in the following decade he was typecast in film noir, horror, and comedy films. He costarred with Boris Karloff and Bela Lugosi in 1940's *You'll Find Out* and gave comic turns to *The Boogie Man Will Get You* (1942) and *Arsenic and Old Lace* (1944).

Lorre was menaced by a disembodied hand in *The Beast with Five Fingers* in 1946, and he in turn harassed Bob Hope in *My Favorite Brunette* in 1947. He wrote, directed, coproduced, and starred in *The Lost One* (1951), a German film about a psychopath who murders several women before World War II and then becomes a physician

Lorre is flanked by Vincent Price and Basil Rathbone in this still from Poe's Tales of Terror *(1962).*

ANSWERS TO ROUTINE DOCTOR EXAMINATIONS

783. Rotwang   **784.** Insane asylum   **785.** Bela Lugosi   **786.** Preston Foster **787.** Humphrey Bogart   **788.** He dug up his father's grave to recover a winning lottery ticket.   **789.** *Dr. Cyclops*   **790.** Boris Karloff   **791.** Lionel Atwill   **792.** To find a beautiful body to attach to his fiancée's severed head   **793.** Bela Lugosi   **794.** He reverts to his true age.   **795.** Lionel Atwill   **796.** Tom Conway, brother of George Sanders   **797.** John Agar   **798.** Dr. Feinstone   **799.** Corbin Bernsen

in a refugee camp. The film flopped, and Lorre's health faltered. He never fully recovered from the fiasco.

The actor returned to Hollywood and showed many different sides in such films as *20,000 Leagues Under the Sea* (1954), *Around the World in 80 Days* (1956), *The Sad Sack* (1957), *The Buster Keaton Story* (1957), and *Voyage to the Bottom of the Sea* (1961).

Lorre's greatest success on the silver screen, however, came in his later years when Roger Corman teamed him with Vincent Price, Basil Rathbone, and Boris Karloff in comedy-horror films such as *Tales of Terror* (1962), *The Raven* (1963), and *The Comedy of Terrors* (1964).

He died March 23, 1964, at the age of fifty-nine, following a heart attack.

JOHN CARRADINE

JOHN CARRADINE WAS born Richmond Reed Carradine on February 5, 1906, in New York City. He studied sculpture and was working his way across the South, peddling sketches, when he made his acting debut in 1925 in a New Orleans production of *Camille*.

Two years later, he migrated to Los Angeles, where he developed a close friendship with John Barrymore and found work in Cecil B. DeMille and John Ford movies. In the early 1930s, Carradine was billed as Peter Richmond and may be glimpsed in uncredited bit parts in Universal classics such as *The Black Cat* (1934) and *The Bride of Frankenstein* (1935).

Probably the high-water mark of Carradine's career was in the late 1930s, when he was given roles in *Stagecoach* (1939), *Drums Along the Mohawk* (1939), and *The Grapes of Wrath* (1940). He also had substantial roles in *The Prisoner of Shark Island* (1937), *Hurricane* (1937), *Jesse James* (1939), *The Hound of the Baskervilles* (1939), and *Blood and Sand* (1941). Although he had more than four hundred films in his repertoire, Carradine became typecast in horror from the 1940s through the end of his career. He played Dracula in *House of Frankenstein* (1944) and *House of Dracula* (1945) for Universal, and his performance as *Bluebeard* (1944) was considered one of his finest.

ANSWERS TO ISLAND OF LOST SOULS (1932)

800. H. G. Wells **801.** False. Wells considered the film "vulgar." **802.** "The House of Pain" **803.** Bela Lugosi **804.** Moreau plans to mate Lota, his greatest success thus far, with Parker. **805.** Parker's fiancée, Ruth (Leila Hyams), and a rescue party **806.** He is tortured to death in the House of Pain by his vengeful creations. **807.** *Terror Is a Man* **808.** Burt Lancaster **809.** Val Kilmer **810.** It was banned.

Hillbillys in a Haunted House (1967), *Blood of Ghastly Horror* (1967), *Terror in the Wax Museum* (1973), *Satan's Cheerleaders* (1976), and *Vampire Hookers* (1977).

In spite of his reputation as a schlocky horror star, Carradine found good supporting roles in mainstream films such as *The Ten Commandments* (1956), *The Man Who Shot Liberty Valance* (1962), *The Shootist* (1976), *The White Buffalo* (1977), and *Peggy Sue Got Married* (1986). In his later years, Carradine returned to a better class of horror films, including *The Sentinel* (1977), *The Monster Club* (1980), *The Howling* (1981), and *The House of the Long Shadows* (1982).

Carradine's more memorable horror credits include *Captive Wild Woman* (1943), *The Mummy's Ghost* (1944), *The Invisible Man's Revenge* (1944), and *The Black Sleep* (1956). Although Carradine possessed a great speaking voice, the actor's list of badly made films is legendary. Among those are *Billy the Kid vs. Dracula* (1966),

The actor was nicknamed the "Bard of the Boulevard" because of his fondness for walking the streets of Hollywood while reciting Shakespeare. Three of his sons—David, Keith, and Robert—also pursued careers on the silver screen. John Carradine died of natural causes on November 27, 1988, at age eighty-two.

MICHAEL GOUGH

IN MANY WAYS, Michael Gough, known for his tall, gaunt frame and inimitable voice, is the British equivalent to John Carradine. He is a talented actor who has played several good supporting roles in some great films, but he is best known for the cheesy horror flicks that were his bread and butter in the 1960s and 1970s.

Born on November 23, 1917, in Malaya to British parents, Gough made his stage debut in 1936, after training at the Old Vic, and made his first film, *Blanche Fury,* in 1947. Among his better early movies were *Anna Karenina* (1948), *The Man in the White Suit* (1951), *Rob Roy* (1953), *The Sword and the Rose* (1953), and *Richard III* (1955).

Gough steered toward the macabre in 1958 when he joined Peter Cushing and Christopher Lee in Hammer's remake of *Dracula*. A year later he continued his wicked film ways in *Horrors of the Black Museum* as the villainous author who commits murders and then writes bestsellers about them. In the 1960s Gough slugged his way through B-grade but fun flicks such as *Konga* (1961), *Black Zoo* (1963), *Berserk*

(1967), and the legendary *Trog* (1970) along with better crafted films such as Hammer's *Phantom of the Opera* (1962) and *Dr. Terror's House of Horrors* (1964).

The actor was better served on the stage and on British television making appearances on *Doctor Who* and *The Avengers,* among others. More legitimate film and television movie roles appeared in the form of *Julius Caesar* (1970), *The Boys from Brazil* (1978), *A Christmas Carol* (1984), *Out of Africa* (1985), *Arthur the King* (1985), *The Serpent and the Rainbow* (1987), and *The Age of Innocence* (1993). More recently, Gough is best known as Alfred the butler in the recent *Batman* films. His most recent role is in Tim Burton's *Sleepy Hollow,* based on the classic Washington Irving tale.

In Konga *(1961), Michael Gough discovers that there's never a Batman around when an oversized ape decides to show you Big Ben.*

TOP 5 MAD DOCTORS AND WEIRD SCIENTISTS MOVIES

The Abominable Dr. Phibes (1971)
Re-Animator (1985)
Island of Lost Souls (1933)
The Invisible Man (1933)
The Flesh and the Fiends (1959)

Harvey Stephens stars as Damien in The Omen *(1976).*

9

DEMONS AND DEVILS

You're telling me I should send my child to a witch doctor?
—Chris MacNeil (Ellen Burstyn) in *The Exorcist* (1973)

ROSEMARY'S BABY (1968)

811. The voice of what famous actor, who is not seen or credited in the film, is heard on the telephone?

812. What foreign director made his American debut with this work and also wrote the script?

813. In what famous New York apartment complex was the film shot?

814. Who plays Rosemary's husband?

815. In what type of commercial is Rosemary's husband seen on television?

816. What is the title of the television series for which Rosemary's husband is up for a leading role?

817. What is the nickname of their apartment building?

818. What actor shows them their apartment?

819. What is their apartment number?

820. What talk-show host-actor plays Dr. Hill?

821. Who portrays Dr. Abe Saperstein?

822. What was the peculiar habit of two spinster sisters who lived in the apartment building at the turn of the century?

823. What was found in the basement in 1959?

824. What gift does Minnie give Rosemary?

825. What food is used to drug Rosemary?

826. What is the title of the book that friend Hutch gives to Rosemary?

827. With what does Rosemary unscramble an anagram to figure out her neighbor is a witch?

828. What does Rosemary do with her necklace?

829. Who is seen smoking a cigar while waiting outside a phone booth?

830. Only what part of Rosemary's baby is seen?

Answers on page 137

When you're carrying the offspring of the devil, your world is bound to get a little off kilter, as Mia Farrow finds out in Rosemary's Baby *(1968). Above, she tries to enlist the aid of John Cassavetes, who plays her husband, and to the right, she decides to take the matter into her own hands.*

CURSE OF THE DEMON (1958)

831. What is the ancient English setting for the opening prologue?

832. Who was the director of this horror classic?

833. What is the name of Dr. Karswell's estate?

834. Dana Andrews's character, Dr. John Holden, is a psychiatrist who studies what?

835. Who is the demon's first victim?

836. Where does Holden first meet Karswell (Niall McGuiness)?

837. What was Karswell's previous occupation?

838. After Karswell passes a magical talisman to Holden, how long does Holden have to live?

839. When Holden sneaks into Karswell's library late one night, into what creature does Karswell's cat Grimalkin change?

840. What does Holden pass on to Karswell that terrifies him and causes his encounter with the demon?

Answers on page 139

THE EXORCIST (1973)

841. How old is Regan MacNeil said to be in *The Exorcist*?

842. Who directed *The Exorcist*?

843. Who provides the voice of the demon in *The Exorcist*?

844. Who won a Golden Globe and an Academy Award for the screenplay for *The Exorcist*?

845. *The Exorcist* is based on an actual possession case in what town?

846. Who was nominated for an Academy Award for the portrayal of Chris MacNeil?

ANSWERS TO ROSEMARY'S BABY (1968)

811. Tony Curtis **812.** Roman Polanski **813.** The Dakota, outside which John Lennon was murdered in 1980 **814.** John Cassavetes **815.** Yamaha motorcycles **816.** *Miami Beach* **817.** Black Branford **818.** Elisha Cook Jr. **819.** 7E **820.** Charles Grodin **821.** Ralph Bellamy **822.** They cooked and ate young children. **823.** The body of an infant **824.** A good-luck necklace filled with tannin root, also known as devil's pepper **825.** Chocolate mousse **826.** *All of Them Witches* **827.** A Scrabble board game **828.** Throws it down a drain **829.** Producer William Castle **830.** The eyes

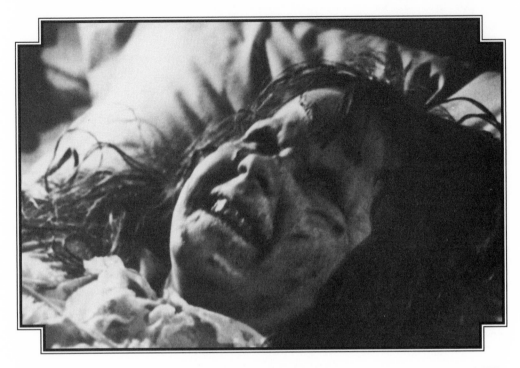

In The Exorcist *(1973), Linda Blair discovers that hosting a demon can wreak havoc on your social life.*

847. Who plays Father Damien Karras?
848. Who plays the lead priest trying to exorcise Regan MacNeil's demon in *Exorcist II: The Heretic* (1977)?
849. What is the name of Mike Oldfield's theme music for *The Exorcist?*
850. Who plays the lead police investigator in 1990's *The Exorcist III?*

Answers on page 140

THE OMEN (1976)

851. Who wrote the Academy Award–winning score for 1976's *The Omen?*
852. What is the name of the child reputed to be the embodiment of the antichrist in *The Omen?*
853. Who are the actors who play the parents of the devil child?
854. In what country does most of *The Omen* take place?
855. How does the young nanny (Holly Palance) die in *The Omen?*

Brad Dourif portrays an evil spirit in The Exorcist III *(1990). This odd-looking actor has specialized in playing eccentrics since 1975, when he received an Oscar nomination for best supporting actor as Billy in* One Flew Over the Cuckoo's Nest. *He followed that memorable part with the lead role in John Huston's* Wise Blood *(1979). Since then Dourif has paid the bills as one of Hollywood's most dependable nut cases, often in fantasy films like* Dune *(1984),* Blue Velvet *(1986),* Spontaneous Combustion *(1989),* Grim Prairie Tales *(1990),* Body Parts *(1991),* Alien Resurrection *(1998),* Urban Legend *(1998), and* Prophecy III: The Ascent *(1999). More mainstream roles came his way in* Ragtime *(1981),* Mississippi Burning *(1988),* Jungle Fever *(1991), and* Murder in the First *(1995), but he will probably always be best remembered as the voice of Chucky in the* Child's Play *movies.*

856. How many daggers are said to be needed to kill the son of Satan in *The Omen?*

857. Who plays Damien in 1978's *Damien: Omen II?*

858. What member of the cast of television's *Designing Women* appears in *Damien: Omen II?*

859. Who plays Richard Thorn, Damien's uncle, in *Damien: Omen II?*

860. Who plays Damien in 1981's *The Final Conflict?*

861. What is the name of Damien's daughter who carries the torch for the devil in 1991's television movie *Omen IV: The Awakening?*

Answers on page 140

ANSWERS TO CURSE OF THE DEMON (1958)

831. Stonehenge **832.** Jacques Tourneur **833.** Lufford Hall **834.** Paranormal psychology, ESP, and the supernatural **835.** Professor Harrington **836.** In the British Museum **837.** A magician. He was billed as Dr. Bobo the Magnificent. **838.** Three days **839.** Leopard **840.** He returns the magic talisman.

GENERALLY DEVILISH QUESTIONS

862. What famous horror studio's last shocker was *To the Devil—A Daughter* (1976)?

863. What was the name of the last silent horror film?

864. In what film does Alan Alda play a classical piano player whose soul is switched with that of Curt Jurgens?

865. Who are the two male stars who find themselves and their wives being chased by a coven in *Race with the Devil* (1975)?

866. Who plays a butler with a lollipop in *The House of Exorcism* (1973)?

867. What was the devil doll in *The Devil Doll* (1963)?

868. Who has *The Devil Within Her* (1975) in the film of that title?

869. Who stars as a goat-headed demon in *The Devil's Rain* (1975)?

870. Who is marked to have the devil's child in *To the Devil—A Daughter*?

871. Who stars as Louis Cyphre (Lucifer) in *Angel Heart* (1987)?

872. Who plays the devil in *The Evil* (1981)?

873. Who plays the son of Kirk Douglas and the antichrist in *The Chosen* (1978)?

874. Who claims to be Satan in *Mr. Frost* (1991)?

Answers on page 142

HAVING A DEVIL OF A TIME

875. In what 1934 film does Dr. Vitus Verdegast (Bela Lugosi) play chess with devil-worshiping Hjalmar Poelzig (Boris Karloff) for the life of a potential sacrifice (Jacqueline Wells)?

ANSWERS TO THE EXORCIST (1973)

841. Twelve years old   **842.** William Friedkin   **843.** Mercedes McCambidge   **844.** William Peter Blatty   **845.** Mount Ranier, Maryland, where a young boy apparently was possessed   **846.** Ellen Burstyn   **847.** Jason Miller   **848.** Sir Richard Burton   **849.** "Tubular Bells"   **850.** George C. Scott

ANSWERS TO THE OMEN (1976)

851. Jerry Goldsmith   **852.** Damien   **853.** Gregory Peck and Lee Remick   **854.** England   **855.** By hanging   **856.** Seven   **857.** Jonathan Scott-Taylor   **858.** Meshach Taylor   **859.** William Holden   **860.** Sam Neill   **861.** Delia

876. *All That Money Can Buy* (1941) is based on what famous short story by Stephen Vincent Benét?

877. By what name does the devil (Walter Huston) go by in *All That Money Can Buy?*

878. In *All That Money Can Buy,* what does the devil trade Jabez Stone (James Craig) in exchange for the farmer's soul?

879. What area of New York City is the home of a group of satanists in *The Seventh Victim* (1943)?

880. Who plays the devil in *The Story of Mankind* (1957)?

881. Name the satanic cult leader played by Charles Gray in *The Devil Rides Out* (1968).

882. How do the Duc de Richleau (Christopher Lee) and his friends protect themselves from an onslaught of evil forces (including a giant spider and the Angel of Death) in *The Devil Rides Out?*

Bruce Campbell looks out for the handyman in The Evil Dead *(1983), a cult classic from writer-director Sam Raimi.*

883. What happens to the members of a satanic cult at the end of *The Devil's Rain* (1975)?

884. In what kind of vehicle do Peter Fonda and friends use to flee angry devil worshipers in *Race with the Devil* (1975)?

885. What happens to Baron Corofax (Peter Cushing) and his satanic group after they are sprinkled with holy water by an Irish priest (Donald Pleasance) in *Land of the Minotaur* (1976)?

886. What does *The Sentinel* (1977) stand guard over in the basement of a Brooklyn apartment building?

887. TRUE OR FALSE: Bill Cosby plays an emissary of hell in *The Devil and Max Devlin* (1981).

888. How does Coopersmith (Clint Howard) contact Satan in *Evilspeak* (1982)?

889. Name the demonic tome used to summon *The Evil Dead* (1983).

890. How are unsuspecting victims transformed into monsters in *Demons* (1986)?

891. Who both wrote and directed *Hellraiser* (1987)?

892. Who is the leader, played by Doug Bradley, of the demonic Cenobites in *Hellraiser*?

893. What alias does Satan (Al Pacino) use in *The Devil's Advocate* (1997)?

894. From what state does satanic victim Kevin Lomax (Keanu Reeves) hail in *The Devil's Advocate?*

Answers on page 143

ANSWERS TO GENERALLY DEVILISH QUESTIONS

862. England's Hammer Films　**863.** *Seven Footprints to Satan* (1927)　**864.** *The Mephisto Waltz* (1971)　**865.** Peter Fonda and Warren Oates; the female costars are Loretta Swit and Lara Parker.　**866.** Telly Savalas　**867.** A ventriloquist's dummy　**868.** Joan Collins　**869.** Ernest Borgnine　**870.** Natassia Kinski　**871.** Robert De Niro　**872.** Victor Buono　**873.** Simon Ward　**874.** Jeff Goldblum

SATAN'S SLOGANS

Match the ad copy to the correct film.

895. "Come in, children."

896. "It will tear your soul apart . . . again."

897. "The first time was only a warning."

898. "Slave to Satan!"

899. "The newest attorney in the world's most powerful law firm has never lost a case. But he's about to lose his soul."

900. "Funnier than *The Omen* . . . Scarier than *Silent Movie*."

901. "Chosen . . . Singled out to die. Victim of his imagination or victim of a demon?"

902. "It will tear your soul apart."

903. "A living nightmare of black magic . . . and unspeakable evil!"

904. "Every corner of the soul is lost to the icy touch of the supernatural!"

A. *The Seventh Victim* (1943)

B. *Curse of the Demon* (1957)

C. *The Blood on Satan's Claw* (1971)

D. *The Brotherhood of Satan* (1972)

E. *Lisa and the Devil* (1974)

F. *Satan's Cheerleaders* (1977)

G. *Damien—Omen II* (1978)

H. *Hellraiser* (1987)

I. *Hellbound: Hellraiser II* (1988)

J. *The Devil's Advocate* (1997)

Answers on page 144

ANSWERS TO HAVING A DEVIL OF A TIME

875. *The Black Cat* **876.** "The Devil and Daniel Webster" **877.** Mr. Scratch **878.** Some gold and a guarantee of seven years of prosperity **879.** Greenwich Village **880.** Vincent Price **881.** Mocata **882.** The group is protected by lying in a pentagram that has been drawn on the floor. **883.** The evildoers melt. **884.** Camper **885.** The satanists explode. **886.** The gateway to hell itself **887.** True **888.** Via computer **889.** *The Book of the Dead* **890.** They watch a possessed horror film. **891.** Clive Barker **892.** Pinhead **893.** John Milton, in homage to the author of *Paradise Lost* **894.** Florida

DAVID CRONENBERG

PERHAPS NO OTHER filmmaker succeeds in conveying an atmosphere of personal horror better than Canadian director David Cronenberg. All of Cronenberg's films pertain in some way to the horror of the human body; diseases don't just kill people in his films—they transform them into new life-forms. The very nature of what constitutes a human and how the outside world influences or reacts to that perception seem to be Cronenberg's main philosophical concerns. Audiences, however, seek out Cronenberg films because they know his nightmarish visions never fail to elicit screams of pure terror.

Born in Toronto on March 15, 1943, Cronenberg began making experimental films while still in college. His first feature, *They Came from Within* (a.k.a. *Shivers,* 1975) featured 1960s horror heroine Barbara Steele in a story of scientifically created parasites that transformed their victims into sexually voracious mutants. Cronenberg followed this with *Rabid* (1977), in which former porn star Marilyn Chambers played a motorcyle accident victim who became a sexual vampire after receiving an experimental skin graft (unbridled scientific experimentation is usually the true menace in a Cronenberg film).

Other Cronenberg offerings include *The Brood* (1979), *Scanners* (1981), *Videodrome* (1983), an adaptation of Stephen King's *The Dead Zone* (1983), a remake of *The Fly* (1986), and *Dead Ringers* (1988). The director brought William S. Burroughs's underground classic *The Naked Lunch* to the screen in 1991. His next two projects, an adaptation of the musical *M. Butterfly* (1993) and the controversial *Crash* (1996), seemed to indicate that Cronenberg was drifting away from his more unrealistic horrors, but *eXistenZ* (1999), about violent video games that

---

ANSWERS TO SATAN'S SLOGANS

895. D   **896.** I   **897.** G   **898.** A   **899.** J   **900.** F   **901.** B   **902.** H   **903.** C   **904.** E

plug directly into a person's body, put him back in familiar territory.

Cronenberg, a bespectacled, mild-mannered sort who looks as if he ought to be teaching English somewhere, has also made appearances in his own movies and those of other directors. In Clive Barker's *Nightbreed* (1990) and Gus Van Sant's *To Die For* (1995), his talent for playing psychotic killers suggests Cronenberg has the potential to become something of a horror star himself.

TOP 5 DEMONS AND DEVILS MOVIES

Curse of the Demon (1957)
Rosemary's Baby (1968)
The Exorcist (1973)
The Devil Rides Out (1968)
The Omen (1976)

Abbott and Costello come unwound when they run into the number-one customer of Band-Aids in Abbott and Costello Meet the Mummy *(1955), with Eddie Parker as the guy who's mum.*

10

SCREAMS OF LAUGHTER

I'm the ghost with the most, babe.

—Betelgeuse (Michael Keaton) in *Beetlejuice* (1988)

ABBOTT AND COSTELLO MEET THE MONSTERS

905. Who plays Count Dracula in *Abbott and Costello Meet Frankenstein* (1948)?

906. What form does Dracula take when he wants to fly in *Abbott and Costello Meet Frankenstein?*

907. At the end of *Abbott and Costello Meet Frankenstein,* whose voice is heard as the Invisible Man?

908. Who portrays the Wolf Man in *Abbott and Costello Meet Frankenstein?*

909. Who plays Dr. Jekyll in *Abbott and Costello Meet Dr. Jekyll and Mr. Hyde* (1953)?

910. What movie star's photo hangs from a wall in an early scene from *Abbott and Costello Meet the Invisible Man* (1951)?

911. Complete the title: *Abbott and Costello Meet the Killer* _____ _____ (1949).

912. What Abbott and Costello "monster" flick takes place in Egypt?

913. What Abbott and Costello film takes place in a haunted house and features the Andrews Sisters?

914. When Lou Costello drinks the potion in *Abbott and Costello Meet Dr. Jekyll and Mr. Hyde,* what does he change into?

915. TRUE OR FALSE: Abbott and Costello never encountered the Creature from the Black Lagoon.

Answers on page 149

The surprise success of Abbott and Costello's first collaboration with Frankenstein, Dracula, and the Wolf Man, initiated a series of Abbott and Costello Meet . . . *films, spanning a decade.*

Little Shop of Horrible Laughs

916. Who stars as the botanist Seymour Krelboin, who creates Audrey Jr., in 1960's *Little Shop of Horrors?*

917. What is carnivorous plant Audrey Jr.'s most famous line (two words) in *Little Shop of Horrors?*

918. How many days did it take producer-director Roger Corman to film *Little Shop of Horrors?*

919. Besides playing the holdup man, what other role did screenwriter Charles Griffith play in the original *Little Shop of Horrors?*

920. What future Oscar winner plays dental patient Wilbur Force in *Little Shop of Horrors?*

921. What is the name of the flower shop where the action occurs in *Little Shop of Horrors?*

922. Who stars as Audrey in the original *Little Shop of Horrors?*

923. Who stars as Seymour Krelboin in the 1986 remake of *Little Shop of Horrors?*

924. Who plays Audrey in the remake of *Little Shop of Horrors?*

925. Who provides the voice of Audrey Jr. in the remake of *Little Shop of Horrors?*

Answers on page 150

Abbott and Costello played opposite some of the icons of the genre, including Lugosi (above) and Karloff (right).

YOUNG FRANKENSTEIN IN THE GENES (1974)

926. Who plays the blind hermit in *Young Frankenstein?*

927. How does Gene Wilder pronounce his last name in *Young Frankenstein?*

928. What is the name of the book Frederick Frankenstein's grandfather wrote?

929. What comedian portrays Igor?

930. What actress marries the Monster?

931. What actress portrays Inga?

932. What musical number do Dr. Frankenstein and his monster perform?

933. Who portrays the Monster in *Young Frankenstein?*

934. Who directed *Young Frankenstein?*

935. What instrument does Frau Blücher (Cloris Leachman) play?

936. What happens every time someone says Frau Blücher's name?

Answers on page 151

ANSWERS TO ABBOTT AND COSTELLO MEET THE MONSTERS

905. Bela Lugosi   **906.** A cartoon bat   **907.** Vincent Price   **908.** Lon Chaney Jr.
909. Boris Karloff   **910.** Claude Rains (star of *The Invisible Man*)   **911.** *Boris Karloff*
912. *Abbott and Costello Meet the Mummy* (1955)   **913.** *Hold That Ghost* (1941)   **914.** A giant mouse   **915.** False. Abbott and Costello met the Creature on their television show.

WHO YOU GONNA CALL? GHOSTBUSTERS (1984)

937. What is the name of the giant marshmallow monster in *Ghostbusters*?

938. What is the name of the Ghostbusters' vehicle?

939. What actress plays Dana?

940. What is the occupation of Rick Moranis's character?

941. The Ghostbusters' office was originally used as what?

942. In front of what building do two stone lions come to life and fly away?

943. Who plays Dr. Peter Venkman?

944. Who portrays Janine, the Ghostbusters' secretary?

945. What ghost ship steers into New York City in *Ghostbusters II* (1989)?

946. What is the name of Sigourney Weaver's baby in *Ghostbusters II*?

Answers on page 152

Bill Murray, Dan Ackroyd, and Harold Ramis (left to right) are paranormal policemen in 1984's ghostly comedy Ghostbusters.

ANSWERS TO LITTLE SHOP OF HORRIBLE LAUGHS

916. Jonathan Haze   **917.** "Feeeeed meeeeeee!"   **918.** Two   **919.** He was the voice of Audrey Jr.   **920.** Jack Nicholson   **921.** Welles' Skid Row   **922.** Jackie Joseph   **923.** Rick Moranis   **924.** Ellen Greene   **925.** Levi Stubbs Jr.

GHOULISH GAGS

Match the humorous dialogue with the film.

947. "Get her! That was your whole plan! Get her! You were scientific!"

948. "I'm so scared even my goose pimples have goose pimples."

949. "I've seen *The Exorcist* about a hundred and sixty-seven times, and it keeps getting funnier every single time I see it. Not to mention the fact that you're talking to a dead guy."

950. "I'm going out for a bite to drink."

951. "In a half an hour the moon will rise and I'll turn into a wolf." "You and 20 million other guys."

952. "What we need today, young blood and brains."

953. "Raise your hands—and all of your flippers."

954. "I can't believe we said no to free beer."

955. "This thing is much too big to be some lost dinosaur."

956. "Sorry, Venkman, I'm terrified beyond the capacity for rational thought."

A. Larry Lawrence (Bob Hope) in *The Ghost Breakers* (1940)

B. Dr. Peter Venkman (Bill Murray) in *Ghostbusters* (1984)

C. Jay (Will Smith) in *Men in Black* (1997)

D. Larry Talbot (Lon Chaney Jr.) and Wilbur (Lou Costello) in *Abbott and Costello Meet Frankenstein* (1948)

E. Count Dracula (George Hamilton) in *Love at First Bite* (1979)

F. Val McKee (Kevin Bacon) in *Tremors* (1990)

G. Betelgeuse (Michael Keaton) in *Beetlejuice* (1988)

H. Count Dracula (Bela Lugosi) in *Abbott and Costello Meet Frankenstein* (1948)

I. Dr. Egon Spengler (Harold Ramis) in *Ghostbusters* (1984)

J. Dr. Nick Tatopoules (Matthew Broderick) in *Godzilla* (1998)

Answers on page 153

ANSWERS TO YOUNG FRANKENSTEIN IN THE GENES (1974)

926. Gene Hackman **927.** Fronk-enstein **928.** *How I Did It* **929.** Marty Feldman
930. Madeline Kahn **931.** Teri Garr **932.** "Puttin' on the Ritz" **933.** Peter Boyle
934. Mel Brooks **935.** Violin **936.** Horses whinny

Above, left, Skid Row foundling Seymour Krelborn (Rick Moranis) has a heart-to-heart talk with Audrey II, the Venus people-trap he discovered during a total eclipse of the sun, in Little Shop of Horrors *(1986). To the right, Peter Boyle has a crackling good time as the singing and dancing creature in* Young Frankenstein *(1974).*

LAUGHING BENEATH THE COVERS

957. Who starred as Mr. Chicken in *The Ghost and Mr. Chicken* (1966)?

958. What is the last line in *The Ghost and Mr. Chicken*—a line that is repeated throughout the film?

959. In what horror comedy can you see John Candy, Bill Murray, Steve Martin, Jim Belushi, and Christopher Guest?

960. What is Jerry Lewis's Mr. Hyde–like character's name in *The Nutty Professor* (1963)?

961. Who plays the coed the nutty professor is nuts over?

962. Who starred in the 1996 remake of *The Nutty Professor*?

ANSWERS TO WHO YOU GONNA CALL? GHOSTBUSTERS (1984)

937. The Stay Puft Marshmallow Man **938.** The Ectomobile **939.** Sigourney Weaver
940. Accountant **941.** Fire station **942.** New York Public Library **943.** Bill Murray
944. Annie Potts **945.** *Titanic* **946.** Oscar

963. How many different characters does the star of *The Nutty Professor* play in the 1996 remake?

964. There is a 1985 film titled *Transylvania 6-5000,* but what character starred in a 1963 cartoon of the same title?

965. Who plays the comely but false vampire in *Transylvania 6-5000*?

966. What film features Bob Hope and Paulette Goddard spending the night in a haunted castle on a Caribbean island?

967. Who plays Bob Hope's butler, Alex, in the film?

968. What famous vaudeville duo star in *Ghost Catchers* (1943)?

969. What famous comedy gang does Bela Lugosi bump into in *Spooks Run Wild* (1943)?

970. Who plays Renfield in *Love at First Bite* (1979)?

971. Who portrays Lydia in *Beetlejuice* (1988)?

972. What is Betelgeuse's profession in *Beetlejuice?*

973. In which Abbott and Costello film do the stars unload two suspicious crates in McDougal's House of Horrors?

974. In what 1939 film do Bob Hope and Paulette Goddard spend the night in a haunted house?

975. What famous director starred as the Schlockthrupus in 1971's *Schlock?*

976. Who directed *Beetlejuice* (1988)?

Answers on page 154

OH, SCARS EH?

Horror films or movies of a similar genre with a penchant to scare have won numerous Academy Awards over the years. Here is a list of those that have picked up the little golden robot. (The year listed is the year the film was released.)

1932:   Fredric March, Best Actor
        for *Dr. Jekyll and Mr. Hyde*

1943:   *The Phantom of the Opera,*
        Cinematography and
        Art-Set Decoration

1949:   *Mighty Joe Young,* Special
        Effects

1951:   *When Worlds Collide,* Special
        Effects

1962:   *Whatever Happened to Baby
        Jane?* Costume Design
        (black-and-white)

1963:   *Occurrence at Owl Creek Bridge,*
        Short Subjects (live-action
        subjects)

1968:   Ruth Gordon, Supporting
        Actress for *Rosemary's Baby*

1973:   *The Exorcist,* Writing (screen-
        play based on material from
        another medium) and Best Sound

1975:   *Jaws,* Sound, Music (original score), and Film Editing

Oscar-winning actor Fredric March poses beside his alter ego in Dr. Jekyll and Mr. Hyde *(1932).*

ANSWERS TO LAUGHING BENEATH THE COVERS

957. Don Knotts   **958.** "Attaboy, Luther!"   **959.** *Little Shop of Horrors* (1986)   **960.** Buddy Love, thought to be a parody of Dean Martin   **961.** Stella Stevens   **962.** Eddie Murphy
963. Seven   **964.** Bugs Bunny   **965.** Geena Davis   **966.** *The Ghost Breakers* (1940)
967. Willie Best   **968.** Olsen and Johnson   **969.** The Bowery Boys (or the East Side Kids)
970. Arte Johnson   **971.** Winona Ryder   **972.** Bio-exorcist   **973.** *Abbott and Costello Meet Frankenstein*   **974.** *The Cat and the Canary*   **975.** John Landis   **976.** Tim Burton

1976: *The Omen,* Music (original score)

1979: *Alien,* Visual Effects

1981: *An American Werewolf in London,* Makeup

1986: *The Fly,* Makeup

      Aliens, Visual Effects and Sound Effects Editing

1987: *Harry and the Hendersons,* Makeup

1988: *Beetlejuice,* Makeup

1989: *The Abyss,* Visual Effects

1990: Kathy Bates, Best Actress for *Misery*

1991: *The Silence of the Lambs,* Best Picture

      Anthony Hopkins for Best Actor

      Jodie Foster for Best Actress

      Jonathan Demme for Director

      Ted Tally, Writing (screenplay based on material previously produced or published)

1992: *Bram Stoker's Dracula,* Best Costume Design, Best Makeup, and Best Effects (sound effects editing)

1993: *Jurassic Park,* Best Sound, Visual Effects, and Best Effects (sound effects editing)

1994: *Ed Wood,* Martin Landau for Best Supporting Actor and Makeup

1996: *Independence Day,* Visual Effects

1997: *Men in Black,* Best Makeup

1998: *Gods and Monsters,* Writing (adapted screenplay)

TOP 5 SCREAMS OF LAUGHTER MOVIES

Abbott and Costello Meet Frankenstein (1948)
Ghostbusters (1984)
Young Frankenstein (1974)
The Ghost and Mr. Chicken (1966)
Love at First Bite (1979)

Simone Simon strikes terror in the hearts of some as a beautiful woman cursed by a Balkan legend in Val Lewton's masterpiece Cat People *(1942).*

II

DEADLIER THAN THE MALE

It was *the boogeyman!*

> —Laurie Strode (Jamie Lee Curtis),
> *Halloween* (1978)

CATTY LADIES

977. What type of big cat can Irena (Simone Simon) turn into in *The Cat People* (1942)?

978. Who was the producer of *The Cat People*?

979. Who directed the film?

980. In what famous park do several scenes take place?

981. What is Simone Simon's character's native country?

982. Where does she meet her demise?

983. Where does Alice Moore (Jane Randolph) find refuge from the Cat Woman?

984. Whom does the Cat Woman kill?

985. What actor loses an arm in *The Cat People* (1982)?

986. What type of big cat does Barbara Shelley share a psychic link with in *Cat Girl* (1957)?

Answers on page 159

CARRIE (1976)

987. Who directed this film based on Stephen King's first published book?

988. What is Carrie's last name?

989. What is the name of the high school Carrie attends (HINT: The name pays homage to a great Hitchcockian character)?

990. When Carrie discovers the book *The Secret Science Behind Miracles* in her school library, what word does she read and utter out loud?

991. Who plays Tommy Ross, the school hunk who takes Carrie to the prom?

992. Who plays bad boy Billy?

993. What is dumped on Carrie at the prom?

994. What is the prom night theme?

995. Which *Carrie* star eventually married the film's director?

996. What is the title of the 1999 sequel to *Carrie?*

Answers on page 160

SCREAM QUEENS

Whoever said that females are "the weaker sex" apparently didn't watch many horror films. Although they've played their share of victims, actresses in many films have demonstrated the ability to portray monsters, villains, and (more recently) monster fighters.

997. For what Fay Wray horror vehicle did Max Factor provide the makeup?

998. What Universal Pictures "scream queen" made her fantasy film debut in the Abbott and Costello comedy *Hold That Ghost* (1941)?

999. In what film does Jane Addams play a mad scientist's hunchbacked assistant?

1000. What transforms Nancy Archer (Allison Hayes) into a giant in *Attack of the 50-Foot Woman* (1957)?

1001. For what purpose does Janice Starlin (Susan Cabot) use the experimental serum that transforms her into *The Wasp Woman* (1959)?

1002. What film features Barbara Steele as a witch burned at the stake after being impaled with a spike-studded mask?

1003. What natural phenomenon triggers Carla's (Barbara Shelley) transformation into *The Gorgon* (1964)?

Piper Laurie plays a slightly obsessed mom in Carrie *(1976).*

1004. Who played Lin Tang, daughter of Fu Manchu (Christopher Lee), in five films?

1005. How does the creature (Susan Denberg) die at the conclusion of *Frankenstein Created Woman* (1967)?

1006. In what film does Ingrid Pitt play the lesbian vampire Carmilla?

1007. How does she meet her demise at the end of the film?

1008. Who play the *Twins of Evil* (1972)?

ANSWERS TO CATTY LADIES

977. A black panther   **978.** Val Lewton   **979.** Jacques Tourneur   **980.** Central Park in Manhattan   **981.** Serbia   **982.** In the zoo with the big cats   **983.** In a swimming pool **984.** Her psychiatrist (Tom Conway)   **985.** Ed Begley Jr.   **986.** A leopard

Joan Crawford (left) and Bette Davis (right) are squabbling siblings in What Ever Happened to Baby Jane? *(1962).*

1009. Who plays the witch-burning Gustav Weil in *Twins of Evil*?

1010. In what film does Jodie Foster play a murderous teenager?

1011. What movie critic unintentionally helped an obscure female revenge movie, *I Spit on Your Grave* (1978), garner a tremendous cult following in the early 1980s?

1012. What silent screen heroine matches wits with Robert Mtchum in *The Night of the Hunter* (1955)?

1013. Why does her brother (Malcolm MacDowell) propose an incestuous union to Irina (Nastassia Kinski) in *Cat People* (1982)?

1014. What is Trash (Linnea Quigley) doing just before being attacked by zombies in *Return of the Living Dead* (1985)?

ANSWERS TO CARRIE (1976)

987. Brian De Palma   **988.** White   **989.** Bates High School (Norman Bates in *Psycho*)
990. Telekinesis   **991.** William Katt   **992.** John Travolta   **993.** Pig's blood   **994.** Love Among the Stars   **995.** Nancy Allen   **996.** *The Rage: Carrie 2*

1015. What board game does Lady Sylvia Marsh (Amanda Donohoe) play in Ken Russell's delirious horror film *The Lair of the White Worm* (1988)?

1016. Name the child actress who played Wednesday in *The Addams Family* (1991) and *Addams Family Values* (1993).

1017. Who filled the bill in the lead role of *Attack of the 50-Foot Woman* when it was remade forty years after the original?

1018. What film had poster copy that read: "She was marked with the curse of those who slink and court and kill by night!"

1019. What actress is *The Bad Seed* (1956)?

1020. Why was Bette Davis's character called "Baby Jane" in *What Ever Happened to Baby Jane?* (1962)?

1021. TRUE OR FALSE: Joan Crawford costarred with Bette Davis in *Hush . . . Hush, Sweet Charlotte* (1964).

Answers on page 163

Allison Hayes played the victimized wife in the original Attack of the 50-Foot Woman *(1957).*

MISS MATCHING

Match the screamer to her film.

1022. Sian-Barbara Allen

1023. Adrienne Barbeau

1024. Meredith Baxter

1025. Olivia de Havilland

1026. Anita Ekberg

1027. Sondra Locke

1028. Lilli Palmer

1029. Barbara Stanwyck

1030. Susan Strasberg

1031. Peggy Weber

A. *Ben* (1972)

B. *The House That Screamed* (1970)

C. *The House That Would Not Die* (TV, 1970)

D. *Scream of Fear* (1960)

E. *Scream Pretty Peggy* (TV, 1973)

F. *Screaming Mimi* (1958)

G. *The Screaming Skull* (1958)

H. *The Screaming Woman* (TV, 1972)

I. *Swamp Thing* (1982)

J. *Willard* (1970)

Answers on page 164

Barbara Steele and John Richardson are on the verge of a tender moment in Black Sunday *(1961).*

SPECIES (1995)

1032. How does the secret research lab directed by Xavier Fitch (Ben Kingsley) fabricate alien DNA?

1033. After escaping from the lab, how does the young Sil (Michelle Williams) travel from Utah to Los Angeles?

1034. Why does Fitch want Dan Smithson (Forrest Whitaker) to join the monster-hunting team, which is otherwise made up of scientists Laura Baker (Marg Hellenberger), Stephen Arden (Alfred Molina), and government-sponsored assassin Preston Lennox (Michael Madsen)?

1035. What is the adult Sil (Natasha Henstridge) attempting to find in Los Angeles?

1036. How does Sil trick the search team into thinking she is dead?

1037. Where is Sil finally destroyed?

1038. In *Species II* (1998), how is new human-alien hybrid Eve (Natasha Henstridge) created?

1039. How does astronaut Patrick Ross (Justin Lazard) bring the alien menace to Earth?

1040. TRUE OR FALSE: Michael Madsen and Marg Hellenberger reprise the same characters they played in the first *Species* film.

1041. Name the famous artist who designed the alien incarnation of Sil.

Answers on page 165

ANSWERS TO SCREAM QUEENS

997. *Dr. X* (1932)   **998.** Evelyn Ankers   **999.** *House of Dracula* (1945)   **1000.** An encounter with radioactive aliens   **1001.** To reverse the aging process   **1002.** *Black Sunday* (1961)   **1003.** The full moon   **1004.** Tsai Chin   **1005.** She commits suicide by jumping off a cliff.   **1006.** *The Vampire Lovers* (1970)   **1007.** She is impaled on a spear and then decapitated by General von Spielsdorf (Peter Cushing).   **1008.** Mary and Madeline Collinson   **1009.** Peter Cushing   **1010.** *The Little Girl Who Lives Down the Lane* (1976)   **1011.** Roger Ebert, who railed against the movie in his column in the *Chicago Sun-Times* and on his television show, *Sneak Previews*   **1012.** Lillian Gish   **1013.** Having sex with each other is the only way to prevent them from turning into killer panthers.   **1014.** Performing a striptease in a graveyard   **1015.** "Snakes and Ladders"   **1016.** Christina Ricci   **1017.** Daryl Hannah   **1018.** *The Cat People* (1942)   **1019.** Patty McCormack   **1020.** She was a child star.   **1021.** False

HUNCHBACK TRIVIA QUIZ

1042. Who wrote the novel *The Hunchback of Notre Dame?*
1043. What is the locale for the films?
1044. What is the hunchback Quasimodo's occupation?
1045. What are the names of the gargoyles in the Disney animated version?
1046. What is the name of the King of Beggars?

Answers on page 166

PLAYING A HUNCH

Match the actor to the film.

1047. Lon Chaney	A. *Hunchback of Notre Dame* (1923)
1048. Anthony Hopkins	B. *Hunchback of Notre Dame* (1939)
1049. Tom Hulce	C. *Notre Dame de Paris* (1956)
1050. Charles Laughton	D. *Hunchback of Notre Dame* (TV, 1982)
1051. Mandy Patinkin	E. *Hunchback of Notre Dame* (1996)
1052. Anthony Quinn	F. *The Hunchback* (TV, 1997)

Answers on page 166

LADIES WITH A HUNCH

Match the actress to the film.

1053. Lesley-Anne Down	A. *Hunchback of Notre Dame* (1923)
1054. Salma Hayek	B. *Hunchback of Notre Dame* (1939)
1055. Gina Lollobrigida	C. *Notre Dame de Paris* (1956)
1056. Patsy Ruth Miller	D. *Hunchback of Notre Dame* (TV, 1982)
1057. Demi Moore	E. *Hunchback of Notre Dame* (1996)
1058. Maureen O'Hara	F. *The Hunchback* (TV, 1997)

Answers on page 166

ANSWERS TO MISS MATCHING

1022. E **1023.** I **1024.** A **1025.** H **1026.** F **1027.** J. **1028.** B **1029.** C **1030.** D
1031. G

GOTCHA!

Match the victim with her tormentor.

1059. Gloria Talbott
1060. Hilary Dwyer
1061. Veronica Carlson
1062. Lee Grant
1063. Kathleen Burke
1064. Hazel Court
1065. Elena Verdugo
1066. Joey Heatherton
1067. Joyce Meadows
1068. Nancy Barrett

A. Jonathan Frid, *House of Dark Shadows* (1970)

B. Lon Chaney Jr., *House of Frankenstein* (1944)

C. Anton Diffring, *The Man Who Could Cheat Death* (1959)

D. Troy Donahue, *My Blood Runs Cold* (1965)

E. Michael Ironside, *Visiting Hours* (1982)

F. Peter Cushing, *Frankenstein Must Be Destroyed* (1968)

G. Vincent Price, *The Conqueror Worm* (1968)

H. John Agar, *The Brain from Planet Arous* (1957)

I. Tom Tryon, *I Married a Monster from Outer Space* (1958)

J. Lionel Atwill, *Murders in the Zoo* (1933)

Answers on page 167

ANSWERS TO SPECIES (1995)

1032. An alien intelligence transmitted the DNA code to Earth.   **1033.** By train
1034. Dan is an "empath"—his psychic powers help him read Sil's thoughts.   **1035.** A suitable mate for reproducing her species   **1036.** Sil fakes her death in an explosive car crash.
1037. She is consumed in a burning pool of oil in the sewers of Los Angeles.   **1038.** Eve is cloned from traces of Sil's DNA.   **1039.** He is contaminated by alien DNA while on a mission to Mars.   **1040.** True   **1041.** H. R. Giger, designer of *Alien* (1979)

FAY WRAY

IF SHE NEVER made another horror film, Fay Wray would still be remembered as the greatest screamer of cinema and as the focus of King Kong's affections in the 1933 classic.

She was born Vina Fay Wray near Cardston, Alberta, Canada, on September 15, 1907. By the time she was a

teenager, the actress was in Hollywood making silent flicks. She went from Hoot Gibson westerns to stardom in the classic romantic drama *The Wedding March* (1928). Four years later, while making *The Four Feathers*, Wray met directors Merian C. Cooper and Ernest Schoedsack, who cast her opposite the tallest, darkest leading man in Hollywood, a guy named Kong.

During this period, Wray appeared in other horror films such as *Doctor X* (1932), *The Most Dangerous Game* (1932), *The Vampire Bat* (1933), *The Mystery of the Wax Museum* (1933), and *The Clairvoyant* (1934). Her non-genre film works include *Viva Villa!* (1934), *The Richest Girl in the World* (1934), *Murder in Greenwich Village* (1937), and *Not a Ladies' Man* (1942), after which she retired—only to return about ten years later for ten more movies in the 1950s, including *Hell on Frisco Bay* (1955), *Rock Pretty Baby* (1956), *Tammy and the Bachelor* (1957), and her last, *Dragstrip Riot*, in 1958.

ANSWERS TO HUNCHBACK TRIVIA QUIZ

1042. Victor Hugo   **1043.** Notre Dame Cathedral in Paris   **1044.** Bellringer   **1045.** Victor and Hugo   **1046.** Clopin

ANSWERS TO PLAYING A HUNCH

1047. A   **1048.** D   **1049.** E   **1050.** B   **1051.** F   **1052.** C

ANSWERS TO LADIES WITH A HUNCH

1053. D   **1054.** F   **1055.** C   **1056.** A   **1057.** E   **1058.** B

Wray starred in a 1953 television series, *The Pride of the Family,* and came out of retirement one last time to costar with Henry Fonda in the 1980 TV movie *Gideon's Trumpet.* Although long retired from the silver screen, Wray remains active in her nineties. She released an autobiography, *On the Other Hand,* in 1989 and declined director James Cameron's invitation to play the role in *Titanic* that brought Gloria Stuart back to the limelight.

EVELYN ANKERS

FOLLOWING IN THE footsteps of Fay Wray came Evelyn Ankers, nicknamed "Queen of the Screamers" in the 1940s. The actress was born on August 17, 1918, in Valparaíso, Chile, to British parents. She appeared in the British films *Rembrandt* (1937) and *Fire over England* (1938), among others, before coming to the States in the early 1940s.

Contracted by Universal in 1941, she immediately hit her stride and loosened her vocal cords in films such as *Hold That Ghost* (1941), *The Wolf Man* (1941), *Ghost of Frankenstein* (1942), *Son of Dracula* (1943), *The Mad Ghoul* (1943), *The Invisible Man's Revenge* (1944), and *The Frozen Ghost* (1945). Although she normally played "good" girls, Ankers could be bad. She plotted against Lon Chaney Jr. in *Weird Woman* (1944) and was nemesis to Basil Rathbone in the Sherlock Holmes feature *The Pearl of Death* (1946).

Among her other credits are *Pardon My Rhythm* (1944), *Black Beauty* (1946), *The Lone Wolf in London* (1947), *Tarzan's Magic Fountain* (1949), and *The Texan Meets Calamity Jane* (1951).

Ankers died of cancer at age sixty-seven on August 29, 1985, in Hawaii, where she had retired with her husband, actor Richard Denning.

ANSWERS TO GOTCHA!

1059. I **1060.** G **1061.** F **1062.** E **1063.** J **1064.** C **1065.** B **1066.** D **1067.** H **1068.** A.

BARBARA STEELE

THE MOST POPULAR scream queen of the sixties, Barbara Steele made most of her horror films in Italy, even though she was English by birth. Born December 29, 1937, in Trenton Wirrall, England, Steele came to prominence in Mario Bava's classic vampire tale *Black Sunday* (1961), in which she played both a bloodthirsty witch and her virginal descendant.

The film capitalized on Steele's striking good looks, particularly her piercing eyes. Over the next few years, she played victims and villains in equal measure, and often in the same movie. Steele costarred with Vincent Price in *The Pit and the Pendulum* (1961) then returned to Europe for *The Horrible Dr. Hitchcock* (1962), *The Ghost* (1963), *The She Beast* (1965), and *The Crimson Cult* (1968), a film in which she costarred with fellow horror vets Boris Karloff, Christopher Lee, and Michael Gough.

Steele also turned up in a few mainstream pictures, most significantly Federico Fellini's classic *8½* (1963), but chillers remained her stock-in-trade. Tired of making horror films and recently married to screenwriter James Poe, she retired from acting in 1970. Steele occasionally emerges from retirement to appear in the films of her admirers. Jonathan Demme cast her in *Caged Heat* (1974), David Cronenberg recruited her for *Shivers* (1975), and Joe Dante gave her a call for *Piranha* (1978).

In the 1980s Steele began working behind the camera for television producer Dan Curtis, which led to her being cast as Dr. Julia Hoffman in the 1991 revival of Curtis's Gothic soap opera *Dark Shadows*.

BRINKE STEVENS

THE PROLIFERATION OF straight-to-video horror films in the 1980s provided many aspiring actresses with a shortcut to stardom. In the pursuit of better things, many of this new generation of scream queens found only disappointment, but some, including Linnea Quigley and Michelle Bauer, have developed their own cottage industries based on their sexy scary screen personas. Brinke Stevens is probably the greatest success story among this group. A keen business savvy and hard work have made her the contemporary empress of scream queens.

Stevens was born Charlene Elizabeth Brinkeman on September 20, 1954, in San Diego, California. The actress originally pursued a career in marine biology, earning a master's degree in that area from the Scripps Institute of Oceanography. The stun-

Her first big role came as a scientist in *Attack of the B-Movie Monster* (1985). Soon she was working on *Slave Girls from Beyond Infinity* and *Sorority Babes in the Slimeball Bowl-a-Rama* (1988), two classics of late 1980s video cheese. Her other horror credits include *Transylvania Twist, Spirits, The Haunting Fear* (all 1990), *Bad Girls from Mars* (1991), *Teenage Exorcist* (1994), *Invisible Mom* (1995), and *Vampirates* (1998).

In addition to her film roles, Stevens has expanded her fan base with a galaxy of marketing techniques, including a newsletter, a set of trading cards, hundreds of glamour stills, and even a comic book, *Brinke of Eternity*. She also writes articles on the B-movie industry and penned the script for *Teenage Exorcist*. Stevens was briefly married to artist Dave Stevens, creator of *The Rocketeer*, in the early 1980s.

ning brunette soon made her way to Hollywood where she alternated bit parts with gigs as a model and a nude body double (a job she performed in the movie *Body Double*).

INGRID PITT

OF ALL THE beautiful women who provided "Hammer Glamour" for England's number-one producer of horror movies, the most memorable is Polish native Ingrid Pitt. Her exotic beauty and sensual, throaty voice earned her a fan following that continues to grow to this day. That's quite an accomplishment for a "scream queen" who, in her prime, appeared in only four horror films!

Pitt was born Ingoushka Petrov on November 21, 1944. While growing up in East Berlin, she studied to be an obstetrician, but she turned to acting after failing her exams. She took jobs as a model, stunt girl, and even a bull fighter before making her debut in *The Sound of Horror*, a Spanish dinosaur flick, in 1964. Following bit parts in *Chimes at Midnight* (1964), *Doctor Zhivago* (1965), and *A Funny Thing Happened on the Way to the Forum* (1966), Pitt landed a good role in *Where Eagles Dare* (1969) opposite Clint Eastwood and Richard Burton. This in turn led her to England's Hammer Films, where she was cast as

Ingrid Pitt (above left, in a 1970 still and, on the right, at an engagement in 1997) played in a variety of films, ranging from Doctor Zhivago *(1965) and* Where Eagles Dare *(1969) to Hammer productions such as* The Vampire Lovers *(1970) and* Countess Dracula *(1971).*

the bloodthirsty Carmilla in *The Vampire Lovers* (1970).

The success of *The Vampire Lovers* convinced Hammer to give Pitt the title role in *Countess Dracula* (1971), and she also appeared in *The House That Dripped Blood* (1970) and *The Wicker Man* (1973). At this point Pitt seemed more than able to succeed as a distaff rival to such established fright-film stars as Peter Cushing and Christopher Lee, but when the horror boom faded in the mid-1970s, she disappeared from the screen. By the early 1980s, however, she was a familiar face on British television, where she guest-starred on such pop-

ular shows as *Doctor Who, The Zoo Gang,* and *Smiley's People.* She also reemerged in mainstream motion pictures, including *Who Dares Wins* (1982), *The Wild Geese II* (1985), and *Hanna's War* (1988).

In recent years Pitt has written novels and appeared in several documentaries about the glory days of Hammer Horror, including *Flesh and Blood: The Hammer Heritage of Horror* (1994). The small but intensely fanatical cult following that has developed around her inspired the actress to launch *Pitt of Horror,* a magazine devoted both to her work and scary entertainment in general.

JAMIE LEE CURTIS

JAMIE LEE CURTIS has made the rare jump from scream queen to mainstream movie star. Born on November 22, 1958, in Los Angeles, Curtis is the daughter of Tony Curtis and Janet Leigh. One of her first jobs as a pro was in the 1977 television series *Operation Petticoat,* which was based on a feature film that starred her dad. The following year John Carpenter cast Curtis (at a salary of $8,000) as terrified baby sitter Laurie Strode in the seminal slasher film *Halloween.*

The flick's surprising success inspired a wave of derivative teen chop-'em-up movies, and Curtis headlined in *Prom Night* (1980), *Terror Train* (1980), *The Fog* (1980), and *Halloween II* (1981). In the title role of *Death of a Centerfold: The Dorothy Stratten Story* (1981), she hinted at her ability to handle weightier material, and the Dan Aykroyd–Eddie Murphy vehicle, *Trading Places* (1983), showed her flair for comedy. She escaped typecasting for good via *A Fish Called Wanda* (1988) and has since proved her worth in a variety of roles in films, such as *Blue Steel* (1990), *My Girl* (1991), *True Lies* (1994), *Forever Young* (1994), *Fierce Creatures* (1997), *Homegrown* (1998), and *Daddy and Them* (1999).

By 1998, Curtis felt comfortable enough to reprise her star-making role in *Halloween H2O: Twenty Years Later,* in which she shared scenes with her mother. Married to actor-writer-director Christopher Guest, Curtis became Baroness Lady Haden-Guest after her husband inherited the barony in 1996. She has written two best-selling children's books.

TOP 5 DEADLIER THAN THE MALE MOVIES

Halloween (1978)
The Lair of the White Worm (1987)
The Mystery of the Wax Museum (1933)
Attack of the 50-Foot Woman (1958)
Hold That Ghost (1941)

King Kong manhandles a flying reptile with one hand and keeps Fay Wray at bay with the other in King Kong *(1933).*

12

MONKEY STARS

I tell you I will prove your kinship with the ape. Erik's blood shall be mixed with the blood of man!

—Dr. Mirakle (Bela Lugosi) in *Murders in the Rue Morgue* (1930)

YOU KNOW THE NAME OF KING KONG

1069. What actor plays the hero, Jack Driscoll, in *King Kong* (1933)?

1070. What island did King Kong inhabit?

1071. How is King Kong billed by promoter Carl Denham (Robert Armstrong)?

1072. What is the first name of the heroine played by Fay Wray?

1073. What is the last line of the original *King Kong*?

1074. What actress calls Kong a "male *chauvinist* ape!" in *King Kong* (1976)?

1075. From what building does King Kong fall in the 1976 film?

1076. What is the color of the star simian in 1933's *Son of Kong*?

1077. What actress stars in *King Kong Lives* (1986) (HINT: She was a beauty who worked with a TV beast)?

1078. What famous makeup man plays the big ape in most of *King Kong* (1976)?

Answers on page 175

MIGHTY JOE YOUNG AT YOUR SERVICE

1079. What cowboy starred as the hero in the original *Mighty Joe Young* (1949)?

1080. Who was the female lead in the original *Mighty Joe Young*?

1081. What song would Jill sing to calm big Joe?

1082. In what American city did Joe perform?

1083. What actor from the original *King Kong* costars in the 1949 *Mighty Joe Young*?

1084. Who is the male star of 1998's *Mighty Joe Young*?

1085. What is Jill's last name in *Mighty Joe Young*?

Answers on page 177

MURDERS IN THE POE MORGUE

1086. Where does Dr. Mirakle (Bela Lugosi) exhibit his ape in *Murders in the Rue Morgue* (1932)?

1087. What television game-show panelist of the 1950s plays a woman of the streets who becomes a victim in *Murders of the Rue Morgue* (1932)?

1088. What actor plays medical student Pierre Dupin in this film?

Answers on page 177

GORILLA MY DREAMS

1089. What is the name of the carnival in *Gorilla at Large* (1954)?

1090. What actress plays the lady who swings over a cage of apes in *Gorilla at Large*?

1091. What one-name actress stars as a woman who changes into a gorilla in *Captive Wild Woman* (1943) and *Jungle Woman* (1944)?

1092. Who plays the hero in *Captive Wild Woman*?

1093. What actress turns into an ape woman in *Jungle Captive* (1945)?

Answers on page 177

GREAT APES AND GORILLAS

Match the film with the plot.

1094. *The Ape* (1940)
1095. *The Ape Man* (1943)
1096. *Bride of the Gorilla* (1951)
1097. *Dr. Renault's Secret* (1942)
1098. *Goliathon* (1977)
1099. *Konga* (1961)
1100. *The Mighty Gorga* (1969)
1101. *Monkey Shines* (1988)
1102. *The Monster Walks* (1932)
1103. *Return of the Apeman* (1944)
1104. *The Unholy Three* (1930)

A. Boris Karloff disguises himself as a gorilla.
B. Circus owner Anthony Eisley finds a giant ape.
C. George Zucco turns J. Carrol Naish from a gorilla into an apeman.
D. Is the haunted house killer a chimp or chump?
E. King Kong gone Hong Kong
F. Michael Gough as a mad doc whose gorilla attacks London
G. Monkey Ella helps quadriplegic Allan.
H. Murder at the circus and Lon Chaney's only talkie
I. Raymond Burr turns into a big ape.
J. Scientist Bela Lugosi turns himself into a killer apeman.
K. Scientist Bela Lugosi transplants John Carradine's brain into the missing link.

Answers on page 177

King Kong strutted about in King Kong Lives *(1986), but he died at the box office.*

ANSWERS TO YOU KNOW THE NAME OF KING KONG

1069. Bruce Cabot **1070.** Skull Island **1071.** "The eighth wonder of the world"
1072. Ann **1073.** "It was beauty killed the Beast." **1074.** Jessica Lange **1075.** The World Trade Center **1076.** White **1077.** Linda Hamilton **1078.** Rick Baker

PLANETS OF THE APES

1105. The 1968 film *Planet of the Apes* was based on what novel?

1106. What is the name of Charlton Heston's astronaut character in *Planet of the Apes*?

1107. Who portrays Dr. Cornelius in *Planet of the Apes*?

1108. What is the name of Linda Harrison's character in *Planet of the Apes*?

1109. What are the names of the doctors played by Kim Hunter and Maurice Evans in *Planet of the Apes*?

1110. Fill in the blank: In *Planet of the Apes*, Julius says, "You know the saying, 'Human see, ____ __.'"

1111. Who stars as human Brent in *Beneath the Planet of the Apes* (1970)?

1112. Fill in the blank: Says an ape in *Beneath the Planet of the Apes*, "The only good human is _ ____ _____."

1113. How many apes escape to twentieth-century Earth in *Escape from the Planet of the Apes* (1971)?

1114. What is the name of the baby ape in *Escape from the Planet of the Apes*?

Charlton Heston is placed on trial for being disruptive to the social order in Planet of the Apes *(1968).*

1115. What is worshiped as a god in *Beneath the Planet of the Apes?*

1116. What is the name of Cornelius's son in *Conquest of the Planet of the Apes* (1972)?

1117. Who portrays General Aldo in 1973's *Battle for the Planet of the Apes* (HINT: He co-starred in *B.J. and the Bear*)?

1118. What actor starred as Galen in the 1974 *Planet of the Apes* television series and was in four of the *Planet of the Apes* feature films?

1119. Which *Planet of the Apes* movie ends with the word "Mama"?

1120. Which of the *Planet of the Apes* movies is considered the most violent?

1121. TRUE OR FALSE: *Planet of the Apes* producer Arthur P. Jacobs's wife, Natalie Trundy, played a human, an ape, and a mutant in the various *Apes* movies.

1122. At the shocking conclusion of *Planet of the Apes,* what does Taylor see half buried in the sand?

Answers on page 178

ANSWERS TO MIGHTY JOE YOUNG AT YOUR SERVICE

1079. Ben Johnson **1080.** Terry Moore **1081.** "Beautiful Dreamer" **1082.** Hollywood **1083.** Robert Armstrong **1084.** Bill Paxton **1085.** Young

ANSWERS TO MURDERS IN THE POE MORGUE

1086. A Paris sideshow **1087.** Arlene Francis **1088.** Leon Ames

ANSWERS TO GORILLA MY DREAMS

1089. The Garden of Evil **1090.** Anne Bancroft **1091.** Acquanetta **1092.** Milburn Stone, "Doc Adams" on television's *Gunsmoke* **1093.** Vicky Lane

ANSWERS TO GREAT APES AND GORILLAS

1094. A **1095.** J **1096.** I **1097.** C **1098.** E **1099.** F **1100.** B **1101.** G **1102.** D **1103.** K **1104.** H

WILLIS H. O'BRIEN

WILLIS H. O'BRIEN was the pioneer of fantasy films and a man with a knack for making dinosaurs come to rip-roaring life on the silver screen.

Born in Oakland, California, on March 2, 1886, cartoonist-sculptor O'Brien began his film career in about 1914, with the Edison Company, where he produced film shorts set in prehistoric days. His early special effects credits include *The Dinosaur and the Missing Link* (1916), *Prehistoric Poultry* (1916), *R.F.D. 10,000 B.C.* (1916), and *The Ghost of Slumber Mountain* (1918).

He practically invented live-action animation (a.k.a. stop-motion animation) by crafting rubber figures with flexible metal skeletons, and then shifting them bit by bit as film was exposed, thus creating the effect of reality and motion. His *Lost World* (1925) was a tremendous success. O'Brien proved even greater prowess with his work as the chief technician on *King Kong*, making the great ape appear to come to life.

He later won an Oscar for his special effects mastery on *Mighty Joe Young* (1949). Over the years he showed his stuff in the films *The Son of Kong* (1933), *The Black Scorpion* (1957), and *Behemoth, The Sea Monster* (1959). O'Brien died on November 8, 1962, at age seventy-six.

RODDY MCDOWALL

RODDY MCDOWALL MADE 150 feature films during a career that spanned seven decades. Born Roderick Andrew Anthony Jude McDowall in London, England, on September 17, 1928, the actor was one of the most successful child stars of the 1940s with such credits as *How Green Was My Valley* (1941), *My Friend Flicka* (1942), *Lassie Come Home* (1943), *The White Cliffs of Dover* (1944), *Keys of the Kingdom* (1944), *Macbeth* (1948), and *Kidnapped* (1949).

During the 1950s McDowall was mostly offscreen, but he became a successful stage and television performer, winning both a Tony and an Emmy in 1960. His film career returned with a flourish in the 1960s, when he show-

---

ANSWERS TO PLANETS OF THE APES

1105. *Monkey Planet,* by Pierre Boulle   **1106.** Col. George Taylor   **1107.** Roddy McDowall
1108. Nova   **1109.** Zira and Zaius   **1110.** "human do."   **1111.** James Franciscus   **1112.** "a dead human"   **1113.** Three   **1114.** Milo   **1115.** An atomic bomb   **1116.** Caesar
1117. Claude Akins   **1118.** Roddy McDowall   **1119.** *Escape from the Planet of the Apes*
1120. *Conquest of the Planet of the Apes*   **1121.** True   **1122.** The ruins of the Statue of Liberty

cased his broad talents in Disney comedies (1966's *The Adventures of Bullwhip Griffin*), war films (1963's *The Longest Day*), dramas (1966's *Inside Daisy Clover*), and costume epics (1966's *Cleopatra*). McDowall's most important adult film role, however, was as an articulate ape in the sci-fi classic *Planet of the Apes* (1968), three sequels, and the television series.

McDowall continued to make all types of films—appearing in *The Life and Times of Judge Roy Bean* (1972), *The Poseidon Adventure* (1972), *Evil Under the Sun* (1982), *Dead of Winter* (1987), and *Overboard* (1989)—and doing voice work for *The Black Hole* (1979) and the animated *A Bug's Life* (1998).

In the meantime, the actor hit his mark in a number of good horror films from the 1960s and into the 1990s, including *It!* (1967), *The Legend of Hell House* (1973), *Arnold* (1974), and *Carmilla* (1989). Perhaps his most fondly remembered role is Peter Vincent, the vampire-hunting horror host of *Fright Night* (1985) and *Fright Night Part II* (1989).

McDowall was also a prolific television actor who guest-starred on everything from *The Twilight Zone* and *Alfred*

Underneath the makeup, Roddy McDowall, (standing) and Kim Hunter (seated) pose with their "son" in Escape from the Planet of the Apes *(1971).*

Hitchcock Presents to *Combat* and *Matlock* to *Batman* (live and animated).

The actor died of cancer at age seventy on October 3, 1998. McDowall was an accomplished photographer who published five books of his works. The Academy of Motion Picture Arts and Sciences named its photographic archives in his honor.

TOP 5 MONKEY STARS MOVIES

King Kong (1933)
Planet of the Apes (1968)
Mighty Joe Young (1949)
Murders in the Rue Morgue (1932)
Captive Wild Woman (1943)

Kevin McCarthy and Dana Wynter are on the run in Invasion of the Body Snatchers *(1956).*

13

THEY CAME FROM ANOTHER PLANET

If they're mortal, they have mortal weaknesses. They'll be stopped—somehow.

—Clayton Forrester (Gene Barry) in *The War of the Worlds* (1953)

GREETINGS, EARTHLINGS

1123. In what 1956 film is it said, "That truck was carrying a load of the strangest-looking seed pods"?

1124. What is the name of the village in 1960's *Village of the Damned*?

1125. Who play the male and female leads in the 1995 remake of *Village of the Damned*?

1126. Who played Dr. Clayton Forrester in 1953's *The War of the Worlds*?

1127. Who wrote the novel on which *The War of the Worlds* is based?

1128. What newsman played himself in 1951's *The Day the Earth Stood Still*?

1129. Who played Klaatu in *The Day the Earth Stood Still*?

1130. What is the name of the robot in *The Day the Earth Stood Still*?

1131. *The Day the Earth Stood Still* won a 1952 Golden Globe for what?

1132. Who played Gen. William Grey in 1996's *Independence Day*?

1133. In *Independence Day*, on what date (day and month) is Washington, D.C., first attacked?

Jean Carson in I Married a Monster from Outer Space *(1958) with Ken Lynch, right, and Tom Tryon, both looking pretty grim. Courtesy of Jean Carson.*

1134. Name two films in which actor Jeff Goldblum says the line, "Faster. Must go faster!"

1135. What is the name of actor Tom Tryon's monstrous character in 1958's *I Married a Monster from Outer Space?*

1136. Who played Dr. Arthur Carrington in *The Thing from Another World* (1951) and Dr. Pryor in 1953's *The War of the Worlds?*

1137. Who played Dr. David Kibner in the 1978 remake of *The Invasion of the Body Snatchers?*

1138. What remake warned, "Man is the warmest place to hide"?

1139. Who plays Martin Cochrane in 1957's *Monolith Monsters?*

1140. What creatures are the first to be made into mush in 1982's *The Thing?*

1141. Who played the Thing in *The Thing from Another World?*

1142. Who played Captain Roth in 1953's *Invaders from Mars?*

Answers on page 184

I DON'T THINK THEY'RE FROM AROUND HERE

1143. Howard Keel was the star of what 1962 film about mutant plants that stalk humans?

1144. In what 1960s television series are the films *Moon Men Invade Venus on Giant Bats* and *The Anteaters from Outer Space* mentioned?

1145. Jimmy Hunt, who plays David Maclean in 1953's *Invaders from Mars,* plays what role in the 1986 remake?

1146. Who is "the weirdest visitor the earth has ever seen"?

1147. What is the special danger that *Kronos* (1957) presents to earthlings?

1148. Who played the Cosmic Man in the 1959 release of the same name?

1149. Who plays Talleah in 1958's *Queen of Outer Space?*

1150. What is the name of the Venusian queen in *Queen of Outer Space?*

1151. *Grave Robbers from Outer Space* was the original title for what "classic"?

1152. What words does Helen Benson (Patricia Neal) say to save Earth in *The Day the Earth Stood Still?*

Answers on page 185

Kevin McCarthy and Dana Wynter flee from a motley crowd in Invasion of the Body Snatchers *(1956).*

What in the World Is This?

1153. What film won the Academy Award in 1954 in the category "Best Effects, Best Special Effects"?

1154. How is *The Thing* of 1951 destroyed?

1155. What color is the hair of the children in 1960's *Village of the Damned*?

1156. What Golden Turkey Award winner is widely acclaimed as "the worst movie of all time"?

1157. In what sci-fi horror film can the Grateful Dead's Jerry Garcia be spotted playing a banjo in a park?

1158. In what sci-fi take on Shakespeare's *The Tempest* does Robby the Robot first appear?

1159. Who was the original choice to play Klaatu in *The Day the Earth Stood Still*?

1160. What film warns, "Earth, take a good look. It could be your last."

1161. Who plays the role of Dr. Alvin Kurtzweil in 1998's *The X Files*?

1162. What effect does pure oxygen have on the aliens in 1958's *I Married a Monster from Outer Space*?

Answers on page 186

And Still They Come . . .

1163. Who plays the role of Tom Jones in 1996's *Mars Attacks!*?

1164. *Mars Attacks Puerto Rico* is better known as what 1965 film?

1165. Who wrote the novel on which 1971's *The Andromeda Strain* is based?

1166. What is Will Smith's character's name in *Independence Day*?

1167. What is the name of the satellite that brings the Andromeda strain down to Earth?

1168. What film was Steve McQueen's first starring role?

ANSWERS TO GREETINGS, EARTHLINGS

1123. *Invasion of the Body Snatchers* **1124.** Midwich **1125.** Christopher Reeve and Kirstie Alley **1126.** Gene Barry **1127.** H. G. Wells **1128.** CBS's Drew Pearson **1129.** Michael Rennie **1130.** Gort **1131.** Best Film Promoting International Understanding **1132.** Robert Loggia **1133.** July 3 **1134.** *Jurassic Park* and *Independence Day* **1135.** Bill Farrell **1136.** Robert Cornthwaite **1137.** Leonard Nimoy **1138.** *The Thing* (1982) **1139.** Les Tremayne **1140.** Huskies **1141.** James Arness, best known as Matt Dillon on television's *Gunsmoke* **1142.** Milburn Stone, best known as Doc Adams on television's *Gunsmoke*

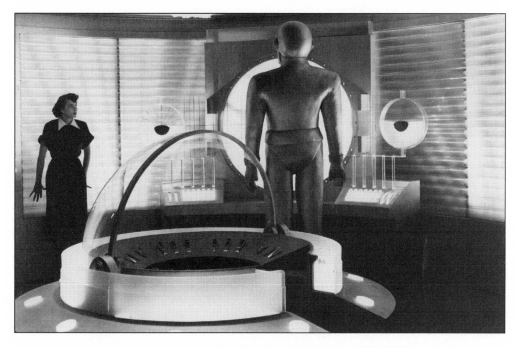

Patricia Neal encounters Gort in The Day the Earth Stood Still *(1951).*

1169. What 1950s space flick is very similar to the plot of *Alien?*

1170. How many eyes does the monster have in 1959's *The Angry Red Planet?*

1171. What is the name of the incredible melting man in 1977's *The Incredible Melting Man?*

1172. In what film are the words "All communications are out, which is why these tape recordings I'm making are for the sake of future history, if any" heard?

1173. Where does the government take its first downed alien in 1996's *Independence Day?*

1174. Who plays Dr. Doug Martin in 1954's *Killers from Space?*

Answers on page 187

ANSWERS TO I DON'T THINK THEY'RE FROM AROUND HERE

1143. *The Day of the Triffids* **1144.** *The Andy Griffith Show* **1145.** Police chief **1146.** *Man from Planet X* **1147.** It saps the earth's energy. **1148.** John Carradine **1149.** Zsa Zsa Gabor **1150.** Yllana **1151.** *Plan 9 from Outer Space* **1152.** "Klaatu barada nikto."

Zsa Zsa Gabor (center) and other stunning female inhabitants of Venus rule supreme in Queen of Outer Space (1958), while Eric Fleming (left) looks as if he's from Mars.

ALIENATED QUIZ

1175. How many sequels were there to *Alien?*

1176. Who directed *Alien* (1979)?

1177. What was the last name of Sigourney Weaver's character in *Alien?*

1178. What was the name of the space vehicle in *Alien?*

1179. Who else survived with Weaver's character in *Alien?*

1180. Who directed *Aliens?*

1181. What is the first name of Sigourney Weaver's character in *Aliens?*

1182. How many characters survived in *Aliens?*

1183. Why does Ripley commit suicide in *Alien 3?*

1184. How is Ripley resurrected in *Alien: Resurrection?*

Answers on page 188

ANSWERS TO WHAT IN THE WORLD IS THIS?

1153. *The War of the Worlds* **1154.** Electrocution **1155.** Blond **1156.** *Plan 9 from Outer Space* **1157.** *The Thing* (1982) **1158.** *Forbidden Planet* **1159.** Claude Rains **1160.** *Independence Day* **1161.** Martin Landau **1162.** It kills them.

COMPANY'S COMING

1185. What actors portray Agent Jay and Agent Kay in *Men in Black* (1997)?

1186. How many earthlings return from Mars in *Angry Red Planet* (1959)?

1187. In *Invaders from Mars* (1953), Jimmy Hunt plays a boy who has nightmarish dreams about what?

1188. The son of what actress has the lead role in the remake of *Invaders from Mars* (1986)?

1189. In *Lifeforce* (1985) a space shuttle brings vampires to London from what destination?

1190. Who plays Dr. Leslie Gaskill in 1957's *Kronos*?

1191. What is the name of the forbidden planet in *Forbidden Planet* (1956)?

1192. Who plays Dr. Edward Morbius in *Forbidden Planet*?

1193. What is the name of Gog's companion robot in *Gog* (1954)?

1194. What is the name of the master computer in *Gog*?

Answers on page 189

Gene Barry and Amy Robinson dodge murderous Martians in War of the Worlds *(1953).*

ANSWERS TO AND STILL THEY COME . . .

1163. Tom Jones   **1164.** *Frankenstein Meets the Space Monster*   **1165.** Michael Crichton
1166. Capt. Steven Hiller   **1167.** *Scoop VII*   **1168.** *The Blob* (his salary was $3,000)
1169. *It! The Terror from Beyond Space*   **1170.** Three   **1171.** Steve West   **1172.** *The War of the Worlds*   **1173.** Area 51   **1174.** Peter Graves

GEORGE ZUCCO

GEORGE ZUCCO WAS born January 11, 1886, in Manchester, England, and made his acting debut in 1908 in Canada. He played vaudeville before going to the stage in London and on Broadway. He began working in films with 1930's *The Dreyfus Case*. For the next thirty years, Zucco specialized in aristocratic archvillains and fiends.

He seesawed between classy A pictures, such as *The Good Companions* (1933), *Marie Antoinette* (1935), *My Favorite Blonde* (1946), *Madame Bovary* (1949), and *David and Bathsheba,* and B time-killers such as *The Mad Monster* (1942), *Dead Men Walk* (1943), *Voodoo Man* (1944), and *The Flying Serpent* (1946). But horror fans best remember Zucco as the high priest of Karnak in three mummy films during the 1940s. His other horror works include *The Hunchback of Notre Dame* (1939), *The Cat and the Canary* (1939), *House of Frankenstein* (1944), and *The Mad Ghoul* (1943). Mystery fans relished his performance as Professor Moriarty in *The Adventures of Sherlock Holmes* (1939). Zucco died in 1960 in Hollywood.

LIONEL ATWILL

LIONEL ALFRED WILLIAM ATWILL was born on March 1, 1885, in Croydon, England. He studied to be an architect, but he fell in love with the stage and made his acting debut in 1905. After appearing on-stage in London and America with such leading ladies as Lily Langtry and Helen Hayes, he made his film debut in 1918 in *Eve's Daughter.*

Atwill, nicknamed "Pinky," was typecast as a villain. In 1932 he made his first

---

ANSWERS TO ALIENATED QUIZ

1175. Three: *Aliens, Alien 3,* and *Alien: Resurrection*   **1176.** Ridley Scott   **1177.** Ripley
1178. *Nostromo*   **1179.** Her cat   **1180.** James Cameron   **1181.** Ellen   **1182.** Three: Ripley, Newt, and Cpl. Dwayne Hicks   **1183.** An alien embryo has been implanted in her body.
1184. She is a clone of the original Ripley.

horror film, playing the mad scientist in *Doctor X.* A year later he appeared as a most memorable madman, Ivan Igor, in *The Mystery of the Wax Museum* (1933). Further roles in *The Vampire Bat* (1933), *Murders in the Zoo* (1933), *Mark of the Vampire* (1935), and *Man Made Monster* (1941) entrenched Atwill as a formidable horror heavy. At the same time, however, he also began appearing in many Universal productions on the right side of the law, usually as a police inspector or government official—for example, in *Son of Frankenstein* (1939), *Frankenstein Meets the Wolf Man* (1943), and both *House of Frankenstein* (1944) and *House of Dracula* (1945).

Lionel Atwill (right) in Mark of the Vampire *(1935)*

Atwill did other roles, villainous and otherwise. Among those credits are *Captain Blood* (1935), *Johnny Apollo* (1940), *Pardon My Sarong* (1942), *The Three Musketeers* (1939), and *The Secret of Dr. Kildare* (1939). Probably his best non-horror role was as Professor Moriarty in *Sherlock Holmes and the Secret Weapon* (1942). He died on April 22, 1946, of pneumonia while making the serial *Lost City of the Jungle.*

TOP 5 THEY CAME FROM ANOTHER PLANET MOVIES

Invasion of the Body Snatchers (1956)
The Day the Earth Stood Still (1951)
The War of the Worlds (1953)
Alien (1979)
The Thing (1951)

ANSWERS TO COMPANY'S COMING

1185. Will Smith and Tommy Lee Jones   **1186.** Two and brainwashing the people, even his mom and dad Carson)   **1189.** Halley's Comet   **1190.** Jeff Morrow **1193.** Novac   **1194.** Magog   **1187.** Martians taking over his town   **1188.** Karen Black (her son: Hunter   **1191.** Altair-4   **1192.** Walter Pidgeon

An incendiary cockroach ravages the face of Patty McCormick in Bug *(1975).*

14

BIG BUGS AND GIANT REPTILES

Eventually, you do *plan to have dinosaurs on your dinosaur tour, right?*

—Ian Malcolm (Jeff Goldblum) in
Jurassic Park (1993)

CREEPY CRAWLIE QUIZ

1195. What is the name of the thirty-six-foot-long gator in *Alligator* (1980)?

1196. In what city's sewers does the gator roam?

1197. What is the name of the sewer worker whom the gator chomps as a victim?

1198. Who stars as the heroine in *The Alligator People* (1959)?

1199. In what does the big bad spider travel from South America to the United States in *Arachnophobia* (1990)?

1200. Who plays exterminator Delbert McClintock in *Arachnophobia*?

1201. What cowboy star finds a tyrannosaurus eating his cattle in *The Beast of Hollow Mountain* (1959)?

1202. What cowboy star puts a dinosaur in a circus in *Valley of the Gwangi* (1969)?

1203. What creatures attack Chicago in *The Beginning of the End* (1957)?

1204. How are the creatures destroyed in *The Beginning of the End*?

1205. Who plays the hero in *The Beginning of the End*?

1206. Where do the scorpions come from that attack Mexico City in *The Black Scorpion* (1957)?

Answers on page 193

MORE CREEPIES AND CRAWLIES

1207. What kind of creature is *The Beast from 20,000 Fathoms* (1953)?

1208. Where does the beast meet its demise?

1209. What character actor kills the beast with a bullet made of an atomic isotope?

1210. How is *The Deadly Mantis* (1957) eliminated?

1211. Who plays the hero in *The Deadly Mantis*?

1212. What city and its landmarks does the mantis attack?

1213. What television star-vixen gets gobbled by giant ants in *Empire of the Ants* (1977)?

1214. How many sequels were there to the original *The Fly* (1958)?

1215. The original *The Fly* was based on a short story that appeared in what magazine?

1216. Who portrays Francois Delambre in two of the earlier *Fly* films?

1217. Who wrote the screenplay for the original *The Fly*?

1218. What are the famous two words cried out (in duplicate) by the scientist in the original *The Fly*?

1219. What actor has the lines "Be afraid. Be very afraid" in *The Fly* (1986)?

1220. What actor turns into a six-foot fly in *The Fly* (1986)?

1221. What actor becomes a pest in *The Fly II* (1989)?

Answers on page 194

AW, BIG AIN'T THE WORD FOR IT

1222. What veteran character actor is the hero in *The Giant Behemoth* (1959)?

1223. What kind of dinosaur is the behemoth?

1224. What city does the behemoth attack?

1225. In what Canadian province does *The Giant Claw* (1957) lay its eggs?

1226. Who plays the main good guy in *The Giant Claw*?

1227. What singing cowboy actor produced *The Giant Gila Monster* (1959)?

1228. What London landmark does *Gorgo* (1960) destroy?

1229. What West Coast landmark is the Creature after in *It Came from Beneath the Sea* (1953)?

1230. What is the Creature in *It Came from Beneath the Sea*?

1231. How is the Creature destroyed?

1232. Who plays the hero in *Kingdom of the Spiders* (1977)?

1233. The different film versions of *The Lost World* are based on a novel by what author?

1234. In the silent film version of *The Lost World* (1925), what kind of dinosaur is brought back to London?

1235. Who plays Professor Challenger in the 1960 version of *The Lost World*?

1236. What was used to portray dinosaurs in 1960's *The Lost World*?

Answers on page 195

Gorgo runs rampant in London in 1961.

ANSWERS TO CREEPY CRAWLIE QUIZ

1195. Ramon **1196.** Chicago **1197.** Ed Norton, named after the *Honeymooners* character **1198.** Beverly Garland **1199.** A coffin **1200.** John Goodman **1201.** Guy Madison **1202.** James Franciscus **1203.** Grasshoppers **1204.** They are drowned in a lake. **1205.** Peter Graves **1206.** A volcano

Mere bullets are harmless to the gigantic ants in Them! *(1954).*

A QUIZ WITH LEGS

1237 In what film did people turn to stone when they looked upon Prudence Hyman's character?

1238. What do Al Rokker, Danny DeVito, Sylvester Stallone, Dionne Warwick, George Lucas, and Steven Spielberg all have in common in *Men in Black* (1997)?

1239. Who plays Professor Challenger in 1925's *The Lost World*?

1240. Who plays Challenger in 1992's *The Lost World*?

1241. Who directed 1960's *The Lost World*?

1242. What *Playboy* centerfold plays Liz Walker in 1959's *Attack of the Giant Leeches*?

1243. What is *Mothra* (1962) before he becomes a giant moth?

1244. How do the two twelve-inch-tall Alilenas attract Mothra to Tokyo?

1245. What crop do the albino inhabitants force the mole men to grow in *The Mole People* (1956)?

1246. Who play the two heroes of *The Mole People*?

Answers on page 196

ANSWERS TO MORE CREEPIES AND CRAWLIES

1207. A rhedosaurus   **1208.** Coney Island   **1209.** Lee Van Cleef   **1210.** Gassed in Holland Tunnel   **1211.** Craig Stevens, best known as Peter Gunn   **1212.** Washington, D.C.   **1213.** Joan Collins   **1214.** Two: *Return of the Fly* and *Curse of the Fly*   **1215.** *Playboy*   **1216.** Vincent Price   **1217.** James Clavell   **1218.** "Help me! Help me!"   **1219.** Geena Davis   **1220.** Jeff Goldblum   **1221.** Eric Stoltz

THIS BUGS ME QUIZ

1247. What creatures wreak terror on an Indian reservation in *Nightwing* (1979)?

1248. What city is destroyed in *Rodan* (1957)?

1249. What type of creatures are the two monsters in *Rodan*?

1250. Who portrays Steve in *Tarantula* (1955)?

1251. Who is the mad scientist in *Tarantula*?

1252. In what film can you see the early talents of James Arness, Fess Parker, and Leonard Nimoy?

1253. What are "them" in *Them!* (1954)?

1254. Where in Los Angeles are the creatures of *Them!* destroyed?

1255. Giant worms attack what town in *Tremors* (1990)?

1256. What singer makes her film debut in *Tremors* as Heather Gummer?

Answers on page 197

It's cowboys and dinosaurs in Ray Harryhausen's Valley of the Gwangi *(1969).*

ANSWERS TO AW, BIG AIN'T THE WORD FOR IT

1222. Gene Evans **1223.** Brontosaurus **1224.** London **1225.** Quebec **1226.** Jeff Morrow **1227.** Ken Curtis **1228.** London Bridge **1229.** Golden Gate Bridge **1230.** A giant octopus **1231.** It is torpedoed. **1232.** William Shatner **1233.** Sir Arthur Conan Doyle **1234.** A brontosaurus **1235.** Claude Rains **1236.** Live lizards and iguanas

MORE QUESTIONS TO MAKE YOUR SKIN CRAWL

1257. Faith Domergue turns into a cobra and goes after David Janssen, Jack Kelly, Marshall Thompson, Richard Long, and William Reynolds in what 1955 Universal flick?

1258. What type of monster is *Gamera the Invincible* (1965)?

1259. Who leads Hugh Beaumont and Whit Bissell in an expedition to a plateau of dinosaurs and Acquanetta in *The Lost Continent* (1951)?

1260. What former child star plays a mad scientist who makes a big spider and king-sized ladies in *Mesa of Lost Women* (1952)?

1261. What cowboy movie star is the hero of *The Monster That Challenged the World* (1957)?

1262. What awakens a giant "dead spider" in *The Spider* (1958)?

1263. Strother Martin turns what Hollywood hunk into a king cobra in *SSSSSSS* (1973)?

Answers on page 198

Strother Martin, left, is a scientist conducting studies on snake life who gets a helping hand from Jack Ging and Heather Menzies in SSSSSSS *(1973).*

ANSWERS TO A QUIZ WITH LEGS

1237. *The Gorgon* (1964)   **1238.** They all play aliens.   **1239.** Wallace Beery   **1240.** John Rhys-Davies   **1241.** Irwin Allen   **1242.** Yvette Vickers   **1243.** A giant caterpillar **1244.** By singing in unison   **1245.** Mushrooms   **1246.** Hugh Beaumont and John Agar

Cesar Romero, front and center, leads a cast of intrepid characters in 1951's Lost Continent.

DINO MIGHT QUIZ

1264. Who directed *Jurassic Park* (1993) and its sequel, *The Lost World: Jurassic Park* (1997)?

1265. How are dinosaurs re-created in *Jurassic Park*?

1266. How does a can of shaving cream play a part in *Jurassic Park*?

1267. In what city does a tyrannosaurus run amok in *The Lost World: Jurassic Park*?

1268. Who is the author of both *Jurassic Park* novels?

Answers on page 199

ANSWERS TO THIS BUGS ME QUIZ

1247. Vampire bats   **1248.** Tokyo   **1249.** Pterodactyls   **1250.** Mara Corday   **1251.** Leo J. Carroll   **1252.** *Them!*   **1253.** Giant ants   **1254.** In the sewers   **1255.** Perfection, Nevada   **1256.** Reba McEntire

Champion swimmer and diver Ricou Browning (and later a director) performed the underwater scenes as the Gill Man in The Creature from the Black Lagoon *(1954).*

The Creature from the Black Lagoon

1269. Who directed *The Creature from the Black Lagoon* (1954)?

1270. Along what river is the Creature discovered?

1271. What is another name given to the Creature?

1272. Who plays the Creature on land?

1273. TRUE OR FALSE: The film was originally released in 3-D.

1274. Who plays the heroine in *The Creature from the Black Lagoon*?

1275. Where is the Creature taken in *Revenge of the Creature* (1955)?

1276. Who plays the hero in the sequel?

1277. Who plays a lab assistant and makes his movie debut in *Revenge of the Creature*?

1278. What multiple Oscar–winner wrote or cowrote all of the original music for *The Creature Walks Among Us* (1956)?

Answers on page 200

ANSWERS TO MORE QUESTIONS TO MAKE YOUR SKIN CRAWL

1257. *Cult of the Cobra*　**1258.** A giant fire-breathing turtle　**1259.** Cesar Romero
1260. Jackie Coogan　**1261.** Tim Holt　**1262.** Rock 'n' roll music　**1263.** Dirk Benedict

THE GODZILLA OF QUIZZES

1279. What is Godzilla's name in Japan?

1280. Who designed Godzilla?

1281. How tall is Godzilla?

1282. What is the English name for one of Godzilla's later foes, Kingu Kongu?

1283. Who or what is Godzilla's first victim?

1284. Who or what is Godzilla's second victim?

1285. Near what island did all of these early encounters with Godzilla take place?

The answer to the first question above is readily apparent to those who can read Japanese in the Godzilla *movie poster below (left). The poster art proved effective and was repeated for* Godzilla, King of the Monsters *(1956)*

ANSWERS TO DINO MIGHT QUIZ

1264. Steven Spielberg **1265.** Dinosaur DNA found in the preserved bodies of insects is scientifically re-created. **1266.** An attempt to smuggle dinosaur DNA is made using the can as a disguise. **1267.** Los Angeles **1268.** Michael Crichton

1286. What do the Japanese scientists believe caused Godzilla to erupt?

1287. Who plays Steve Martin in *Godzilla?*

1288. What is Martin's vocation?

1289. Martin is on his way to what international city when he stops in Tokyo?

1290. Martin reports that eight ships have been obliterated by what?

1291. What is the first weapon the Japanese use against the colossal, fire-breathing lizard?

1292. Where does Godzilla lurk just before he begins his crushing assault on Tokyo?

1293. How is the country rid of Godzilla?

1294. What was the title of the first *Godzilla* sequel?

1295. What city does Godzilla attack in the original *Godzilla, King of the Monsters* (1956)?

1296. What is the last name of the Japanese director of *Godzilla, King of the Monsters?*

1297. In *Godzilla Raids Again* (1959) Godzilla comes to terms with an Angilas. What is this fire monster's name?

1298. After his first fight with Godzilla in *Kong Kong vs. Godzilla* (1963), what force of nature brings King Kong's strength back?

1299. Where does the battle between King Kong and Godzilla take place in the finale of *King Kong vs. Godzilla* (1963)?

1300. What two creatures polish off Godzilla in *Godzilla vs. Mothra* (1964)?

1301. In what film does Godzilla first team with Mothra and Rodan?

1302. What American actor stars in *Godzilla vs. Monster Zero* (1965)?

1303. Who is the bad guy behind all the mayhem in *Godzilla vs. Monster Zero* (1966)?

1304. In what film does a boy dream he goes to Monster Island?

1305. What kind of creature does Godzilla fight in *Godzilla vs. the Sea Monster* (1967)?

1306. What is the name of the sea monster in *Godzilla vs. the Sea Monster?*

1307. What happens to the evil island of Letchi in the exciting conclusion of *Godzilla vs. the Sea Monster?*

ANSWERS TO THE CREATURE FROM THE BLACK LAGOON

1269. Jack Arnold **1270.** Amazon **1271.** Gill Man **1272.** Ben Chapman **1273.** True
1274. Julie Adams **1275.** A Florida aquarium **1276.** John Agar **1277.** Clint Eastwood
1278. Henry Mancini

1308. What is the name of the offspring in *Son of Godzilla* (1968)?

1309. In 1968's *Destroy All Monsters,* what specific city does each of the following monsters nuke, blast, level, and trample: Godzilla, Mothra, Rodan, and King Ghidorah?

1310. What is the name of the little boy in *Godzilla's Revenge* (1969)?

1311. What remarkable feat does Godzilla debut in *Godzilla vs. Gigan* (1969)?

1312. In a 1969 short, what famous woodlands cartoon creature does Godzilla stomp?

1313. What creates the monster Hedorah in *Godzilla vs. Hedorah* (1971)?

1314. In what film does Godzilla team with Jet Jaguar, a robot, to battle Gigan and Megalon?

1315. Who fights on Godzilla's side in *Godzilla vs. Mechagodzilla* (1974)?

1316. What is the name of the subterranean beings who unleash Megalon against those bomb-bursting earthlings in *Godzilla vs. Megalon* (1976)?

1317. What is the name of the wicked professor with a cyborg daughter in *Terror of Mechagodzilla* (1978)?

1318. What gigantic amphibious dinosaur is Mechagodzilla's ally in *Terror of Mechagodzilla?*

1319. In what latter-day *Godzilla* film does Raymond Burr return for a visit?

1320. In what film do we discover Godzilla was born in 1944 after a dinosaur mutated when a Bikini H-bomb went off?

1321. Aliens from what century warn the citizens of Tokyo that Godzilla will soon be awake and on the warpath in *Godzilla vs. King Ghidrah* (1991)?

1322. How many heads does King Ghidrah have?

1323. What are the two tiny women on Infant Island called in *Godzilla vs. Mothra* (1992)?

1324. In *Godzilla and Mothra: The Battle for Earth* (1992), Battra and Mothra team up against Godzilla. What is another name Battra is called?

1325. In *Godzilla vs. Gigan* (1993), aliens from another nebula settle in what entertaining locale?

1326. Godzilla's foe in *Godzilla vs. Space Godzilla* (1994) is a mutated form of what monster?

1327. Who lives with Godzilla on Birth Island in *Godzilla vs. Destroyer* (1995)?

1328. In *Godzilla vs. Destoroyah* (1998) Godzilla, Godzilla Junior, and what other monster get into a three-way melee?

1329. Who thought he needed a bigger box to catch Godzilla in 1998?

1330. What city does Godzilla attack in 1998's *Godzilla*?

1331. Which two stars of TV's *The Simpsons* have major roles in *Godzilla* (1998)?

1332. In 1998, what famous sports venue does Godzilla lay eggs?

1333. What is the tagline for 1998's *Godzilla*?

1334. What beverage does Jean Reno have a hard time finding in *Godzilla* (1998)?

Answers on pages 204–5

BIG AND LITTLE PEOPLE

1335. Who had the title role in *The Amazing Colossal Man* (1957)?

1336. What city does the colossal man attack?

1337. At what famous site is the Amazing Colossal Man stopped?

1338. Who starred in the title role of *The Attack of the 50-Foot Woman* (1957)?

1339. Who starred in the 1993 television movie *Attack of the 50-Foot Woman*?

1340. What film is showing at the drive-in as Daryl Hannah makes an appearance in the 1993 television movie?

Some days it just doesn't pay to be the biggest man in town. Lack of clothes can lead you to contemplate your state, like the title character in The Amazing Colossal Man *(1957).*

And of course, at the opposite end of the spectrum, there's something to be said about bigness. This topic was explored in The Incredible Shrinking Man *in the same year as* The Amazing Colossal Man.

1341. Who stars as *Dr. Cyclops* (1940)?

1342. How many explorers does Dr. Cyclops shrink?

1343. Who has the title role in *The 30-Foot Bride of Candy Rock* (1959)?

1344. Who plays groom to the 30-Foot Bride?

1345. Who plays the lead in *The Incredible Shrinking Man* (1957)?

1346. What two creatures does he flee from?

1347. What midget actor appears in *The Incredible Shrinking Man*?

1348. Who stars as *The Incredible Shrinking Woman* (1981)?

1349. What is the title of the sequel to *The Amazing Colossal Man*?

1350. In *Attack of the Puppet People* (1958), what film do hero John Agar and his girlfriend see at a drive-in?

1351. In what other film besides *Cyclops* (1957) can you find Dean Parkins playing a bad big, big man?

1352. In 1936's *The Devil-Doll*, who plays the madman who shrinks people to twelve inches in order that they can rob and kill for him?

Answers on page 205

RAY HARRYHAUSEN

ON THE SAME stop-motion animation plateau as Willis H. O'Brien's creations is the imaginative work of Ray Harryhausen. Born in Los Angeles on June 29, 1920, Harryhausen was awed when he saw *King Kong* on the big screen in 1933. Already a photography enthusiast, he was soon experimenting at home in his garage with puppets while studying art and drama in school. During World War II, he served in the Signal Corps in the navy, where he produced training films.

Afterward he worked on George Pal's *Puppetoons* and then joined his hero O'Brien in 1946, with whom he served ably on *Mighty Joe Young* (1949). Harryhausen went on to bigger projects from there, like *The Beast from 20,000 Fathoms* (1953) and, after pairing with producer Charles H. Schneer, turned out such products as *Jason and the Arg-* *onauts* (1963), *One Million Years B.C.* (1966), *The Valley of the Gwangi* (1969), *The Golden Voyage of Sinbad* (1974), and *Clash of the Titans* (1981).

ANSWERS TO THE GODZILLA OF QUIZZES

1279. Gojira **1280.** Eiji Tsuburaya **1281.** Over 400 feet tall **1282.** King Kong **1283.** A Japanese ship **1284.** The ship sent to rescue the first one **1285.** Oto Island **1286.** Experiments with H-bombs **1287.** Raymond Burr **1288.** Correspondent for United World News **1289.** Cairo **1290.** "Mysterious, blinding flash of light" **1291.** Depth bombs **1292.** Tokyo Harbor **1293.** Godzilla is destroyed with a new oxygen-based weapon. **1294.** *Godzilla Raids Again* (1959) **1295.** Tokyo **1296.** Honda (Inoshiro Honda) **1297.** Gigantis **1298.** Thunderbolts from a rainstorm **1299.** Mount Fuji **1300.** Giant caterpillars **1301.** *Ghidrah, the Three-headed Monster* (1965) **1302.** Nick Adams **1303.** The Controller of Planet X **1304.** *Godzilla's Revenge* (1969) **1305.** A giant lobster **1306.** Ebirah **1307.** Letchi is nuked into oblivion **1308.** Minya **1309.** In order: New York, Beijing, Moscow, and Tokyo **1310.** Ichiro **1311.** He talks. **1312.** Bambi **1313.** Smog or pollution **1314.** *Godzilla vs. Megalon* (1974) **1315.** Kingseesar **1316.** The Seatopians **1317.** Professor Mafuni **1318.** Titanosaurus **1319.** *Godzilla 1985* **1320.** *Godzilla vs. King*

No one was better at mixing actors and animated creatures on film. Harryhausen had skeletons dueling with good guys, like Jason and Sinbad, and made it look real. Along the way he developed his own processes, which he dubbed Dynamation and then Superdynamation.

In 1972, Harryhausen authored *Film Fantasy Scrapbook*. Twenty years later, the stop-motion animator and special effects genius was awarded the Gordon E. Sawyer Special Achievement Award from the Academy of Motion Pictures Arts and Sciences.

TOP 5 BIG BUGS AND GIANT REPTILES MOVIES

Jurassic Park (1993)
Them! (1954)
The Incredible Shrinking Man (1957)
The Fly (1958)
Godzilla, King of the Monsters (1954)

ANSWERS TO THE GODZILLA OF QUIZZES (CONTINUED)

Ghidrah **1321.** The twenty-third century **1322.** Three **1323.** The Cosmos **1324.** Black Mothra **1325.** Children's Land Amusement Park **1326.** Mothra **1327.** Little Godzilla **1328.** The Oxygen Destroyer **1329.** The Taco Bell chihuahua in popular television commercials **1330.** New York City **1331.** Hank Azaria and Harry Shearer **1332.** Madison Square Garden **1333.** "Size does matter." **1334.** A good cup of coffee

ANSWERS TO BIG AND LITTLE PEOPLE

1335. Glenn Langan **1336.** Las Vegas **1337.** Hoover Dam **1338.** Allison Hayes **1339.** Daryl Hannah **1340.** The original *Attack of the 50-Foot Woman* **1341.** Albert Dekker **1342.** Five people . . . and one burro **1343.** Dorothy Provine **1344.** Lou Abbott **1345.** Grant Williams **1346.** A cat and a spider **1347.** Billy Curtis **1348.** Lily Tomlin **1349.** *War of the Colossal Beast* (1958) **1350.** *The Amazing Colossal Man* **1351.** *War of the Colossal Beast* **1352.** Lionel Barrymore

Michael Landon, before he turned into Little Joe Cartwright, turned into a juvenile werewolf in I Was a Teen-age Werewolf *(1957).*

15
THOSE HORRIBLE TEEN YEARS

*You get a letter? I got run over, Helen gets her hair
chopped off, Julie gets a dead body in her trunk, and you
get a letter? Oh, that's balanced!*

—Barry (Ryan Phillipe) in *I Know What You
Did Last Summer* (1997)

WE ALL SCREAM FOR SCREAM QUIZ

1353. In 1996's *Scream,* the last name of Skeet Ulrich's character, Billy Loomis, is a tip of the hat to what two other horror classics?

1354. Who plays Fred, the janitor, in *Scream?*

1355. Who is the first victim in *Scream?*

1356. What is the name of Courtney Cox's character in *Scream?*

1357. In what town do the events in *Scream* take place?

1358. Name two actresses who have played the character Sidney Prescott in the *Scream* movies.

1359. In 1997's *Scream 2,* where do Sidney and Randy attend college?

1360. What star of television's *Ally McBeal* plays a sorority girl named Murphy in *Scream 2?*

1361. What actor or actors with the name Arquette play police officers in one or more of the *Scream* movies?

1362. What is the name of the movie within a movie in *Scream 2?*

Neve Campbell finds terror on the line in Scream *(1996).*

1363. What is the name of the sequel to the movie within a movie in *Scream 2* that is revealed in *Scream 3* (1999)?

1364. What is the name of the book written by Gale Weathers that is the basis for the movie within a movie in *Scream 2*?

1365. Where do the murders in *Scream 3* take place?

Answers on page 209

I Know What You Did Last Summer and the Next

1366. What *Scream* writer also helped pen 1997's *I Still Know What You Did Last Summer*?

1367. Who plays Helen Shivers in *I Know What You Did Last Summer*?

1368. What is the weapon of choice in *I Know What You Did Last Summer* and the sequel?

1369. Who is the first person left for dead in *I Know What You Did Last Summer*?

1370. Where does the killing in 1998's *I Still Know What You Did Last Summer* take place?

1371. Who won the free trip for four to the tropics in *I Still Know . . . ?*

1372. What words flash on the karaoke screen to let Julie (Jennifer Love Hewitt) know there's trouble in *I Still Know . . . ?*

1373. Who plays Melissa (Missy) Egan in *I Know What You Did . . .* ?

1374. What is the name of Freddie Prinze Jr.'s character in *I Know . . .* and *I Still Know . . .* ?

1375. Who is Julie's boyfriend in *I Still Know . . .* ?

Answers on page 211

YOU'RE NOTHING BUT AN ANIMAL QUIZ

1376. What young actor plays the sickly boy befriended by a rat in *Ben* (1972)?

1377. What breed of dog was Cujo in *Cujo* (1983)?

1378. What star of a *Frankenstein* sequel is seen in *Willard* (1970)?

1379. What *Gunsmoke* star is under attack by oversized hairy dogs in *The Killer Shrews* (1959)?

1380. What legendary actor is croaked to death by hundreds of croakers in *Frogs* (1972)?

1381. What type of birds does Tippi Hedren's character purchase in the beginning of *The Birds* (1963)?

1382. In what town is *Jaws* (1975) set?

1383. On what river does *Anaconda* (1997) take place?

1384. What type of beast preys on Tom Skerritt in *Savage Harvest* (1981)?

1385. In what Irwin Allen film do killer bees put the sting on Henry Fonda, Olivia de Havilland, Richard Widmark, Fred MacMurray, Richard Chamberlain, and Slim Pickens?

1386. What type of critters go berserk in *Night of the Lepus* (1972)?

1387. What 1978 film about hungry little fish, directed by Joe Dante and starring Bradford Dillman, Kevin McCarthy, and Barbara Steele, spoofed *Jaws*?

1388. What causes the leeches in 1959's *Attack of Giant Leeches* to mutate into monsters?

1389. Who played the title role in *The Wasp Woman* (1959)?

Answers on page 211

ANSWERS TO WE ALL SCREAM FOR SCREAM QUIZ

1353. *Psycho* (1960) and *Halloween* (1978), both of which feature characters named Loomis
1354. Wes Craven   **1355.** Casey Becker (Drew Barrymore)   **1356.** Gale Weathers
1357. Woodsboro   **1358.** Neve Campbell and Tori Spelling   **1359.** Windsor College
1360. Portia de Rossi   **1361.** David Arquette (as Deputy Dwight "Dewey" Riley) and Lewis Arquette as Chief Louis Hartley   **1362.** *Stab*   **1363.** *Stab 2*   **1364.** *The Woodsboro Murders*
1365. Hollywood

THE BLOB (1958)

1390. What are Steve and Jane looking for in the night skies when they see the first sign of the Blob?

1391. What is the racing "crown" Steve wins during a drag race?

1392. What is Jane's father's occupation?

1393. What movie is playing at the local theater during this film?

1394. What horror star's name is on the theater marquee for the Midnight Spook Show?

1395. The poster for what movie is on the wall outside of the theater?

1396. The Blob traps Steve and Jane and others in what local eatery?

1397. What was taken from the high school to defeat the Blob?

1398. Where was the Blob's final destination in this film?

1399. What was the price of admission for Steve's friends to the Midnight Spook Show?

Answers on page 212

Jane Martin (Aneta Corsaut) and Steve Andrews (Steve McQueen) try to help an old man (Olin Howlin) as a doctor checks out a victim of The Blob *(1958).*

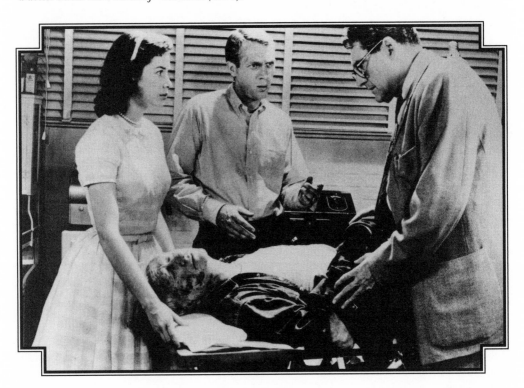

MORE TEEN ANGST

1400. What was the alternate title to 1972's *Beware! The Blob*?

1401. Who directed *Beware! The Blob* (HINT: It was nicknamed "the film that J.R. shot")?

1402. What actor, also seen in *Them!* is the first victim of the Blob in the original *The Blob*?

1403. What former cowboy star played the sheriff in *Gremlins* (1984)?

1404. Who was the voice of Gizmo in *Gremlins*?

1405. Who played Kate in *Gremlins*?

1406. Who portrayed the giant teenage caveman in *Eegah* (1962)?

1407. Who played the hero in *The Blob* (1988)?

1408. Who rescues the heroine from Eegah and sings bad rock 'n' roll in *Eegah*?

1409. Guess who directed *Eegah*?

1410. Where does Eegah meet his demise?

1411. What does Whit Bissell's Professor Frankenstein keep in a pit beneath the house in *I Was a Teenage Frankenstein* (1957)?

1412. In what 1959 cheapo flick about hot rods, teenagers, and a haunted house would you see the conclusion read "The Endest, Man"?

1413. Who plays Jamie Lee Curtis's dad in *Prom Night* (1980)?

1414. What was the alternate title for *Hello Mary Lou: Prom Night II* (1987)?

1415. What *Dawson's Creek* actor and *Hyperion Bay* actor appears in *Prom Night III: The Last Kiss* (1989)?

ANSWERS TO I KNOW WHAT YOU DID LAST SUMMER AND THE NEXT

1366. Kevin Williamson **1367.** Sarah Michelle Gellar **1368.** A hook **1369.** Benjamin Willis **1370.** The Bahamas **1371.** Karla Wilson (Brandy Norwood) **1372.** "I Still Know" **1373.** Anne Heche **1374.** Ray Bronson **1375.** Will Benson

ANSWERS TO YOU'RE NOTHING BUT AN ANIMAL QUIZ

1376. Lee Harcourt Montgomery **1377.** St. Bernard **1378.** Elsa Lanchester **1379.** Ken Curtis **1380.** Ray Milland **1381.** Love birds **1382.** Amityville **1383.** Amazon River **1384.** Lions **1385.** *The Swarm* (1978) **1386.** Rabbits **1387.** *Piranha* **1388.** Radiation from Cape Canaveral **1389.** Susan Cabot

1416. What is the occupation of the killer in *Prom Night IV: Deliver Us from Evil* (1992)?

1417. What acting kin of Jamie Lee Curtis appears with her in both *The Fog* (1980) and *Halloween H20* (1998)?

1418. In what teen flick are Tommy Kirk, Johnny Crawford, and Beau Bridges adolescents who grow thirty feet tall?

1419. What daughter of a superstar warbler sings in the film *Ghost in the Invisible Bikini* (1966)?

1420. What hot band from the early 1960s performs in the 1966 film *Ghost in the Invisible Bikini*?

1421. On what H. G. Wells novel was *Village of the Giants* supposedly based?

1422. What Oscar-winning actor plays the conductor in *Terror Train* (1980)?

1423. What world-famous magician wishes he could disappear from *Terror Train*?

1424. Who wrote the novel on which *The Other* (1972) is based?

Answers on page 214

TEENAGE CAVEMAN (1959)

1425. Who starred in the title role in *Teenage Caveman*?

1426. Who directed *Teenage Caveman*?

1427. How old was the actor in real life when he played the cave teen?

1428. What was the cave teen's father's position in the clan?

1429. What was the "god symbol"?

1430. What was their name for the land beyond the river?

1431. What new weapon does the teen invent?

1432. What does the clan find in the possession of a strange beast in the end?

Answers on page 214

ANSWERS TO THE BLOB (1958)

1390. Shooting stars (which Steve McQueen became)   **1391.** A hubcap   **1392.** High school principal   **1393.** *Daughter of Horror*   **1394.** Bela Lugosi   **1395.** *The Vampire and the Robot*   **1396.** The Downington Diner   **1397.** Fire extinguishers (the cold from the CO_2 was its nemesis)   **1398.** The Arctic   **1399.** 80 cents

Michael Landon tackled his first starring role in I Was a Teenage Werewolf *(1957) and reprised the role in "I Was a Middle-Aged Werewolf" during a 1988 episode of* Highway to Heaven.

I WAS A TEENAGE WEREWOLF (1957)

1433. What high school does Michael Landon's hirsute Tony attend?

1434. What does Tony do at the gym after observing the female gymnast practicing?

1435. How many victims fall prey to the teen werewolf?

1436. Who hypnotizes Tony and takes him back to mankind's primitive state?

1437. What tune does Vic sing at the percolating party where 7-Up is served?

1438. What character is the first to recognize that the victims have been killed by a werewolf?

1439. What type of animal chases the Werewolf in the woods only to be killed by the monster?

1440. What television star of *Zorro* and *Lost in Space* plays a cop in this film?

1441. What is the name of Tony's girlfriend?

1442. What lesson did the world learn from this tragic ordeal of young Michael Landon that was expressed in the last line of the movie?

1443. TRUE OR FALSE: Michael Landon played a werewolf again in *How to Make a Monster* (1958).

Answers on page 215

JOHN CARPENTER

DIRECTOR-WRITER-MUSICIAN John Carpenter was born January 16, 1948, in Carthage, New York, and grew up in Bowling Green, Kentucky, where his father was head of the music department at Western Kentucky University. As a youth, Carpenter absorbed sci-fi films and haunted the local movie theaters. By the age of eight he was making eight-millimeter films with his dad's camera.

After attending Western Kentucky he transferred to the USC Film School in Los Angeles and made a number of short films before giving birth to *The Resurrection of Bronco Billy,* a project that won him a 1970 Oscar for Best Short Subject in Live Action.

After his work on *Dark Star* (1975), a cult hit, and *Assault on Precinct 13* (1976), he was handed the reins to a $300,000 budget-flick called *The Baby-Sitter Murders.* With Donald Pleasance and Jamie Lee Curtis, Carpenter styled it into *Halloween* and watched it rake in more than $60 million.

He has since gone on to bigger budgets and films such as *The Fog* (1980), *The Thing* (1982), *Escape from New York* (1982), *Christine* (1983), *Big Trouble in Little China* (1984), *They Live* (1987), *Memoirs of an Invisible Man* (1991), *Village of the Damned* (1995), *Escape from L.A.* (1996), and *Vampires* (1999), while hooking up with actor Kurt Russell on several of these projects, including television's *Elvis* (1979).

Carpenter occasionally appears in his own films under the name of Rip Haight. He is a huge fan of the NBA, a major Elvis Presley devotee, and enjoys vintage Cadillacs. He is also a great admirer of the late director Sergio Leone.

ANSWERS TO MORE TEEN ANGST

1400. *Son of Blob* **1401.** Larry Hagman **1402.** Olin Howlin **1403.** Scott Brady
1404. Howie Mandell **1405.** Phoebe Cates **1406.** Richard Kiel, who later portrayed "Jaws" in two James Bond films **1407.** Kevin Dillon **1408.** Arch Hall Jr. **1409.** Arch Hall Sr.
1410. In a swimming pool **1411.** Alligators **1412.** *The Ghost of Dragstrip Hollow*
1413. Leslie Nielsen **1414.** *The Haunting of Hamilton High* **1415.** Dylan Neal **1416.** Priest
1417. Janet Leigh, her mother **1418.** *Village of the Giants* (1965) **1419.** Nancy Sinatra
1420. The Bobby Fuller Four **1421.** *Food of the Gods* **1422.** Ben Johnson **1423.** David Copperfield **1424.** Tom Tryon

ANSWERS TO TEENAGE CAVEMAN (1959)

1425. Robert Vaughn **1426.** Roger Corman **1427.** Twenty-five **1428.** Symbol maker
1429. A meteorite **1430.** "The land of the god that kills with its touch" **1431.** A bow and arrow **1432.** A book of photographs from the twentieth century, the atomic era

WES CRAVEN

FOR THREE DECADES, director-writer-producer Wes Craven has been giving moviegoers "nightmares." Born August 2, 1939, in Cleveland, Craven began writing and drawing while in high school. He earned an English degree from Wheaton College in Illinois, and then studied writing and philosophy at Johns Hopkins University. While teaching college, he started making sixteen-millimeter movies and soon left his original profession to pursue filmmaking.

The director struck first with *Last House on the Left* in 1972 and hit a scary lick again in 1977 with *The Hills Have Eyes*. He opened the 1980s with *Deadly Blessing* and *Swamp Thing* and then created the first of seven in a series, the prolific and profitable *Nightmare on Elm Street* (1984) with its evil Freddy Krueger.

Craven directed other spooky winners in *Shocker* (1989), *The People Under the Stairs* (1989), *The Serpent and the Rainbow* (1993), and *Vampire in Brooklyn* (1993). He then struck horror gold again with 1996's *Scream,* which he followed up with *Scream 2* in 1997 and *Scream 3* in 1999. He also created the television series *Nightmare Cafe* and directed several episodes of the 1985 *Twilight Zone* television series. Occasionally, the filmmaker shows up in minor roles in his films.

TOP 5 HORRIBLE TEEN YEARS MOVIES

Carrie (1976)
Scream (1996)
The Blob (1958)
I Was a Teenage Werewolf (1957)
Friday the 13th (1980)

ANSWERS TO I WAS A TEENAGE WEREWOLF (1957)

1433. Rockdale High (not to be confused with Archie Andrews's Riverdale High)   **1434.** He transforms into a werewolf and then kills the girl.   **1435.** Four (a teenage boy, a girl gymnast, two doctors)   **1436.** Dr. Brandon (Whit Bissell)   **1437.** "Eenie, Meenie, Minie, Mo"   **1438.** Peppe, the janitor at the police station (he was from the old country)   **1439.** A German shepherd   **1440.** Guy Williams   **1441.** Arlene   **1442.** "It's not for man to interfere in the ways of God."   **1443.** False. Landon once again played the Werewolf in an episode of *Highway to Heaven.*

Rod Serling, host and creator of TV classic The Twilight Zone.

16

TELEVISION HORROR SHOWS

As sure as my name is Boris Karloff, this is a thriller.
—Boris Karloff's introduction to *Thriller* (1960–62)

JUST BEGINNING TO SCARE YOU

1444. What television show began with the introduction, "Man lives in the sunlit world of what he believes to be reality. But there is unseen by most an underworld, a place that is just as real, but not as brightly lit, a dark side"?

1445. What television series began with the words, "There is nothing wrong with your television set. Do not attempt to adjust the picture. . . . For the next hour sit quietly and we will control all that you see and hear"?

1446. What television series opened with these words: "There is a fifth dimension beyond that which is known to man. It is a dimension as vast as space and as timeless as infinity. It is the middle ground between light and shadow, between science and superstition, and it lies between the pit of man's fears and the summit of his knowledge. This is the dimension of imagination"?

1447. What 1970s television character who stalked creatures of the night said, "So, when you have finished this bizarre account, judge for yourself its believability, and then try to tell yourself, wherever you may be, it couldn't happen here"?

1448. What television series opened with the host's shadow filling his own silhouette?

1449. What famous filmmaker directed the pilot episode of *Night Gallery*?

1450. In what spooky form did the Cryptkeeper on *Tales from the Crypt* appear (HINT: He's a common Halloween apparition)?

1451. What was the 1960s American gothic horror show that became the first television series the Sci-Fi Channel purchased and began running daily on its network?

1452. What was the first daytime horror serial?

1453. What 1987–90 syndicated series was set in a store named Curious Goods, which was filled with cursed antiques?

1454. Who was the host of *The Twilight Zone*?

1455. What *Twilight Zone* episode had already won an Oscar before it was broadcast?

1456. In an episode of *Twilight Zone* featuring William Shatner, "Nightmare at 20,000 Feet," what type of creature is seen on the wing of a jet?

1457. Who is the voice of the Cryptkeeper on *Tales from the Crypt*?

1458. With what two words did Alfred Hitchcock open his show?

1459. What was the name of the theme to *Alfred Hitchcock Presents*?

1460. What series was based on the short stories of British writer Roald Dahl?

1461. Who hosted *Night Gallery*?

1462. Who was the host of the 1960s NBC anthology *Thriller*?

1463. Who was the host of *Freddy's Nightmares*?

Answers on page 220

STARS THAT GO BUMP IN THE NIGHT

1464. What horror flick director produced *Eerie, Indiana*?

1465. What is the real name of television horror host Elvira?

1466. In an episode of what 1960s television series did Boris Karloff wear his Frankenstein monster makeup for the final time of his career?

1467. Who starred as the ghostly Capt. Daniel Gregg in *The Ghost and Mrs. Muir*?

1468. Who portrayed host Winston Essex in NBC's 1972 anthology *Ghost Story*?

1469. Who starred as the count in *The Curse of Dracula* in 1979?

1470. In what series did Geraint Wyn Davies play Detective Nick Knight, a detective who is also an eight-hundred-year-old vampire?

1471. In what 1958–60 television series, loosely based on a Universal horror classic, is the face of the star never seen nor his name revealed (HINT: A new version of this subject appeared in a 1975 series by the same title)?

Karloff and Hitchcock were proofs of the old adage "Old horror masters never die, they show up on television."

1472. Stuntman Dick Durock was the star of what television show about a doctor who had been changed into a creature by an environmental disaster?

1473. What famous cowboy actor starred as the mysterious Capt. Janos Skorzeny in *Werewolf*?

Answers on page 221

MADE-FOR-TELEVISION HORROR MOVIES

1474. What chases Karen Black in the "Prey" episode of *Trilogy of Terror* (1975)?

1475. What Oscar winner plays the Beast in the 1976 television movie *Beauty and the Beast*?

1476. What is the name of the farm where Hope Lange and Paul Burke are bothered by witches and warlocks in a 1970 movie?

1477. Who stars as the evil matriarch Widow Fortune in 1978's *Dark Secret of Harvest Home*?

1478. Who portrays Satan in 1972's *The Devil's Daughter*?

1479. What actor-singer, in the only horror role of his career, stars in 1971's *Dr. Cook's Garden*?

1480. What television star plays the owner of an extremely wicked canine in 1978's *Devil Dog: The Hound of Hell*?

Kolchak (left) was a hard-nosed, down-on-his-luck newspaper reporter who barely survived from episode to episode. Barry Atwater (right) was the first threat to Kolchak's safety in the television movie The Night Stalker *(1972).*

1481. What type of vehicle chases after Dennis Weaver in 1971's *Duel?*

1482. How does the possessed vehicle come to an end in *Duel?*

1483. In a 1972 movie, anthropologist Cornel Wilde and his daughter go to Mexico in search of what ancient creatures (HINT: They are also the title of the movie)?

1484. What actor portrays the murderous phantom who lives on a Hollywood film company's back lot in *The Phantom of Hollywood* (1975)?

ANSWERS TO JUST BEGINNING TO SCARE YOU

1444. *Tales from the Darkside*   **1445.** *The Outer Limits*   **1446.** *The Twilight Zone*
1447. Kolchak   **1448.** *Alfred Hitchcock Presents*   **1449.** Steven Spielberg (at age twenty-one)   **1450.** A skeleton   **1451.** *Dark Shadows* (1966–71)   **1452.** *Dark Shadows*
1453. *Friday the 13th—The Series*   **1454.** Rod Serling   **1455.** *An Occurrence at Owl Creek Bridge,* a short film from France   **1456.** A gremlin   **1457.** John Kassir   **1458.** "Good evening"   **1459.** Gounod's "Funeral March of a Marionette"   **1460.** *Tales from the Darkside*
1461. Rod Serling   **1462.** Boris Karloff   **1463.** Robert Englund

1485. Fill in the blank: Kay Lenz stars as a girl with psychic powers who joins a sorority of losers in 1978's *The Initiation of* _____.

1486. Name the two young actresses who oppose one another in 1981's *Midnight Offerings* (HINT: One starred in *The Waltons* and the other in *Little House on the Prairie*).

Answers on page 222

KOLCHAK: SCOOP OF SCARE

1487. Who starred as *Kolchak: The Night Stalker*?

1488. What is Kolchak's first name?

1489. What city did Kolchak operate in as a reporter when it became a weekly series?

1490. What is the title of the sequel to the television movie *The Night Stalker*?

1491. In what city is the 1972 television movie *The Night Stalker* set?

1492. In what city is the sequel, the 1973 television movie, set?

1493. What type of creature does Kolchak chase in the television movie *The Night Stalker*?

1494. What actor played Kolchak's boss, city editor Tony Vincenzo?

Answers on page 223

BY THE DARK SHADOWS OF THE MOON

1495. In what state was *Dark Shadows* set?

1496. What *Charlie's Angels* star played Daphne Harridge on *Dark Shadows*?

1497. What was the name of the gloomy manor on *Dark Shadows*?

1498. What was the name of the vampire played by Jonathan Frid?

1499. What animal's head decorated the top of the vampire's cane?

1500. What was the name of the werewolf played by David Selby?

1501. What tune from *Dark Shadows* made the Billboard Top 20 in 1968?

1502. What were the titles of the two feature film spinoffs from *Dark Shadows*?

ANSWERS TO STARS THAT GO BUMP IN THE NIGHT

1464. Joe Dante **1465.** Cassandra Peterson **1466.** *Route 66* **1467.** Edward Mulhare **1468.** Sebastian Cabot **1469.** Michael Nouri **1470.** *Forever Knight* **1471.** *The Invisible Man* **1472.** *The Swamp Thing* **1473.** Chuck Connors

1503. When *Dark Shadows* became the first daytime soap to be resurrected into a prime-time show in 1991, what British actor took up the cloak as Barnabas Collins?

1504. Who was the producer of the series *Dark Shadows* and television movie *The Night Stalker*?

Answers on page 224

SITCOM SPOOKINESS

1505. With what physical feat did Samantha Stephens begin her magic tricks?

1506. Anne Jeffreys, as Marian Kirby, was known as "the ghostess with the mostess" on what 1950s television comedy?

1507. What is the name of *Sabrina the Teen Age Witch*'s chatting cat?

1508. In the short-lived sitcom *Highcliffe Manor*, Christian Marlowe played Bram Shelley, a handsome monster that took on what form?

1509. Name Fred Gwynne's character in *The Munsters*.

1510. What was the name of the hand in the black box on *The Addams Family*?

1511. In what 1979 sitcom did cowboy character actor Jack Elam play "Frank," the Frankenstein monster?

Answers on page 224

X MARKS THE SUPERNATURAL SPOT

1512. On *The X-Files*, what are the first names of agents Mulder and Scully?

1513. At the conclusion of the first season of *The X-Files*, what are the dying words of "Deep Throat" (actor Jerry Hardin)?

1514. In the pilot episode of *The X-Files*, in what state does most of the action occur?

1515. What role does William B. Davis play on *The X-Files*?

1516. What happened to Mulder's sister when he was twelve years old?

Answers on page 225

ANSWERS TO MADE-FOR-TELEVISION HORROR MOVIES

1474. A Zuni fetish doll   **1475.** George C. Scott   **1476.** Crowhaven Farm   **1477.** Bette Davis   **1478.** Joseph Cotten   **1479.** Bing Crosby   **1480.** Richard Crenna   **1481.** An oil tanker   **1482.** It plunges off a cliff and explodes.   **1483.** Gargoyles   **1484.** Jack Cassidy **1485.** *Sarah*   **1486.** Mary McDonough and Melissa Sue Anderson

Jonathan Frid (above, left) played the leading role in daytime TV's Dark Shadows. *Karen Black (above, right), star of the very scary* Trilogy of Terror *(1975), has also been spooked in* Burnt Offerings *(1976),* Invaders from Mars *(1986), and* Evil Spirits *(1992).*

WITCHY WOMEN

Match the actress to the witch she played.

1517. Melissa Joan Hart

1518. Lara Parker

1519. Catherine Hicks

1520. Elizabeth Montgomery

1521. Agnes Moorehead

1522. Lisa Hartman

A. Amanda on *Tucker's Witch*

B. Endora on *Bewitched*

C. Sabrina on *Sabrina*

D. Samantha on *Bewitched*

E. Tabitha on *Tabitha*

F. Angelique on *Dark Shadows*

Answers on page 225

ANSWERS TO KOLCHAK: SCOOP OF SCARE

1487. Darren McGavin **1488.** Carl **1489.** Chicago **1490.** *The Night Strangler* **1491.** Las Vegas **1492.** Seattle **1493.** A vampire **1494.** Simon Oakland

BUFFY'S BUFFET

1523. Who plays Buffy in *Buffy the Vampire Slayer*?

1524. What is Buffy's last name in *Buffy the Vampire Slayer*?

1525. In what town does Buffy the vampire slayer live?

1526. What actor portrays Angel in the Buffy series as well as in his own series?

1527. What is the name of the gate over the top of the school library that serves as a partition between Earth and the netherworld?

Answers on page 226

LEFTOVER TV DINNERS

1528. Who starred in the title role of NBC's 1975 series *The Invisible Man*?

1529. What actor could change into all sorts of beasts in *Manimal*?

1530. What was the nickname of the van on Scooby-Doo?

1531. Who sang "Could It Be Magic?" the theme song to *Tabitha* (HINT: Her husband is country music star Clint Black)?

1532. A horror flick called *The Bloodening* was once featured at the local drive-in movie theater of what popular 1990s television series?

Answers on page 226

CARTOONY CREATURES

1533. What is the name of the pet blob of *The Real Ghostbusters*?

1534. What late-night talk-show host is the voice of Winston Zeddmore on *The Real Ghostbusters*?

1535. FILL IN THE BLANK: The 1965 cartoon set on Horror Hill, Transylvania, featuring Professor Weirdo and Count Kook, is titled _____ *the Monster*.

ANSWERS TO BY THE DARK SHADOWS OF THE MOON

1495. Maine   **1496.** Kate Jackson   **1497.** Collinwood   **1498.** Barnabas Collins   **1499.** A wolf   **1500.** Quentin Collins   **1501.** "Quentin's Theme"   **1502.** *House of Dark Shadows* and *Night of Dark Shadows*   **1503.** Ben Cross   **1504.** Dan Curtis

ANSWERS TO SITCOM SPOOKINESS

1505. A twitch of her nose   **1506.** *Topper*   **1507.** Salem   **1508.** The Frankenstein monster   **1509.** Herman Munster   **1510.** Thing   **1511.** *Struck by Lightning*

1536. *Sabrina the Teen-Age Witch* was inspired by what comic book?

1537. What 1970s cartoon features Frankie, Wolfie, Orville Mummy, Ghouli-hand, Tom Drac, Dr. Jekyll-Hyde, Bella La Ghostly, Boneapart, and the Ask It Casket?

1538. In what 1980s cartoon do Mummy Man, Vampira, Dr. Dred, Dracula, Frankie, and Drak Jr. hold their right hands together and say "Wacko" to receive special powers as crime fighters?

1539. What Great Dane teams with Freddy, Daphne, Velma, and Shaggy to track down criminals as well as spooky creatures?

1540. Who's "the friendliest ghost you know"?

Answers on page 227

MORE KIDS STUFF

1541. What two stars of *F-Troop* teamed up again as the stars of Saturday morning's *The Ghost Busters*?

1542. What Saturday morning show featured *The Love Boat*'s Fred Grandy as the teen caretaker of a museum who puts together a team of crime fighters composed of Count Dracula, the Frankenstein monster, and the Wolf Man?

1543. What 1990s television series followed young teens Marshall Teller's and Simon Holmes's efforts to track down the weirdness going on in their very peculiar hometown?

1544. What R. L. Stine book series became a Saturday morning series for kids?

1545. What Nickelodeon series features "The Midnight Society" as kids gathered around a campfire and told scary tales?

Answers on page 227

ANSWERS TO X MARKS THE SUPERNATURAL SPOT

1512. Fox and Dana **1513.** "Trust no one." **1514.** Oregon **1515.** The Cigarette-Smoking Man **1516.** She was abducted by aliens

ANSWERS TO WITCHY WOMEN

1517. C **1518.** F **1519.** A **1520.** D **1521.** B **1522.** E

A home run . . . or a run home? In a particularly spooky episode of The Andy Griffith Show, *called "The Haunted House," Gomer Pyle, Andy Taylor, and Barney Fife go looking for a baseball.*

WE'RE NOT IN MAYBERRY ANYMORE

On the facing page, the column on the left lists other roles played by actors who were either regular cast members, appeared in at least four episodes, or were featured guest stars in at least two episodes of The Andy Griffith Show. *Match the scary movie character on the left with the Mayberry actor (character) on the right. Not all of the actor names will have matches.*

ANSWERS TO BUFFY'S BUFFET

1523. Sarah Michelle Gellar   **1524.** Summers   **1525.** Sunnydale, California   **1526.** David Boreanaz   **1527.** Hellmouth

ANSWERS TO LEFTOVER TV DINNERS

1528. David McCallum   **1529.** Simon McCorkindale   **1530.** The Mystery Machine   **1531.** Lisa Hartman   **1532.** *The Simpsons*

1546. Mrs. Gilmore in *Rosemary's Baby* (1968)

1547. RAF pilot Winston Havelock in 1999's *The Mummy*

1548. Luther Heggs in *The Ghost and Mr. Chicken* (1966)

1549. Coopersmith in *Evilspeak* (1981)

1550. Helen Benson in *I Married a Monster from Outer Space* (1958)

1551. Jane Martin in *The Blob* (1958)

1552. Ben Cully in *It Came from Outer Space II* (1996)

1553. Amaryllis Trumbull in *The Comedy of Terrors* (1963)

1554. Maj. Martin Fielding in *Cult of the Cobra* (1955)

1555. Mr. Lowery in 1998's *Psycho*

1556. Mrs. Barley in *The Day the Earth Stood Still* (1951)

1557. "Radar man" in *The Beast from 20,000 Fathoms* (1953)

1558. Member of the Tribe in *Teenage Caveman* (1958) (two correct answers)

1559. Watchman in *The Monster That Challenged the World* (1957)

1560. Orphanage Woman in *Freddy's Dead: The Final Nightmare* (1988)

1561. Genius in *Village of the Giants* (1965)

A. Aneta Corsaut (Helen Crump)

B. Howard Morris (Ernest T. Bass)

C. Clint Howard (Leon)

D. Don Knotts (Barney Fife)

E. Jean Carson ("fun girl" Daphne from Mount Pilot)

F. Hope Summers (Clara Edwards/ Clara Johnson)

G. James Best (Jim Lindsey)

H. Frances Bavier (Aunt Bee Taylor)

I. Elinor Donahue (Ellie Walker)

J. Bernard Fox (Malcolm Merriweather)

K. Olan Soule (choir director John Masters)

L. George Lindsey (Goober Pyle)

M. Andy Griffith (Andy Taylor)

N. Rance Howard (various roles: bus driver, governor's chauffeur, etc.)

O. Ron Howard (Opie Taylor)

P. Joyce Jameson ("fun girl" Skippy from Mount Pilot)

Q. Charles P. Thompson (security guard Asa Breeney and Doc Roberts)

R. Joe Hamilton (Choney, Jase, Chester Jones, and other town loafers)

Answers on page 228

ANSWERS TO CARTOONY CREATURES

1533. Slimer   **1534.** Arsenio Hall   **1535.** *Milton*   **1536.** Archie Comics   **1537.** *The Groovie Goolies*   **1538.** *Drak Pack*   **1539.** Scooby-Doo   **1540.** Casper

ANSWERS TO MORE KIDS STUFF

1541. Larry Storch and Forrest Tucker   **1542.** *Monster Squad*   **1543.** *Eerie, Indiana*   **1544.** Goosebumps   **1545.** *Are You Afraid of the Dark?*

RICHARD MATHESON

HAILED BY RAY BRADBURY as "one of the most important writers of the twentieth century," author Richard Matheson easily ranks as dean emeritus of American fantasists. Born in New Jersey in 1926, Matheson published his forst short story, "Born of Man and Woman," in a 1950 issue of *The Magazine of Fantasy and Science Fiction*. Although only three pages long, this chilling tale has earned a place as one of the greatest horror stories of all time and provided the title for a 1954 collection of the author's short stories.

After he moved to California in 1951, Matheson tried his hand at mystery novels but returned to the sci-fi genre with *I Am Legend* (1954) and *The Shrinking Man* (1956). When Universal studios expressed an interest in buying the film rights to the latter title, Matheson agreed only if he wrote the screenplay. The effort became *The Incredible Shrinking Man* (1957), and Matheson was transformed from novelist to screenwriter.

In short order Matheson became a screenwriter for American International Pictures and united with director Roger Corman and actor Vincent Price for a series of Edgar Allan Poe adaptations: *House of Usher* (1960), *The Pit and the Pendulum* (1961), *Tales of Terror* (1962), and a hilarious version of *The Raven* (1963). The team also produced an interesting version of Jules Verne's *Master of the World* (1961) and *The Comedy of Terrors* (1964), a ghoulish laughfest. Matheson's other screenwriting ventures included *Burn, Witch, Burn* (1962), *Die! Die! My Darling* (1965), *The Devil Rides Out* (1968), and *DeSade* (1969). He also adapted two of his own fantasy novels for the screen: *I Am Legend* was released as *The Last Man on the Moon* (1964) and *Hell House* was released as *The Legend of Hell House* (1973).

He had left his mark on several classis episodes of Rod Serling's *The Twilight Zone* and in the early 1970s returned to television writing. Matheson adapted his own short story *Duel* in 1971 for an up-and-coming Steven Spielberg. Then he allied himself with *Dark Shadows* creator Dan Curtis, the leading producer of made-for-television horror movies at the time. Matheson scripted both *The Night Stalker* (1972) and its sequel, *The Night Strangler* (1973), and *Dracula* (1974), *Scream of the Wolf* (1974), *Trilogy of Terror* (1975), and *Dead of the Night* (1977). For other producers, Mathe-

---

ANSWERS TO WE'RE NOT IN MAYBERRY ANYMORE

1546. F   **1547.** J   **1548.** D   **1549.** C   **1550.** E   **1551.** A   **1552.** B   **1553.** P
1554. K   **1555.** N   **1556.** H   **1557.** G   **1558.** Q and R   **1559.** R   **1560.** I   **1561.** O

son worked on *The Strange Possession of Mrs. Oliver* (1977), *The Martian Chronicles* (1980), and *Dreamer of Oz* (1990).

Lately he adapted his 1975 time travel romance *Bid Time Return* as *Somewhere in Time* (1980) and contributed to 1983's *Twilight Zone, The Movie.* Matheson's son, Richard Christian Matheson, developed a following among fans of the "splatterpunk" movement and wrote scripts of his own. Father and son united for the script for *Loose Cannons,* a Gene Hackman–Dan Aykroyd buddy comedy that flopped in 1990. Recently Matheson has turned to the western genre. Some of his early fantasy work has been revived on-screen, including the Robin Williams vehicle *What Dreams May Come* (1998) and *A Stir of Echoes* (1999), starring Kevin Bacon. *I Am Legend* was remade in 1971 as *The Omega Man,* with Charlton Heston, and a third version is rumored to be in the works.

GEORGE A. ROMERO

THE FILMS OF George A. Romero are among the most interesting and influential in the horror genre. His first film, *Night of the Living Dead* (1968), virtually created the modern horror film; its use of gore established new boundaries of explicitness for filmmakers interested in terrifying audiences. Eleven years later, Romero wrote and directed a sequel, *Dawn of the Dead,* which shattered those boundaries and opened the door for the "blood and guts" horror movies of the 1980s. Yet in spite of his image as a wizard of gore, Romero imbues his films with a degree of intelligence and sophistication almost unknown in the works of other contemporary terror specialists.

George Andrew Romero was born in New York City on February 4, 1940. Obsessed with movies of all kinds, he made 8-millimeter films as a child, then enrolled at Pittsburgh's prestigious Carnegie-Mellon University and later formed a production company called The Latent Image. Romero and friends made commercials and industrial films for years before he decided to focus on feature films.

When it was released in the fall of 1968, *Night of the Living Dead* had cost

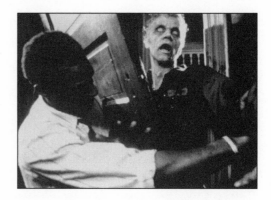

Duane Jones greets an unwelcome visitor in Night of the Living Dead *(1968).*

about $114,000 to make and had been shot at night and on weekends. Amateur and semiprofessional actors played the parts, and Romero shot the film in black and white so as to save money. The low budget forced the filmmakers to be inventive, so grisly shots of ghouls feeding on their victims and a downbeat ending—one of the first in an American horror movie—were added. These elements helped make *Night of the Living Dead* a surprise hit on the drive-in circuit and stimulated a cult following.

Romero's next three pictures–*There's Always Vanilla* (1972), *Jack's Wife* (1973), and *Code Name: Trixie* (1973)— were barely distributed. The director had better luck with *Martin* (1978), the odd tale of a disturbed young man who may or may not have been a vampire. *Dawn of the Dead* (1979) found favor with both audiences and critics,

mixing lowbrow gore and highbrow social satire. Sadly, only the latter element seemed to catch on with the scores of imitations that followed.

Another attempt to break away from horror, the interesting motorcycle drama *Knightriders* (1981), received good reviews but scanty distribution. Since then Romero has concentrated on shockers, including *Creepshow* (1982, the first of several team-ups with Stephen King), *Day of the Dead* (1985), *Monkey Shines* (1988), *Two Evil Eyes* (1990, co-directed by Italian horrormeister Dario Argento), and *The Dark Half* (1993). More recently Romero's name has been associated with plans to make a film version of *Resident Evil,* a popular but gruesome video game inspired by the director's work. A biography of George Romero, Paul R. Gagne's *The Zombies That Ate Pittsburgh,* appeared in 1987.

ROGER CORMAN

ROGER CORMAN IS to low-budget horror what Col. Harland Sanders is to fried chicken. If anyone could be said to have kept drive-in pictures in business in the late 1950s and early 1960s, it was Corman.

Born April 5, 1926, in Detroit, the "King of the B Pictures" began his one-man assault on the movie business after receiving backing from American International producers Samuel Arkoff and James Nicholson with 1954's *The Monster from the Ocean Floor.*

Corman's mark was quick and cheap as he churned out rock 'n' roll, horse operas, sci-fi, and horror with liberal helpings of comedy and social commentary. But along the way he hit pay dirt with favorable teamings of Poe stories and Vincent Price theatrics as well as some cult hits such as *Little Shop of Horrors* (1960).

Besides his record number of profitable cheap flicks, Corman nursed dozens of actors and directors into the business before they were stars. Neophytes who cut their teeth on Corman projects include Jack Nicholson, William Shatner, Ron Howard, James Cameron, Francis Coppola, Joe Dante, Martin Scorsese, and Peter Bogdanovich.

Corman, who is still going strong with more than 250 films as a producer, has appeared in more than twenty of his creations—mostly in cameo spots. Among his box-office brood are *Attack of the Crab Monsters* (1957), *Teenage Cave Man* (1958), *A Bucket of Blood* (1958), *The Pit and the Pendulum* (1961), *Tales of Terror* (1962), *X—The Man with X-Ray Eyes* (1963), *The Raven* (1963), *Bloody Mama* (1970), *The St. Valentine's Day Massacre* (1971), *Death Race 2000* (1976), *Piranha* (1978), and *Frankenstein Unbound* (1990).

Corman released his autobiography, *How I Made a Hundred Movies in Hollywood and Never Lost a Dime,* in 1990.

TOP 5 TELEVISION HORROR MOVIES

Salem's Lot (1979)
Gargoyles (1972)
Trilogy of Terror (1975)
Duel (1971)
Dark Secret of Harvest Home (1978)

Bela Lugosi and Mary Frey make an eerie pair as Degar and Sika, East Indian servants accused of crime, in Night of Terror *(1933).*

17

CAULDRON OF HEEBIE-JEEBIES

I have here a collection of the world's most astounding horrors!
> —Bruno Lampini (George Zucco) in *House of Frankenstein* (1944)

EDGAR ALLAN POE IN MOTION PICTURES

1562. In what year was an Edgar Allan Poe work first adapted to film?
    A. 1900
    B. 1909
    C. 1919
    D. 1924

1563. What is the title of the first film based on a Poe literary work?
    A. *The Bells*
    B. *The Black Cat*
    C. *The Raven*
    D. *The Sealed Room*

1564. Who directed the first film based on works by Poe?
    A. Tod Browning
    B. D. W. Griffith
    C. Fritz Lang
    D. George Melies

1565. What actress was the most famous star of this first Poe film?
    A. Tallulah Bankhead
    B. Clara Bow
    C. Lillian Gish
    D. Mary Pickford

1566. What 1934 film marked the first pairing of Boris Karloff and Bela Lugosi?
    A. *The Black Cat*
    B. *Murders in the Rue Morgue*
    C. *The Raven*
    D. *The Tell-Tale Heart*

1567. What two Poe film adaptations of the same title did Boris Karloff star in twenty-eight years apart?
    A. *The Black Cat*
    B. *The Fall of the House of Usher*
    C. *The Pit and the Pendulum*
    D. *The Raven*

1568. How many film-television versions have been made of Poe's *Murders in the Rue Morgue*?
    A. Three
    B. Five
    C. Eight
    D. Ten

1569. What actor starred in the 1993 feature *The Mummy Lives*?
    A. Tony Curtis
    B. Kirk Douglas
    C. Burt Lancaster
    D. Gregory Peck

1570. Who played a college kid in *The Phantom of the Rue Morgue* (1954)?
    A. Art Carney
    B. Merv Griffin
    C. Leonard Nimoy
    D. Carroll O'Connor

Barbara Steele rises from the dead, much to the chagrin of Vincent Price, in The Pit and the Pendulum *(1961).*

1571. Who directed eight films based on tales by Poe during the 1960s?

        A. Roger Corman

        B. John Frankenheimer

        C. Alfred Hitchcock

        D. Ed Wood

1572. Who plays Edgar Allan Poe in *Web of the Spider* (1970)?

        A. Vincent Price

        B. Peter Cushing

        C. Klaus Kinski

        D. Udo Kier

1573. Which Poe-inspired film also contains elements of Poe's story "Morella"?

        A. *Murders in the Rue Morgue* (1932)

        B. *Tomb of Ligeia* (1964)

        C. *Cry of the Banshee* (1970)

        D. *Two Evil Eyes* (1990)

Answers on page 237

FILMING POE HEAD TO TOE

Match the Poe-based film to the clue.

1574. *The Black Cat* (1934)

1575. *The Black Cat* (1941)

1576. *Fall of the House of Usher* (1982)

1577. *Haunting Fear* (1990)

1578. *House of Usher* (1960)

1579. *House of Usher* (1988)

1580. *Masque of the Red Death* (1964)

1581. *Masque of the Red Death* (1989)

1582. *Murders in the Rue Morgue* (1932)

1583. *Murders in the Rue Morgue* (1971)

1584. *Murders in the Rue Morgue* (TV, 1986)

1585. *The Oblong Box* (1969)

1586. *Phantom of the Rue Morgue* (1954)

1587. *The Pit and the Pendulum* (1961)

1588. *The Pit and the Pendulum* (1990)

1589. *Premature Burial* (1962)

1590. *The Raven* (1935)

1591. *The Raven* (1963)

1592. *The Tomb of Ligeia* (1965)

1593. *The Tell-Tale Heart* (1953)

A. Animated Poe tale

B. Donald Pleasence and Oliver Reed tangle

C. Herbert Lom is up to no good.

D. George C. Scott is Auguste Dupin.

E. Karl Malden goes ape.

F. Lance Henriksen is the Grand Inquisitor.

G. Price, Lorre, and Karloff

H. Lugosi is the mad doctor.

I. Lugosi confronts Basil Rathbone.

J. Jan-Michael Vincent gets dark with Karen Black.

K. Martin Landau plays Roderick Usher.

L. Ray Milland digs Hazel Court.

M. Lugosi and Karloff have a second date.

N. Mr. Karloff meets Mr. Lugosi.

O. Adrian Paul is Prospero.

P. Vincent Price buries his brother alive.

Q. Vincent Price buries his sister alive.

R. Vincent Price has two wives and a black cat.

S. Vincent Price is Prospero.

T. Vincent Price disses Barbara Steele.

Answers on page 238

LOVECRAFT ON FILM

1594. *The Haunted Palace* (1964) and *The Resurrected* (1991) were both inspired by what short novel written by H. P. Lovecraft?

1595. Which two horror stars are united to stalk *The Haunted Palace?*

1596. TRUE OR FALSE: *Die, Monster, Die!* (1965), based on Lovecraft's *The Colour out of Space,* features Bela Lugosi in a starring role.

1597. What 1967 Lovecraft adaptation stars Gig Young, Carol Lynley, and Oliver Reed?

1598. What former teen movie queen wound up being impregnated by Lovecraftian demons in *The Dunwich Horror* (1970)?

1599. What does Wilbur Whatley (Dean Stockwell) steal from the Miskatonic University library in *The Dunwich Horror?*

1600. Who plays Lovecraftian protagonists Herbert West in *Re-Animator* (1985) and Crawford Tillinghast in *From Beyond* (1986)?

1601. What dead animal is resurrected by Herbert West in *Re-Animator?*

1602. Name the 1990 sequel to *Re-Animator.*

1603. In what state was *The Curse,* a 1987 version of *The Colour out of Space,* filmed?

Answers on page 239

THE SHINING (1980)

1604. What word does Danny repeat over and over?

1605. What is the name of the Colorado resort?

1606. What vehicle does Danny drive through the corridors of the hotel?

1607. What has Jack Nicholson been writing on page after page?

1608. What is Nicholson's most famous line from the film?

1609. What actress plays Nicholson's wife?

1610. Where does Nicholson's character die?

1611. Besides Danny, who possesses the shining?

1612. Who directed *The Shining?*

1613. What television network remade *The Shining* as a miniseries in 1997?

Answers on page 239

ANSWERS TO EDGAR ALLAN POE IN MOTION PICTURES

1562. B   **1563.** D (based on "The Cask of the Amontillado")   **1564.** B   **1565.** D   **1566.** A
1567. D   **1568.** B   **1569.** A   **1570.** B   **1571.** A   **1572.** C   **1573.** D

Stephen King (above, left) is the modern master of horror fiction. Jack Nicholson (above, right) says the magic words in the film version of King's The Shining *(1980).*

ROYAL FLUSHED OUT

Match Stephen King's film with the character that King himself played in that film.

1614. *Creepshow* (1982)   A. Cemetery caretaker
1615. *Creepshow 2* (1987)   B. Dr. Bangor
1616. *Knightrider* (1981)   C. Gage Creed
1617. *Pet Sematary* (1989)   D. Hoagie man
1618. *The Shining* (TV, 1998)   E. Jordy Verrill
1619. *Sleepwalker* (1992)   F. Minister
1620. *The Stand* (TV, 1994)   G. Tedy Weizak
1621. *Thinner* (1996)   H. Truck driver

Answers on page 241

ANSWERS TO FILMING POE HEAD TO TOE

1574. N   **1575.** I   **1576.** K   **1577.** J   **1578.** Q   **1579.** B   **1580.** S   **1581.** O   **1582.** H
1583. C   **1584.** D   **1585.** P   **1586.** E   **1587.** T   **1588.** F   **1589.** L   **1590.** M   **1591.** G
1592. R   **1593.** A

KING OF TV

Match the television movie or miniseries with its plot.

1622. *The Langoliers* (1998)
1623. *It* (1991)
1624. *Salem's Lot* (1979)
1625. *Sometimes They Come Back* (1991)
1626. *The Stand* (1994)
1627. *Storm of the Century* (1999)
1628. *The Tommyknockers* (1990)

A. Passengers in a plane discover they are really alone.

B. Plague wipes out most of the world while survivors dream of two mysterious figures.

C. A schoolteacher returns to his hometown where he finds the ghosts of thugs who were killed in a train wreck when he was a boy.

D. Seven people combat a clown-suited demon.

E. A stranger comes to town and knows the deepest secrets of all of the inhabitants.

F. UFO in the woods changes town-folks into alien mutants.

G. A writer returns to small New England town to find vampirism.

Answers on page 241

ANSWERS TO LOVECRAFT ON FILM

1594. *The Case of Charles Dexter Ward*   **1595.** Vincent Price and Lon Chaney Jr.   **1596.** False. Boris Karloff plays the leading role.   **1597.** *The Shuttered Room*   **1598.** Sandra Dee, in her last feature film performance   **1599.** He steals a copy of the *Necronomicon*, the infamous book of the dead frequently mentioned in Lovecraft's stories.   **1600.** Jeffrey Combs   **1601.** A cat **1602.** *Bride of the Re-Animator*   **1603.** Tennessee

ANSWERS TO THE SHINING (1980)

1604. "Redrum" ("murder" backward)   **1605.** Overlook Hotel   **1606.** His Big Wheel bike **1607.** "All work and no play makes Jack a dull boy."   **1608.** "Here's Johnny!"   **1609.** Shelly Duvall   **1610.** In a maze in the snow   **1611.** Dick Halloran (Scatman Crothers) **1612.** Stanley Kubrick   **1613.** ABC

PLOTS OF PLOTS

Match the King film to its plot.

1629. *Apt Pupil* (1998)
1630. *The Boogeyman* (1984)
1631. *Carrie* (1976)
1632. *Children of the Corn* (1984)
1633. *Christine* (1983)
1634. *Creepshow* (1982)
1635. *Cujo* (1982)
1636. *The Dark Half* (1993)
1637. *The Dead Zone* (1983)
1638. *Dolores Claiborne* (1995)
1639. *Graveyard Shift* (1991)
1640. *The Green Mile* (1999)
1641. *The Mangler* (1994)
1642. *Maximum Overdrive* (1986)
1643. *Misery* (1990)
1644. *Needful Things* (1993)
1645. *Night Flier* (1998)
1646. *Silver Bullet* (1985)
1647. *Sleepwalkers* (1992)
1648. *Stand by Me* (1986)
1649. *Thinner* (1996)

A. Death-row guards find a convicted killer has the power to heal.
B. Devilish old man opens curiosity shop in Maine village.
C. Father loses his children and begins to fear for himself.
D. Five tales of homage to 1950s horror comic books
E. A gypsy curse causes a lawyer to lose weight.
F. Iowa town is taken over by youngsters.
G. Laundry equipment eats humans alive.
H. Man survives accident and discovers he has power to predict a person's fate.
 I. Mom and son prey on teenage virgins in midwestern town.
J. Pitiful teen uses her telepathic powers to wreak havoc at prom.
K. 1958 Plymouth driven by demons
L. People disappear in rat-infested mill.
M. Rabid dog terrorizes mother and son.
N. Romance writer is taken hostage by his "number-one fan."
O. A student of the Holocaust befriends a Nazi war criminal.
P. Tabloid reporter tracks a vampire that flies a Cessna.
Q. Trucks o' terror
R. Werewolf terrorizes town.
S. Woman is accused of murdering her employer, which brings her estranged daughter home.
T. A writer kills off his pseudonym, which then comes to life and murders.
U. Four boys search for a dead body.

Answers on page 242

BEFORE THEY WERE MON-STARS

Many of Hollywood's most successful actors paid their dues by appearing in horror films. Although some of these flicks are fondly remembered by fans, most of the stars below would rather leave these early roles off their résumés. Can you match the star with the film?

1650. Jack Nicholson

1651. Tom Hanks

1652. Humphrey Bogart

1653. Daryl Hannah

1654. Kevin Bacon

1655. Clint Eastwood

1656. Charles Bronson

1657. Ed Harris

1658. Roy Scheider

1659. Demi Moore

1660. Donald Sutherland

1661. John Travolta

1662. Angela Bassett

1663. Michael Landon

1664. Tom Selleck

1665. Angela Lansbury

1666. Kate Jackson

1667. Dennis Hopper

1668. Nastassia Kinski

1669. Hugh Grant

A. *I Was a Teen-Age Werewolf* (1957)

B. *Friday the 13th* (1980)

C. *House of Wax* (1953)

D. *The Devil's Rain* (1975)

E. *The Fury* (1978)

F. *The Curse of the Living Corpse* (1964)

G. *Night Tide* (1962)

H. *Daughters of Satan* (1972)

I. *Night of Dark Shadows* (1971)

J. *The Return of Dr. X* (1939)

K. *To the Devil a Daughter* (1976)

L. *He Knows You're Alone* (1980)

M. *The Picture of Dorian Gray* (1945)

N. *Dr. Terror's House of Horrors* (1964)

O. *Parasite* (1981)

P. *Creepshow* (1982)

Q. *The Lair of the White Worm* (1987)

R. *The Raven* (1963)

S. *Critters 4* (1990)

T. *Revenge of the Creature* (1955)

Answers on page 242

ANSWERS TO ROYAL FLUSHED OUT

1614. E   1615. H   1616. D   1617. F   1618. C   1619. A   1620. G   1621. B

ANSWERS TO KING OF TV

1622. A   1623. D   1624. G   1625. C   1626. B   1627. E   1628. F

ALTERNATE TITLES

The first column contains the most common American release titles of various horror films; the second column lists alternate titles—usually foreign or working titles but also some re-release titles. Can you match them?

1670. *Horror of Dracula*	A. *Zombie*
1671. *What* (1964)	B. *The Twelfth Hour*
1672. *Black Sunday*	C. *Dark Eyes of London*
1673. *I Spit on Your Grave*	D. *Satan's Skin*
1674. *Zombie*	E. *Day of the Woman*
1675. *The Grim Reaper*	F. *The Hollywood Strangler*
1676. *The Return of Dracula*	G. *The Night Walk*
1677. *Witchcraft Through the Ages*	H. *Dracula*
1678. *Vampyr*	I. *House of Doom*
1679. *Dawn of the Dead*	J. *Zombie 2*
1680. *Burn, Witch, Burn*	K. *Revenge of the Vampire*
1681. *The Human Monster*	L. *Fanatic*
1682. *Deathdream*	M. *Anthropophagus*
1683. *Mania*	N. *Night of the Eagle*
1684. *Don't Answer the Phone*	O. *Psycho-A-Go-Go*
1685. *Blood on Satan's Claw*	P. *Castle of Doom*
1686. *Die! Die! My Darling*	Q. *The Flesh & The Fiends*
1687. *The Black Cat* (1934)	R. *Night Is the Phantom*
1688. *Nosferatu* (1922)	S. *Haxan*
1689. *Blood of Ghastly Horror*	T. *The Fantastic Disappearing Man*

Answers on page 244

ANSWERS TO PLOTS OF PLOTS

1629. O   **1630.** C   **1631.** J   **1632.** F   **1633.** K   **1634.** D   **1635.** M   **1636.** T   **1637.** H
1638. S   **1639.** L   **1640.** A   **1641.** G   **1642.** Q   **1643.** N   **1644.** B   **1645.** P   **1646.** R
1647. I   **1648.** U   **1649.** E

ANSWERS TO BEFORE THEY WERE MON-STARS

1650. R   **1651.** L   **1652.** J   **1653.** E   **1654.** B   **1655.** T   **1656.** C   **1657.** P   **1658.** F
1659. O   **1660.** N   **1661.** D   **1662.** S   **1663.** A   **1664.** H   **1665.** M   **1666.** I   **1667.** G
1668. K   **1669.** Q

THE SOUND OF HORROR: FILM SCORES

Match the film to the composer of its musical score.

1690. *The Silence of the Lambs* (1961) A. James Bernard
1691. *Psycho* (1960) B. Wojciech Kilar
1692. *Bram Stoker's Dracula* (1992) C. Danny Elfman
1693. *Beetlejuice* (1988) D. Howard Shore
1694. *Fright Night* (1985) E. Bernard Herrmann
1695. *Halloween* (1978) F. Elliot Goldenthal
1696. *Horror of Dracula* (1958) G. Jerry Goldsmith
1697. *Poltergeist* (1983) H. Brad Fiedel
1698. *Creature from the Black Lagoon* (1954) I. Hans J. Salter
J. John Carpenter
1699. *Interview with the Vampire* (1994) K. John Barry
1700. *Séance on a Wet Afternoon* (1964) L. Robert Cobert
1701. *Burnt Offerings* (1976)

Answers on page 244

WHITE HOUSE WHITE-KNUCKLERS

Match the actor at left to the thriller (at right) in which he plays a U.S. president.

1702. Forrest J Ackerman A. *Attack of the Killer Tomatoes* (1978)
1703. Ernie Myers B. *Blood Suckers from Outer Space* (1984)
1704. Jack Nicholson C. *Howling III* (1987)
1705. Michael Pate D. *Deep Impact* (1998)
1706. Dick O'Neill E. *Red Planet Mars* (1952)
1707. Pat Paulsen F. *Amazon Women on the Moon* (1987)
1708. Richard Belzer G. *My Uncle the Alien* (1996)
1709. Willis Bouchey H. *Mars Attacks!* (1996)
1710. Morgan Freeman I. *Independence Day* (1996)
1711. Bill Pullman J. *Species II* (1998)
1712. E. G. Marshall K. *Tentacles* (1977)
1713. Henry Fonda L. *Superman II* (1981)

Answers on page 245

THE SOUND OF TERROR

1714. Name the horror-comedy musical in which rocker Meat Loaf plays Eddie the Biker.

1715. On what film is Michael Jackson's 1982 *Thriller* video based?

1716. What horror great can be heard on *Thriller*?

1717. Who wrote the title song for *The Blob* (1958)?

1718. What country music star sings "I've Come to Kill" in *Door-to-Door Maniac* (1961)?

1719. Who had a graveyard smash with "The Monster Mash"?

1720. What rock band took its name from a 1960s Boris Karloff film?

1721. What was the title of the rock song that put the squash on the killer tomatoes in *Attack of the Killer Tomatoes* (1978)?

1722. What 1959 smash hit, written and performed by Sheb Wooley, became a 1988 film?

1723. What movie, full of rock music, does Charlton Heston's character watch over and over again in *The Omega Man* (1971)?

1724. What rock group wrote songs titled "Godzilla" and "Nosferatu"?

1725. What rock group's first album, *Tales of Mystery and Imagination*, was inspired by the works of Poe?

1726. TRUE OR FALSE: Rock star Ringo Starr makes an appearance in *Son of Dracula* (1974).

1727. For what movie about voracious rats did Michael Jackson record the theme song?

1728. What group ignited the "Goth" movement in the 1980s with its song "Bela Lugosi's Dead"?

Answers on page 246

ANSWERS TO ALTERNATE TITLES

1670. H 1671. R 1672. K 1673. E 1674. J 1675. M 1676. T 1677. S 1678. P
1679. A 1680. N 1681. C 1682. G 1683. Q 1684. F 1685. D 1686. L 1687. I
1688. B 1689. O

ANSWERS TO THE SOUND OF HORROR: FILM SCORES

1690. D 1691. E 1692. B 1693. C 1694. H 1695. J 1696. A 1697. G 1698. I
1699. F 1700. K 1701. L

MISCELLANEOUS MISCHIEF

1729. Who plays the psychic-powered John Morlar in 1977's *The Medusa Touch?*

1730. What is the name of Jennifer Jason Leigh's character in 1999's *eXistenz?*

1731. Who directed 1999's *eXistenz?*

1732. What star of the 1968 film *Romeo and Juliet* plays Nurse Wharton in 1995's *Ice Cream Man?*

1733. What former Golden Glove–winning Los Angeles Dodgers first baseman plays Mr. Spodak in *Ice Cream Man?*

1734. What is the Ice Cream Man's name?

1735. Where did the Ice Cream Man reside just prior to his starting to wield a scoop?

1736. Who directed 1982's *The Evil Dead* and 1987's *Evil Dead II?*

1737. Passages from what tome attract the dead in *The Evil Dead* and *Evil Dead II?*

1738. In what town does *The Birds* (1963) take place?

1739. What Hammer film does James Mason take Sue Lyons and Shelley Winters to see in *Lolita?*

1740. Who plays Sarge in 1981's *Evilspeak?*

1741. What is the name of the fort where Capt. John Boyd is stationed in 1999's *Ravenous?*

1742. Around what war does the action in *Ravenous* take place?

1743. Who plays Cleaves in 1999's *Ravenous?*

1744. In what year does the action in 1961's *Mysterious Island* take place?

1745. What is unusual about Alam Smithere, director of *The Birds II: Land's End* (1994)?

1746. Who plays the psychotic Frank Booth in *Blue Velvet* (1986)?

1747. What two words does Robert Mitchum have tattooed on his knuckles in *The Night of the Hunter* (1955)

1748. What was the final film directed by Alfred Hitchcock?

Answers on page 247

ANSWERS TO WHITE HOUSE WHITE-KNUCKLERS

1702. F **1703.** A **1704.** H **1705.** C **1706.** G **1707.** B **1708.** J **1709.** E **1710.** D **1711.** I **1712.** L **1713.** K

Titles of Terror

Ten of the following twenty titles are actual movies—some are good, but most are very bad. The other ten titles are movies we'd like to see. Can you distinguish the real movies from the fake ones?

1749. *Calling Dr. Death* (1943)

1750. *The Devil and William Walker* (1944)

1751. *Bela Lugosi Meets a Brooklyn Gorilla* (1952)

1752. *Teenage Ghosts* (1958)

1753. *King Kong in the Lost World* (1961)

1754. *The Incredibly Strange Creatures Who Stopped Living and Became Crazy Mixed-Up Zombies* (1964)

1755. *The Slime People* (1964)

1756. *Jesse James Meets Frankenstein's Daughter* (1965)

1757. *Godzilla vs. Gorgo* (1967)

1758. *Nightmare in 3-D* (1972)

1759. *Children Shouldn't Play with Dead Things* (1972)

1760. *Deafula* (1975)

1761. *Morgue of the Vampires* (1976)

1762. *Satan's School for Stewardesses* (1981)

1763. *Bookstore of the Living Dead* (1984)

1764. *Frankenstein's Great Aunt Tillie* (1984)

1765. *Frankenstein General Hospital* (1988)

1766. *Pogs of Dracula* (1998)

1767. *Vampire Accountants* (1994)

1768. *Killer Klowns from Outer Space* (1988)

Answers on page 248

ANSWERS TO THE SOUND OF TERROR

1714. *Rocky Horror Picture Show*　**1715.** *Night of the Living Dead*　**1716.** Vincent Price
1717. Burt Bacharach and Hal David　**1718.** Johnny Cash　**1719.** Bobby "Boris" Pickett
1720. Black Sabbath　**1721.** "Puberty Love"　**1722.** "Purple People Eater"　**1723.** *Woodstock*　**1724.** Blue Oyster Cult　**1725.** Alan Parsons Project　**1726.** True　**1727.** *Ben*
1728. Bauhaus

HANDS-ON HORROR

1769. How does pianist Mel Ferrer lose his hands in *The Hands of Orlac* (1961)?

1770. Who blackmails Mel Ferrer for murder in *The Hands of Orlac* (1961)?

1771. Who plays the mad scientist in *The Hands of Orlac* (1925)?

1772. How does pianist Colin Clive lose his hands in *Mad Love* (1935)?

1773. Whose hands does Dr. Gogol (Peter Lorre) graft on to Colin Clive in *Mad Love?*

1774. How does Eric Landor (Michael Gough) lose his hand in 1965's *Dr. Terror's House of Horrors?*

1775. Who tries to nail a crawling hand to a table in *The Beast with Five Fingers* (1946)?

1776. Who portrays a teen who helps an astronaut's hand to kill in *The Crawling Hand* (1963)?

1777. What happens to the hand in *The Crawling Hand?*

1778. What is Jon Lansdale's (Michael Caine) occupation in *The Hand* (1981)?

1779. How does Jon Lansdale lose his right hand in *The Hand?*

1780. Who wrote and directed *The Hand?*

1781. In what bad horror flick do people possessed by a severed hand attempt to dispose of their left hand?

1782. Who has the idle hands in 1999's *Idle Hands?*

1783. How old is the lead character in *Idle Hands?*

1784. Which hand is evilly "idle" in *Idle Hands?*

Answers on page 249

ANSWERS TO MISCELLANEOUS MISCHIEF

1729. Richard Burton   **1730.** Allegra Geller   **1731.** David Cronenberg   **1732.** Olivia Hussey   **1733.** Steve Garvey   **1734.** Gregory   **1735.** Wishing Well Sanatorium   **1736.** Sam Raimi   **1737.** *The Book of the Dead*   **1738.** Bodega Bay, California   **1739.** *The Curse of Frankenstein*   **1740.** R. G. Armstrong   **1741.** Fort Spencer   **1742.** Mexican War   **1743.** David Arquette   **1744.** 1865   **1745.** Alan Smithee is not a real person   **1746.** Dennis Hopper   **1747.** "Love" and "Hate"   **1748.** *Family Plot* (1976)

CARNIVAL TIME

1785. What was the promotional line for *Carnival of Souls* (1962)?

1786. Where was this cult classic mostly filmed?

1787. Where do the three girls crash their car?

1788. Whose "dead eyes" does heroine Mary Henry see following her?

1789. Who produced a new version of this film in 1998?

Answers on page 252

OUT WITH A BANG

The last six months of the first century of horror saw a flurry of frightening films come to fruition. Here's a tantilizing quiz to test your most recent horror knowledge.

1790. Where did *The Blair Witch Project* (1999) make its world premiere?

1791. When and where was *The Blair Witch Project* filmed?

1792. How many actors auditioned for the three starring roles?

1793. How many people did it take to make this film?

1794. What town is the setting for *The Blair Witch Project*?

1795. What are the first names of the three young filmmakers?

1796. Who wrote the script for *Lake Placid* (1999)?

1797. What is the name of the lake in *Lake Placid*?

1798. What TV sitcom star spewed profanity in the film?

1799. Who plays Kelly Scott's (Bridget Fonda) boyfriend in *Lake Placid*?

1800. What is the locale for *The Haunting* (1999)?

1801. Who stars as Dr. Jeffrey Marrow in *The Haunting*?

1802. Who plays Eleanor *The Haunting*?

1803. Who plays Theodora *The Haunting*?

1804. Who directed *Sleepy Hollow* (1999)?

1805. Who stars as Ichabod Crane in *Sleepy Hollow*?

1806. Who portrays Katrina Van Tassel in *Sleepy Hollow*?

ANSWERS TO TITLES OF TERROR

1749. Real	**1750.** Fake	**1751.** Real	**1752.** Fake	**1753.** Fake	**1754.** Real	**1755.** Real
1756. Real	**1757.** Fake	**1758.** Fake	**1759.** Real	**1760.** Real	**1761.** Fake	**1762.** Fake
1763. Fake	**1764.** Real	**1765.** Real	**1766.** Fake	**1767.** Fake	**1768.** Real	

1807. Who plays the Headless Horseman in *Sleepy Hollow?*

1808. How much money were the survivors of a night in *The House on Haunted Hill* (1999) to receive?

1809. Who takes on the role originally filled by Vincent Price in *The House on Haunted Hill* (1999)?

1810. Who plays Dudley in *Deep Blue Sea* (1999)?

1811. What *Jurassic Park* victim is "Doc" in *Deep Blue Sea?*

1812. Who directed *The Ninth Gate* (1999)?

1813. Who stars as Malcolm Crowe in *The Sixth Sense* (1999)?

1814. Who stars as Cole in *The Sixth Sense?*

Answers on page 252

Future Ice Cream Man Clint Howard. Now, we ask you, Who would ever suspect that a young fellow with a face this innocent could portray warped evil so convincingly? An even better question to ask might be: Will he make you one scoop or two?

ANSWERS TO HANDS-ON HORROR

1769. Plane crash   **1770.** Christopher Lee   **1771.** Conrad Veidt   **1772.** Train crash   **1773.** Those of a knife thrower   **1774.** Franklyn Marsh (Christopher Lee) runs over it in his automobile.   **1775.** Hilary Cummins (Peter Lorre)   **1776.** Peter Breck   **1777.** A cat eats it   **1778.** Newspaper cartoonist   **1779.** Car wreck   **1780.** Oliver Stone   **1781.** Demonoid   **1782.** Anton Tobias (Devon Sawa)   **1783.** Seventeen years old   **1784.** Right

Boris Karloff shows Myrna Loy his deadliest device in The Mask of Fu Manchu *(1932)*

BIBLIOGRAPHY

Although not exhaustive, the following list provides a good introduction to the many horror film studies published over the years. Anyone who wishes to learn more about screen terror or who just wants to start a collection of horror movie books will find plenty of interest here.

Ackerman, Forrest J. *Forrest J Ackerman, Famous Monsters of Filmland.* Pittsburgh: Imagine, 1986.

————. *Mr. Monster's Movie Gold.* Norfolk, Va.: Donning, 1981.

Badley, Linda. *Film, Horror, and the Body Fantastic.* Contributions to the Study of Popular Culture, no. 48. Westport, Conn.: Greenwood, 1995.

Beck, Calvin Thomas. *Heroes of the Horrors.* New York: Collier, 1975.

Bojarski, Richard. *The Films of Bela Lugosi.* Secaucus, N.J.: Citadel, 1980.

————, and Kenneth Beals. *The Films of Boris Karloff.* Secaucus, N.J.: Citadel, 1974.

Borst, Ronald V. *Graven Images.* New York: Grove, 1992.

Brosnan, John. *The Horror People.* New York: St. Martin's, 1976.

Butler, Ivan. *Horror in the Cinema.* Third edition. New York: Barnes, 1979.

Castle, William. *Step Right Up! I'm Gonna Scare the Pants Off America.* New York: Putnam, 1976.

Clarens, Carlos. *An Illustrated History of the Horror Film.* New York: Capricorn, 1967.

Clover, Carol J. *Men, Women, and Chain Saws: Gender in the Modern Horror Film.* Princeton, N.J.: Princeton University Press, 1991.

Cushing, Peter. *An Autobiography* and *Past Forgetting.* 1986, 1988, Reprint, Baltimore: Midnight Marquee, 1999.

Daniels, Les. *Living in Fear: A History of Horror in the Mass Media.* New York: Scribner's, 1975.

Del Vecchio, Deborah, and Tom Johnson. *Peter Cushing: The Gentle Man of Horror and His 91 Films.* Jefferson, N.C.: McFarland, 1992.

Everson, William K. *Classics of the Horror Film.* Secaucus, N.J.: Citadel, 1974.

———. *More Classics of the Horror Film.* Secaucus, N.J.: Citadel, 1986.

Eyles, Allen, et al. *The House of Horror: The Complete Story of Hammer Films.* Second edition. London: Lorrimer, 1984.

Flynn, John L. *Cinematic Vampires: The Living Dead on Film and Television, from The Devil's Castle (1896) to Bram Stoker's Dracula (1992).* Jefferson, N.C.: McFarland, 1992.

Frank, Alan. *Horror Movies.* London: Octopus, 1974.

———. *Monsters and Vampires.* London: Octopus, 1976.

———. *Horror Films.* London: Hamlyn, 1977.

Gifford, Denis. *A Pictorial History of Horror Movies.* London: Hamlyn, 1973.

Hardy, Phil, ed. *The Encyclopedia of Horror Movies.* New York: Harper & Row: 1986.

Hearn, Marcus, and Alan Barnes. *The Hammer Story.* London: Titan, 1997.

Hogan, David J. *Dark Romance: Sexuality in the Horror Film.* Jefferson, N.C.: McFarland, 1986.

Huss, Roy, and T. J. Ross, eds. *Focus on the Horror Film.* Englewood Cliffs, N.J.: Spectrum, 1972.

ANSWERS TO CARNIVAL TIME

1785. Is there life after death? **1786.** Lawrence, Kansas **1787.** On a bridge, and then the car plunges into the river. **1788.** Those of Herk Harvey, the director of the film **1789.** Wes Craven

ANSWERS TO OUT WITH A BANG

1790. Sundance film festival **1791.** In 1997 in Maryland **1792.** Two thousand **1793.** 10, three actors and seven crew members **1794.** Burkittsville, Maryland **1795.** Heather, Michael and Joshua **1796.** David E. Kelley **1797.** Black Lake **1798.** Betty White **1799.** Adam Arkin **1800.** The Berkshires **1801.** Liam Neeson **1802.** Lili Taylor **1803.** Catherine Zeta-Jones **1804.** Tim Burton **1805.** Johnny Depp **1806.** Christina Ricci **1807.** Christopher Walken **1808.** One million dollars apiece **1809.** Geoffrey Rush **1810.** LL Cool J **1811.** Wayne Knight **1812.** Roman Polanski **1813.** Bruce Willis **1814.** Haley Joel Osment

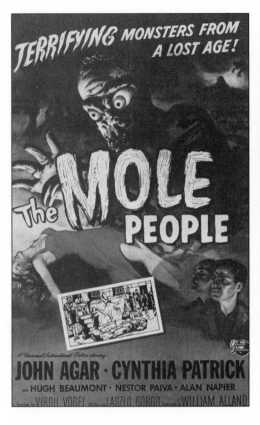 

Jensen, Paul M. *Boris Karloff and His Films*. New York: Barnes, 1974.

———. *The Men Who Made the Monsters*. New York: Twayne, 1996.

King, Stephen. *Danse Macabre*. New York: Everest, 1981.

Lee, Christopher. *Tall, Dark and Gruesome*. 1977. Reprint, Baltimore: Midnight Marquee, 1999.

Lee, Walt. *Reference Guide to Fantastic Films*. 3 volumes. Los Angeles: Chelsea-Lee, 1972–74.

Manchel, Frank. *Terrors of the Screen*. Englewood Cliffs, N.J.: Prentice-Hall, 1970.

Maxford, Howard. *Hammer, House of Horror: Behind the Screams*. Woodstock, N.Y.: Overlook, 1996.

McCarty, John. *The Modern Horror Film*. Secaucus, N.J.: Citadel, 1990.

———, ed. *The Fearmakers*. New York: St. Martin's, 1994.

Charles Ogle (above, left) was the first man-made monster and appeared in Thomas A. Edison's production of Frankenstein *(1910). Lon Chaney (above, right) disguises himself as "The Red Death" in* The Phantom of the Opera *(1925).*

McGee, Mark Thomas. *Fast and Furious: The Story of American International Pictures.* Jefferson, N.C.: McFarland, 1984.

———. *Roger Corman: The Best of the Cheap Acts.* Jefferson, N.C.: McFarland, 1988.

Meikle, Denis. *A History of the Horrors: The Rise and Fall of the House of Hammer.* Lanham, Md.: Scarecrow, 1996.

Miller, Mark A. *Christopher Lee and Peter Cushing and Horror Cinema.* Jefferson, N.C.: McFarland, 1995.

Naha, Ed. *Horrors! From Screen to Scream.* New York: Avon, 1975.

O'Neill, James. *Terror on Tape: A Complete Guide to over 2,000 Horror Movies on Video.* New York: Billboard, 1994.

Parish, James Robert, and Steven Whitney. *Vincent Price Unmasked.* New York: Drake, 1974.

Pattison, Barrie. *The Seal of Dracula.* New York: Bounty, 1975.

Pirie, David. *A Heritage of Horror: The English Gothic Cinema, 1946–1972.* London: Fraser, 1973.

———. *The Vampire Cinema.* London: Hamlyn, 1977.

Silver, Alain, and James Ursini. *The Vampire Film: From Nosferatu to Bram Stoker's Dracula.* Second edition. New York: Limelight, 1993.

Skal, David J. *Hollywood Gothic: The Tangled Web of Dracula from Novel to Stage to Screen.* New York: Norton, 1990.

———. *The Monster Show: A Cultural History of Horror.* New York: Penguin, 1993.

Svehla, Gary, and Susan Svehla, eds. *Bela Lugosi.* Baltimore: Midnight Marquee, 1995.

———. *Boris Karloff.* Baltimore: Midnight Marquee, 1996.

———. *Vincent Price.* Baltimore: Midnight Marquee, 1998.

———. *We Belong Dead: Frankenstein on Film.* Baltimore: Midnight Marquee, 1997.

Weaver, Tom. *Attack of the Monster Movie Makers.* Jefferson, N.C.: McFarland, 1994.

Weldon, Michael. *The Psychotronic Encyclopedia of Film.* New York: Ballatine, 1983.

Wiater, Stanley. *Dark Visions: Conversations with the Masters of the Horror Film.* New York: Avon, 1992.

Williams, Kucy Chase. *The Complete Films of Vincent Price.* Secaucus, N.J.: Citadel, 1995.

Wright, Bruce Lanier. *Nightwalkers: Gothic Horror Movies—The Modern Era.* Dallas: Taylor, 1995.

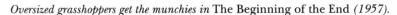

Oversized grasshoppers get the munchies in The Beginning of the End *(1957).*

WHERE TO FIND HORROR VIDEOS

If you're having a hard time finding classic horror films or your favorite cult flick is never available at the nearest video store, there are some alternatives via the mail, telephone, and the Internet. The following list is a short sample of options for your ticket to a night of fright:

Movies Unlimited
3015 Darnell Road
Philadelphia PA 19154
(800) 4-MOVIES
moviesunlimited.com

Facets
1517 W. Fullerton Avenue
Chicago IL 60614
(800) 331-6197
facets.org

Science Fiction Continuum
P.O. Box 154
Colonia NJ 07067
(800) 232-6002
sfcontinuum.com/sjvideo

Sinister Cinema
P.O. Box 4369
Medford OR 97501
(541) 773-6860
cinemaweb.com/sinister

Captain Bijou
P.O. Box 87
Toney AL 35773
(256) 837-0049
captainbijou.com

Videoflicks.com
1654 Avenue Road
Toronto, Ontario, Canada M5M 3Y1
(800) 690-2879
info@videoflicks.com